Coaching Writing

Coaching Writing

The Power of Guided Practice

William Strong

Utah State University

HEINEMANN
Portsmouth, NH

Heinemann
A division of Reed Elsevier Inc.
361 Hanover Street
Portsmouth, NH 03801–3912
www.heinemann.com

Offices and agents throughout the world

The author and publisher wish to thank those who have generously given permission to reprint borrowed material:

Poem #1212 is reprinted by permission of the publishers and the Trustees of Amherst College from *The Poems of Emily Dickinson* edited by Thomas H. Johnson. Copyright © 1951, 1955, 1979, by the President and Fellows of Harvard College. Published by the Belknap Press of Harvard University Press.

"Street Scene," "Pumped Up," and "Parable 1" are reprinted from *Sentence Combining: A Composing Book, Third Edition* by William Strong, Copyright © 1994. Published by Random House / McGraw-Hill, New York. Reprinted by permission of McGraw-Hill.

Figure 2.1 is reprinted from *Teaching Writing as Reflective Practice* by George Hillocks, Jr. Copyright © 1995 by Teachers College, Columbia University. Published by Teachers College Press, New York. Reprinted by permission of the publisher. All rights reserved.

Credit lines continue on p. vi.

Library of Congress Cataloging-in-Publication Data
Strong, William, 1940–
    Coaching writing : the power of guided practice / William Strong.
      p. cm.
    Includes bibliographical references and index.
    ISBN 0-86709-507-5 (alk. paper)
    1. English language—Rhetoric—Study and teaching.   2. Report writing—Study and teaching (Higher).   3. Tutors and tutoring.   I. Title.

    PE1404 .S846 2001
    808'.042'071—dc21

                               2001024542

Editor: Leigh Peake
Production: Lynne Reed
Cover design: Jenny Jensen Greenleaf
Cover photograph: W. Garrett Scholes
Manufacturing: Steve Bernier

Printed in the United States of America on acid-free paper

05 04 03 02   RRD   3 4 5

for
Donald Murray, a hero of the profession,
Lloyd Johnson, an English teacher par excellence,
and my father, William R. Strong, for his lifelong coaching

CONTENTS

FOREWORD

In 1965 I took my driver's test in a black Coupe DeVille, a wide-wheeled, overlong whale of a vehicle with real presence on the highway. It was comfortable, spacious, and, most important to my mother, safe. What that Cadillac was not, however, was a car a sixteen-year-old ought to try to parallel park during his driving test.

But I did. I'd practiced parallel parking for weeks, repeatedly working on a parallel parking exercise the driver's education teacher had taught me earlier that summer. I paid attention to angle and distance and speed as I pulled alongside an imaginary car, shifted into reverse and backed up, cut the steering wheel hard to the right, and backed up farther until I achieved a forty-five-degree angle in the space. I stopped, straightened the wheels, backed up more, then cut the steering wheel hard to the left, and swung the Caddy back beside the curb. I passed the driver's test that August day. And I still use that method of parallel parking when I find a tight space on campus that students can't bother with.

Bill Strong knows the value of guided practice in learning to write. And he's put that career's worth of knowledge together in *Coaching Writing*, a compelling, wise, and readable book that advocates the use of language exercises to teach middle school and high school students to develop as writers.

"Exercising language," Bill writes, "is the work of a lifetime—a cradle-to-grave adventure in which we extend and refine our oral and written skills . . . The point of a good language exercise is to help *students pay attention* to text and *assume increasing control* over their own planning, drafting, and revising processes."

I'm sure Bill knew that he would raise writing process hackles with this book: Exercises? Guided practice? In the name of achieving fine writing by students, you want *me* to engage *them* in *exercises*?

If your mind is moving in that direction, you need to touch the brakes and listen: Bill Strong simply knows that students grow as writers when their teachers couple meaningful writing with purposeful language work. Students may, for example, practice the creation of appositives to gain conciseness in their writing. They may wear the mask of other voices to generate language and ways of seeing they didn't know were in them. They may use sentence-combining exercises to learn to habitually incorporate punctuation as part of the entire symbol system of their writing.

I've known Bill well since 1991 when I began four stimulating years teaching at Utah State University. Bill taught in the Department of Secondary Education, I in English. I worked and played often with Bill during those years. I came to know him as a lover of language. He loves thinking it, saying it, writing it, playing with it, and, of course, teaching it—and thus the main title: *Coaching Writing*.

"The coaching of writing may usefully be considered a lifetime sport," Bill writes, "one that causes suffering to teach us humility and then offers unexpected moments of joy to teach us hope and commitment and professional perseverance."

Whenever I encounter the metaphor of writing teacher as coach, I think of two football coaches I had in high school. The first one kept us psychologically off balance and physically exhausted. Practices were two-and-a-half hour gauntlets each day after school. Our aim was to survive them. With great pause do I imagine such a coach as a writing teacher: up and down the aisles I see him hounding young writers, kicking them in the seat of the pants, screaming in their ears, "Show, don't tell! Show, don't tell!"

My junior and senior years, however, I experienced another kind of coach. Mr. Pardee was so different in demeanor and philosophy from our first coach that we players were suspicious of him. Mr. Pardee took care of us. He insisted that we rest when we were injured. He showed us new plays and maneuvers, then set us to practicing them until making the moves was as easy as breathing. In teachable moments, Mr. Pardee delivered mini-lectures about playing smart, eating right, studying in school, and practicing sexual responsibility. He nudged us to reflect upon our performance both on the field and off. Our practices after school were short and focused. Our aim was to learn. And we did. My senior year, we won the league championship.

Mr. Pardee was the kind of teacher I imagine Bill Strong would want to coach writing. Teachers such as him keep their eyes on the long road, but help students examine the steps they take on the journey and refine the way they walk. *Coaching Writing* will get you and your students to pay attention to language. *"Real writing offers a context for 'hands-on' exercises; but exercises, in turn, can help students approach composing tasks, such as revision, with fresh strategies."*

This book recommends itself to you in many ways: plenty of teaching ideas to make your classroom an active learning environment, useful theory to help shape your philosophy of language, poems about teaching and learning at the head of each chapter, wisdom that has come from decades of experience and thinking.

But what recommends this book most is the fine writing of the author. Bill Strong is a wordsmith of the first order. Whether narrating a bit of memoir, or making fundamental theory accessible through lucid explanation, or persuading with reasonable argument, Bill writes prose that is vivid, economic, direct, and elegant. In sum, *Coaching Writing* is written the way a book about teaching writing ought to be.

Here is a passage that ends a section in which Bill describes himself as a young teacher reluctantly attending a Saturday professional language arts meeting during the height of skiing season. His life changed when he understood the usefulness of language exercises in teaching writing:

> That night, as powder snow fell in the Idaho mountains, I added new paragraphs to my gestating novel and wrote my first exercise using kernel sentences. And the next day I skied the wide-open trails of new terrain until my legs burned.

Bill Strong will go on to write other books. *Coaching Writing*, however, stands, I think, as a capping achievement to his career. The book's contents are a lifetime accumulation of lessons and wisdom gathered through his teaching, learning, and writing.

When I see Bill next, I'll quibble with him about one thing. He argues convincingly for a "path of balance" in teaching writing, "a path of fluency *and* discipline." Such a path means "sustaining the flow of language" amid "meaningful skill building, the kind that would develop voice, stimulate imagination, add vocabulary, teach conventions, internalize genre, and increase language confidence."

That is a noble path, indeed, but let me tell you, Reader, this book did not arise from balance. This book was born of unequivocal, unbalanced passion. Regardless of what he is writing about, this teacher, this writer, this man, Bill Strong, is anything but balanced. He is passionate about language and writing and teaching and living. And, Bill, it shows. It surely does.

Tom Romano
Miami University
Oxford, Ohio

INTRODUCTION

THE GAME OF TEACHING

A word is dead
When it is said,
Some say.

I say,
It just begins
To live that day.

—Emily Dickinson

Exercising Language

Fifteen years after I left high school teaching to work with language arts teachers on the wild, windswept outback of eastern Idaho, there came a summer evening phone call from South Dakota. The Voice had a question. Was I the same person who had taught sophomore English in Portland, Oregon, and then moved out of state?

"I was in your class," the Voice said.

"No grade changes," I joked. "How did you track me down?"

"That's a long story."

The hillside behind my house settled into twilight, and I heard some of the story. Getting through college after Vietnam had been tough. But now the Voice worked in special education and school counseling, doing good work with kids at the margins. Coaching at-risk students in an alternative school was work that truly mattered. After all, he'd been just like them at the same age, without voice and without much hope.

"Maybe it takes one to know one," I offered.

"It helps."

For the life of me, I wasn't remembering this kid from my early teaching days. I hoped the school yearbook would jog my memory after I got off the phone.

As the conversation turned in my direction, I sketched a few personal facts, including my work with beginning and experienced teachers in Utah. My career had been one happy accident after another, I explained. By paying attention to students of all ages and listening to expert teachers across the country, I had learned a little about using language exercises as scaffolding for writing instruction.

A pause. The backyard shadows deepened.

"So what do you coach?" I asked.

"That's *how* I teach," the Voice said. "Or try to."

"Really."

"Yeah. And maybe why I called."

He talked some more about the trauma of Vietnam—how afterward he had read and reread my words in his journal and papers saved from high school. I thanked him for thinking of me after all this time. It was good to hear his voice so strong and clear.

"Well, if you ever get to South Dakota," the Voice said.

"I'll do that," I replied.

That night, after finding a yearbook photo to match up with the Voice, I was more perplexed than ever. A single silent face in a field of forgotten faces. What did this mean, the fact that my long-ago teaching—or coaching—had been remembered by one student, even though I had forgotten his voice and hundreds of others?

Later, I leaned back beneath a canopy of stars and listened to crickets stir the canyon wind. To have an unequivocal sign of intelligent life out there in the universe—language reaching out across many years of separation—was a miracle and a mystery to give me pause.

Coaching Writing

Exercising language is the work of a lifetime—a cradle-to-grave adventure in which we extend and refine our oral and written skills—and the coaching of writing may usefully be considered a lifetime sport, one that causes suffering to teach us humility and then offers unexpected moments of joy to teach us hope and commitment and professional perseverance.

It has taken me sixty years to write the preceding sixty words. It is a good, strong sentence, I think, and not just because it contains two appositives to define the themes of this book or a single word for each year of my life. Rather, it is good and strong because it is true. In beginning with it, I hope to pursue the miracle and mystery of the South Dakota phone call and those scraps of language that mattered to one learner.

I use the metaphor of coaching because Donald Murray used it in *A Writer Teaches Writing* (1968, 1985) to help launch the writing process revolution. As enacted by Murray, coaching is a teaching style that values conversation over correction, praise over criticism. Because it invites dialogue and reflection, coaching draws upon the documented language strengths of women in particular (Tannen 1991). To the extent that it becomes "an active pastime" or a "recreation"—terms used in the *American Heritage Dictionary* (1985)—classroom coaching achieves the status of a lifetime sport.

On a personal level, I still recall the words Murray wrote in response to a draft of my young adult novel, a story within a story that I had worked on for years:

> To attempt the impossible and have a narrative within the narrative. Impossible. Can't be done. You did it—and I have no idea how. I never mixed up the stories, always kept them separate and understood how they connected . . . I cared about all of your characters.

Murray then went on to raise questions, hints for revision. I returned to my writing with renewed hope, and eighteen months later the manuscript won a first prize in the Utah Literary Arts Competition. By encouraging potential and leaving room for my problem-solving initiative, he *showed* me, one-on-one, how good coaching can work.

Some readers, I know, will resist the coaching metaphor because they oppose our culture's preoccupation with sports and athletics. To those kindred spirits, I confess that I regularly boycott Superbowl telecasts since these occasions are always the best skiing days of the year in Utah—bright sunshine, fresh powder, and a nearly deserted mountain. And to further establish my credentials, let me also reveal that my very first article in a national magazine satirized the politics of faculty golf tournaments in the merit-pay district where I taught, one with a rich tradition of administrator brownnosing.

This book is written for beginning and experienced teachers alike, especially those who simply like sentences as much as writer Annie Dillard (1989). It is not for those who think of language as rules and prescriptions, nor is it for those who have given up on the dream of teaching from a place of personal truth, a center of authentic self. Most of all, I write for apprentice and expert teachers at risk for burnout, teachers who may need to be reminded that in working smarter, not just harder, and in taking care of first things first—themselves—they can also take care of their students.

Who are these teachers? They are bright-eyed young idealists, still in college, who understand that classroom coaching has the empowerment of individuals as its democratic goal. They are veteran coaches whose players don't always show up for practice and whose teams sometimes panic in high-stakes situations like districtwide writing assessments or standardized tests. And they are curriculum coordinators who face daily abuse from politicians and press because they know what can happen if they throw in the towel and let special interest groups have their way with instruction.

My message is that good coaching *enables* writers, whatever their skill level, to pay attention to language and to trust their meaning-making instincts. Language itself is an infinitely patient teacher, for us and for our students, if we can attend to its lessons. The human effects of coaching are written in the shorthand of memory:

> Until ninth grade, reading had always come easier to me than writing. That was until I met Mr. O. He was my ninth grade English teacher, and he was also the wrestling coach. Mr. O. was an older man with a few gray hairs left. Short and stout, he looked like a typical coach, but he was anything but typical. Most of the coach/teachers cared more about their sport than anything. This was not the case with Mr. O. He taught me that I could write a great paper if I put my mind to it. I remember going to him several times frustrated about the assignment we were working on. After talking with him for a few minutes, he had my confidence built back up. He always knew what I needed to hear so I could finish writing.
>
> —Kerry Moody

> There was a small waste basket located in the corner of the room. It was a good ten feet away and after ripping pages off my yellow pad I could cast a bank shot off my closet door. If my writing didn't improve, then my field goal percentage would. Every night I could be found in that room, rewording, revising, editing. I was really sweating it out. I wanted this paper to show how I really felt. The feeling of pride and satisfaction was overwhelming to me when in my Composition class, Ms. B. read aloud my paper to the students. My heart was pounding and my stomach muscles were contracting so rapidly that I thought I was going to fall out of my desk. "My Dad, My Hero," was the best paper in the class. A few weeks later I learned Ms. B. had sent a copy of my paper to my dad.
>
> —Jody Roe

Mrs. M.'s sophomore history class had a great impact on my ability to take a stand on an issue. Mrs. M. taught us the techniques that are needed to persuade others. Although I don't
remember what I wrote about, I do remember stating my point of view as I wrote a paper,
then giving several supporting reasons why I believed this certain way. Once I had given reasons or evidence in the body of the paper, I remember summarizing whatever points I had
made as the conclusion of my paper. Mrs. M. complimented me on my ability to write persuasively. I hadn't received too many compliments up to that point in my life, and I haven't
received many since. This experience, however, of learning to write persuasively greatly increased my confidence in writing with a purpose.

—Seth Bingham

Coaching exists in the relationship between young people and the mentors who get
paid (or underpaid) to promote language learning. From the learner's viewpoint, small
incidents get interwoven to create patterns of belief, habit, and feeling toward oneself and
written text. From the teacher's viewpoint, many incidents blur together over a week, a
month, a year—or a lifetime. So coaching is a lifetime sport in two closely related senses:
It is the central activity in the game of teaching, a pursuit with lifelong challenges; and it
is an activity with lifetime effects on language learners, both positive and negative. A teacher
affects eternity, as the old saying goes. Listen.

It seemed that no matter how hard I tried or what I wrote about my papers would be returned,
ripped to pieces. Either the teacher didn't like my style of writing or the topic I wrote about
or they thought my punctuation and sentence structure weren't correct. There was no way I
could please a writing teacher; they could always find something wrong. I felt trapped when
I was assigned to write a paper. There was no way to get out safely. I wasn't in control. Everything depended on what someone else thought. I felt that my teachers didn't care how hard
I tried. They would still crush me. The iron fist would crash down on me time and time again.
Why try? Why work hard to do your best only to be crushed as they tried to mold you into
something you were not? To this day I get a claustrophobic feeling when I am assigned to
write a paper in school. I feel it is impossible to put on paper my true knowledge and feelings
when the reader's (teacher's) purpose is to judge my writing.

—Joyce Fleming

I share these excerpts to center our attention on the conundrum of coaching: that
although it typically occurs in a large-group setting—with each of us trying to work with
150 (or more) learners a day—the effects are always individual. And it is this fact that
puts hardworking teachers, both apprentice and expert, at risk of professional burnout.
It is simply not possible—even if it were desirable—for any sane human being to monitor and nurture 150 (or more) volatile relationships each day. Rather, it makes far more
sense to invest energy in creating what George Hillocks (1995) has called "active learning
environments." Such classrooms invite students to engage actively in writing, encouraged
by teammates and by a coach who sets high, reasonable standards.

Environments for active learning give students authority and responsibility to define
productive relationships with teachers. Recall the lament of the student quoted earlier who
claimed to feel "trapped" and "crushed" and "claustrophobic" because of teachers she
couldn't please. "I wasn't in control," she wrote. Of course, to author a text—or a relationship—is to have some say, or authority, in charting its direction. Therefore, Donald
Murray always insisted that students speak first in writing conferences because "it is their
job to read the text, to evaluate it, to decide how it can be improved so that they will be

able to write when I am not there" (1982, 69). Because students write in many different ways—and have differing approaches to problems—Murray's advice was to be a "responsive teacher," one who "listens to the students first and then to the text" (70). Paradoxically, underteaching can lead to overlearning.

And why, you may ask, is the support of teammates so important in an active learning environment? The answer, of course, is that coaches need all the help they can get to meet a tremendous range of learning needs. Listen.

> I just sat there scared to death and I could feel tears welling up in my eyes. Matt happened to look over at my blank sheet of paper and asked why I hadn't started. I explained that I didn't understand the assignment. He slid his desk next to mine and helped me get started. He told me just to think about one of my favorite fishing trips and tell about it. Soon Terry slid his desk over and helped me too. I finally finished a pretty good story but I still wished I was back in the lower class. My story didn't get hung up with the best ones, but that was O.K. Even though it wasn't that great, I had done it and it made me feel better. I had a hard time for the rest of the year, but I survived and learned a lot more than I ever could have in the other class.
>
> —C. J. DUNLAP

For our model, we might look to colleagues down the hall—in athletics, fine arts, music, drama, science labs, business, and many other areas. Working with students of vastly different abilities, these teachers have long known that peer coaching can help all students, regardless of natural ability or background, acquire skills and knowledge.

The Goal of Balance

Balance is basic to all sports but especially basic to our work in classrooms and computer labs and reading and writing centers. The concept implies wellness, strength, and flexibility—qualities essential for the complex adult activity of coaching writing. To feel balance is to feel physically alert and spiritually centered.

In the classroom, balance enables teachers to be relaxed and surefooted when leading a literature discussion or insisting on civility or responding to a student essay. Outside the classroom, balance enables the best among us to remain resilient and smiling in the face of underfunded programs, legislative mandates, and teacher-bashing editorials. Simply put, balance refers to clear-eyed self-acceptance—a sense of equanimity and perspective—so that even with questionable decisions from school officials who should know better, or lackluster teaching from down the hall, or rudeness from fans who don't value their free admission, we still feel okay about the game.

For writing coaches, it is not always easy to achieve a balanced perspective. Typical rookie teachers feel overwhelmed by the expectations of student teaching or the first year's position. Veterans often feel guilty without a set of papers in the airline carry-on bag and may come to doubt their own standards for homework and grading. And the profession's leaders cannot help feeling harried as they take on poetry festivals, drama production, and the literary magazine—or the requests to mentor student teachers, review curriculum, write technology grants, and present inservice workshops.

But to have any hope of achieving balance—and the sense of centeredness so essential to classroom success—we need to remind ourselves, continually, that our main coaching challenge lies in setting up engaging environments for active learning, not merely in managing crises. For example, we can tap real-world contexts by using bulletin boards, desktop publishing, and the Internet to get students to care about the content and the form of their writing. We can set clear, explicit objectives for written performance by sharing evaluation rubrics and analyzing model papers, both strong and weak. We can ensure helpful, immediate feedback by organizing read-around groups, peer response workshops, and editing conferences. And we can expect students to improve performance skills by tracking their spelling and usage errors, setting goals for themselves, and finding resources to address areas of need.

Put another way, a coherent context is just as important for us as teachers as it is for students as writers. For coaches, context provides the physical, intellectual, and emotional playing field for the game of teaching. How do we want our classroom organized to facilitate our game plan? What materials will we use to further the ends we have in mind? How will we engage the class and coach individuals? For students, context is the game of language learning, and their questions—sometimes voiced, sometimes not—are many: What will I learn? Why is this important? Will it be fun? Will it interest me? How will I be graded? What's the deadline? May I work with friends? How long does it have to be? Does spelling count?

In *Teaching Writing as Reflective Practice*, George Hillocks offers a helpful overview of an active learning environment in which quality coaching can occur:

> First, not only are task objectives clear to teachers, but they are operationally clear to students. Second, the materials and problems engage students because they have been selected in view of (1) what students are able to do, (2) the likelihood of their interest to students, and (3) their power to engage students as real-world problems. Third, students engage in complex tasks with the support from materials, teachers, and/or peers before they proceed to independent work with such tasks. Fourth, students develop a stake or sense of ownership in the classroom proceedings because their ideas and opinions become the focus of classroom activity. (1995, 58)

Hillocks' blueprint is more than merely another opinion about instruction in writing for middle school and high school grades. As one of the nation's premier researchers in writing—and an outstanding teacher in his own right—Hillocks knows what works. In this book, I focus attention on the key issue of "support from materials, teachers, and/or peers" *preceding* independent work. For teachers who are professionally serious about the contexts for coaching, Hillocks' work deserves follow-up reading.

Finally, we need to remind ourselves that the game of teaching is only part of the game of life. Because the coaching of writing is work that drains us emotionally and spiritually, it needs to be balanced, on a regular basis, with the satisfaction and language learning we find in other arenas, such as our own literacy pursuits.

On this point, there is a sad little joke about two teachers headed for the parking lot on a Friday afternoon. One turns to the other and asks, "Say, have you read—?"

"Read it?" comes the reply. "I haven't even *taught* it yet."

At the end of the concluding chapter, I offer to anyone who needs it my official permission to get a life. But now let me forecast what follows more immediately.

Seeking Balance

In this book I outline a coaching approach to instruction in written language at middle school and high school levels. The approach is eclectic, pragmatic, synthetic. As I hinted earlier, it centers on finding balance—ways of working smarter, not harder—and thus reducing the risk of burnout in teaching. I invite members of our professional club, both newcomers and veterans alike, to consider or revisit practical activities, tasks, and methods for exercising language and coaching writing.

If balance is a desirable goal for us as individuals, what about the curriculum we teach? According to research on how students actually spend their time in many secondary English classrooms, about 50 percent is devoted to literature, 27 percent is devoted to writing, and only 10 percent is devoted to language (Applebee 1989, 10). Sad but true, language study in general, and skill instruction in particular, can sometimes be demonized by overly zealous advocates of whole language instruction who eschew exercises of any kind. For some, the only game in town centers on a liberationist pedagogy, and this goal is advanced with truly unbalanced fanaticism.

Let me emphasize, as strongly as possible, that I am not the apostle of a New Busywork Curriculum. And mine is *not* an argument for underlining subjects once and verbs twice or for nonsensical fill-in-the-blank activities that frustrate students, impede their acquisition of performance skills, and deflect attention from real language learning. Instead, I speak for methods that might support active learning environments, including those for whole-class and small-group teaching. I argue for *judicious* and *deliberate* use of language exercises of many kinds but especially those with research-proven track records or strong rationales in theories of language development.

In my view, few teachers feel nostalgia for the mindless skill-and-drill of yesteryear or for classroom games in which star students strutted in the spotlight while everyone else, but especially students of color, practiced spectator skills. Therefore, my advocacy is for a more thoughtful stance toward instruction in written language, one less strident in its ideology and more inclusive in its rhetoric. Linguist John Mellon sums up well the case for a balanced approach to coaching:

> Self-selected reading, writing, and discussing represent one kind of language use. Other learning activities, such as sentence-combining exercises, looking up word meanings, writing essays on assigned topics, reading teacher-suggested material the child might never choose on his or her own, and answering a teacher's instructional questions, while not usually self-sponsored, constitute another equally natural kind of language use, whose only contrivance lies in their having been selected by the teacher on grounds that they bring into use the *particular forms* of language whose processing triggers the acquisition and development of specific performance skills.
>
> Again and again we must stress a central truth: the learning of performance skills occurs in an integrated, wholistic, and largely nonconscious way, as a result of the child's organic predisposition toward such learning. . . . As already suggested, however, planned school-wide programs of in-school language use do serve important functions. One is to insure that students experience the right *forms* of language use, organized in the right *sequences*, and followed up by the right kinds of corrective *feedback*. (1981, 54–55)

So my questions are these: If exercising language is the work of lifetime, as I asserted earlier, do most of us routinely encourage middle school and high school learners to pursue language inquiries—simple at first, then more complex—focused on questions that can genuinely instruct and interest them? And do we regularly use our own language learnings, whatever they may be, as authentic live demonstrations?

I ask such questions because attention to language is out of fashion in many schools—Applebee's research tells us that—and because the novice and veteran teachers who emphasize such work are sometimes viewed as Neanderthal throwbacks by their more highly evolved colleagues. Regrettably, in my opinion, an unbalanced curriculum can lead some of us to disengage from teaching or to feel alienated.

How does this estrangement occur? It occurs when brand-new teachers are made to feel uneasy or guilty about having their students do anything that might be labeled an exercise—say, focusing on syntax, punctuation, paragraph structure, word etymologies, or dozens of other language-related topics. It occurs when hardworking veterans are patronizingly reminded, by visiting consultants with coiffed hair and gleaming Italian loafers, that language should be taught *only* in context, as the need arises. It occurs when supervisors are frustrated in their efforts to orchestrate curriculum consensus because of teacher apathy or overt resistance to Mellon's premise of "planned school-wide programs of in-school language use."

I contend that all good teachers, regardless of differences in cultural background, experience, and coaching styles, seek two basic goals: simple respect from learners, the public, and one another; and a sense of larger meaning in their work. Personally and professionally, we hope that our coaching makes a positive human difference and relates in useful, far-reaching ways to the game of life.

An Overview

This book weaves together three strands of development. With the first strand, its threads combed from the underbrush of memory, I describe coaching situations from my own experience. The second strand connects my story to broader principles of language and literacy instruction, offering commentary as well as professional references. For the third strand, I explain or demonstrate practical applications for middle school and high school teaching. The chapters are intended as *resources* for beginning and experienced teachers, not as a curriculum sequence. I advocate the active learning environment alluded to earlier (Hillocks 1995).

In this book, I begin with sentence-level issues and work up to larger matters of discourse coaching. Why? Because the strand of narrative has been so important in writing these chapters. In other words, I begin with coaching lessons from early in my career and move toward those learned later on. I also assume that readers will imagine local contexts of instruction—students, classrooms, curriculum—as they pursue answers to a wide range of questions. So let me emphasize, again as strongly as possible, that the sequence of chapters is not my advocacy for starting with sentences in September and ending with genre in June. Of the many ways to go wrong in coaching, a simpleminded skills approach seems the sure path to disappointment. And no self-respecting coach aspires to failure.

- Chapter 1, "Coaching Basics," centers on my work with basic writers and their needs—and how I came to field-test and use sentence-combining exercises during the late 1960s.
- Chapter 2, "Coaching Syntax," provides a research-based rationale for given-language activities and illustrates many activities for connecting such work to instruction in writing and literature.
- Chapter 3, "Coaching Usage," explores the tricky issue of error in written language and outlines ideas for securing student involvement and useful methods for teaching proofreading.
- Chapter 4, "Coaching Style," offers ideas for helping students develop increased control of stylistic options through the enabling constraint of sentence modeling and given-language exercises.
- Chapter 5, "Coaching Paragraphs," examines paragraphs as miniatures of instruction and discusses how showing, not telling and other types of practice develop paragraph schema.
- Chapter 6, "Coaching Voice," deals with the influence of a high school teacher whose exotic coaching methods encouraged me to experiment with voice lessons and literacy autobiographies.
- Chapter 7, "Coaching Imagination," explores the concepts of spectator and participant texts and makes a case for increased emphasis on imaginative work in language-learning exercises.
- Chapter 8, "Coaching Collaboration," describes how peer response groups and scaffolded activities in coauthoring help students internalize conventions of writing and learn various skills.
- Chapter 9, "Coaching Genre," focuses on ways to use given-language exercises, crafted writing assignments, and rubrics to help students understand a variety of discourse strategies.
- Chapter 10, "Coaching Assessment," builds on the genre chapter to focus on self-assessment strategies as well as methods for responding to student texts and managing the paper load.
- The Conclusion, "The Zen of Coaching," deals with coaching conferences, recaps key themes related to coaching and language exercises, and acknowledges the many individuals who have coached me.

Following each chapter is a brief section called "Learning Through Language." This feature invites beginning and experienced teachers to reflect on the ideas, advice, and demonstrations within the chapter. The prompts encourage oral and written responses in order to extend, apply, or challenge the text. Such responses can become a vital part of preservice or inservice classes and National Writing Project summer institutes.

Discerning readers will note that my plan does not include a stand-alone chapter on coaching speakers of limited English, sometimes called English Language Learners (ELL). That I believe in such instruction will be clear from Chapter 1 as well as from other chapters of this book. But I also believe that we must stop viewing students with limited English as separate or different from mainstream English speakers.

Literacy Club

Pants dey baggy, an' mouth be cruel;
Our sneer hidin' hurt from dey ridicule.
Caps flip back—we lookin' so bored—
Ignorin' dey word 'cause we be ignored.
Dey say we lazy, an' dey say we rude—
But maybe we learnin' dey attitude.

The central issues for ELL instruction are ones of inclusion and accommodation. Will we as coaches welcome second language learners and try to accommodate their needs—for example, by offering temporary scaffolds for our assignments and having mainstream students serve as our assistant coaches? Or will we sigh and shake our heads and hope that their needs are met by other, "more specialized" teachers?

In brief, then, this book revisits some of my learning about the coaching of written language. I share pieces of my story because I am convinced that what matters most is personal knowledge—an understanding developed from experience and linked to other forms of vicarious or intellectual knowing. It is shared teacher knowledge that has long interested me, as a veteran director of the Utah Writing Project, and that I hope interests you.

Three broad themes underlie the chapters that follow. First, as I have already hinted, I assert that the game of teaching is only part of the game of life. For those of us who are mere mortals, with large classes of students who would often prefer to be somewhere else, the challenge is to design environments for active learning (Hillocks 1995) that will help us work smarter, not harder, and give us breathing room to balance work and play in our busy lives. Although our work may often go unappreciated, most of us earnestly seek *practical* ways to help learners exercise language in several arenas—reading and writing, listening and speaking, critical viewing, and computer-based imaging.

Second, I contend that pursuing some sporting life passion enables us not only to extend and refine our own learning about written language—worth doing for its own sake—but also to feel a sense of balance as we approach day-to-day coaching. In sharing our pursuits with students, we build classroom community and demonstrate a powerful truth: that language learning—"a life of sport"—is the work of a lifetime. If all of us coach *who* we are, in ways large and small, perhaps it is time to give a curriculum of self-disclosure increased visibility. "One of teaching's great rewards," writes Parker Palmer, "is the daily chance it gives us to get back on the dance floor" (1998, 25).

Third, I suggest that the work of daily coaching is informed by a theory of social language learning. Basic to this theory is the idea of club membership—that learners can naturally and easily apprentice themselves to experts (adults, peers, or texts that demonstrate expertise), provided that learners view the club members as being like themselves and the activities as worth doing. Coaches of written language welcome and encourage learners, demonstrate skills, design exercises and practices, help connect activities to larger goals, oversee student performance, and model adult learning. As coaching professionals, we also belong to a professional club, or forum for discourse. This book, I hope, is part of the professional conversation.

To conclude this Introduction, let me add that I remember small victories—the phone call from South Dakota, say—but I also recall the losses. In particular, I still keep an old letter from another high school student, a young man whose prowess with written language was a little like Mark McGwire in the batter's box: enough to give a pitcher (or an insecure teacher) pause. Today this letter reminds me of the need to exercise language and coach writing with a *human* touch. "Work is love made visible," as Kahil Gibran [1923] 1975, 28) once put it.

So in addition to being for Donald Murray, a hero of our profession, and for Lloyd Johnson, my high school English teacher, and for my father, whose lifelong coaching centered on quiet demonstrations of courage in the face of daunting adversity, this book is for all my former students, especially those I never quite reached.

As they often quipped, "Hey, better late than never!"

And they were right.

CHAPTER 1

COACHING BASICS

Pep Talk

A hint of smile helps me look cool:
Such are the games we play in school.
"Learning together, we each can teach—"
So go the words of my pre-game speech.
Their faces and eyes belie their fear:
What, they ask, am I doing here?

Game Time

I heard them before I saw them. Humidity hung like a gray veil in the unlit, echoing corridors of the field house. Drenched in sweat, I followed shouts and the noise of scraping, banging desks until I found my freshman composition class, twenty or so students in a bare, dark room like the inside of a bass drum.

It was chaos enacted deep in the concrete bowels of the building—their faces and moods as dark as my fear—and not an auspicious beginning for a bearded young honky with a peace symbol on his belt and a smug, earnest attitude toward teaching. These students, part of an Educational Opportunity Program in the early 1970s, had left the mean streets of Chicago for a first taste of higher education at the University of Illinois in Urbana. Paralleling this roundup was another for first-year doctoral students like me, whose job was to provide writing and language instruction in teams of two. Each team was expected to "figure something out," offering a class and follow-up tutoring. Beyond that, the program managers had wished us good luck.

I clicked on the lights and settled things down. After arranging the desks in a circle, I handed out markers and name cards and distributed a syllabus designed to put these "disadvantaged" youth on a fast track to academic socialization. Inspired by the loftiest liberal sentiments of the day, it centered on Erich Fromm's *The Art of Loving* (1956). The class, I emphasized, would be student-centered but rigorous. "Any questions?" I asked. We stared at each other and sweated. My gaze slid away from theirs as I went on and on, hoping to coax, challenge, inspire.

When the vacuum of our first class ended, African American and other students shuffled off in their separate directions, and I told myself that things would work out as they always had before. Secretly, however, I wondered why they seemed so unlike the adult basic education students, mostly Mexican Americans, whom I had helped tutor in downtown Denver two summers earlier.

I was edgy—and with good reason, I would learn. Sweating through the first few weeks in the field house, I led nondiscussions on assigned reading, showed and analyzed prose models, and offered prescriptions for success, mostly centered on hard work. Outside the class, I faced another challenge. I had enrolled in Introductory Spanish, a noncredit course that would prepare me for the required foreign language exam. My knowledge of Spanish was limited to a few Mexican food items, but I was supremely motivated. At stake was an advanced degree and the dream of an English education career. So I sat in the front row, attended every class, and studied hard.

The Spanish instructor was a severe-looking woman with arched eyebrows, apparently an honors graduate of the Marquis de Sade School of Language Education. Part of her method was to pace the room restlessly, her high-heel shoes clicking on the tile, as she explained language concepts in staccato, no-nonsense fashion. Then she would square her shoulders, direct us to close our texts and notebooks, and begin to snap her fingers in fierce metronome fashion, pointing at individuals to elicit memorized conjugations and vocabulary. Wrong responses were met with a withering glance and immediate correction. Most of the time I felt like a rabbit frozen in its tracks, paralyzed by the blinding headlights of her unrelenting expectations. My heart pounded fearfully.

Five weeks into the semester, I was more discouraged than ever. My teaching partner and I agreed that the breakthroughs we had envisioned for the field house—our students' liberation from their backgrounds of oppression—were long overdue. Some students remained sullen and unresponsive; others made only halfhearted attempts to develop and revise their essays; still others were not showing up for class or for tutoring sessions. And in my Spanish class, I dreaded the feeling of rising panic each day, my fear erasing whatever faint neural traces had been laid down the night before. Although I tried to breathe deeply and relax, my neocortex filled with static whenever the finger snapping began. About all I was learning was how to hate Spanish and how to feel stupid.

Something had to give. So I switched responsibilities with my partner—she agreed to do the field house work so I could coach individuals and small groups—and I gave up on Spanish. Licking my wounds, I recalled a short story that I had written with advice from my high school students and published two years earlier, one depicting the evasions and blame-game tactics of a teacher not able to relate to his students (Strong 1969). The title, drawn from the first act of *Hamlet*, now echoed with irony: "Why, What Should Be the Fear?"

My first instincts, of course, were to blame students and the shameless lack of direction from program managers, and if these targets seemed too transparently self-serving, I could always blame the system that produced marginally literate young men and women and sent them, like sheep to slaughter, to a world-class university campus that prided itself on its high standards and academic reputation. With just a little effort, I knew I could puff myself up with self-righteous indignation. Models for such discourse were everywhere around me, part of the cultural currency for the era.

I had just begun to understand the reality I faced, and my smugness was long gone. Left behind was my ignorance about language learning. I had played the role of teacher, pontificating from the platform of my vast experience about the virtues of "trying hard" and "putting emphasis on organization" and "making sure to proofread." While perhaps good advice, such platitudes had badly missed the mark on at least two counts: first, they kept basic writers at arm's length—or even further; and, second, they failed to address the real questions of students. What students wanted to know was how to get started and find ideas, how to sequence and develop their points, how to sound knowledgeable and correct their mistakes.

My dramatic failures at both teaching and learning language forced me to reflect on how I might approach my new coaching assignment. I tried to imagine the pressures that minority students probably felt, as perhaps the first people in their families to even have a *chance* at higher education. In terms of risks to self-esteem, they clearly had as much at psychological stake as I did—and maybe more. Did they have the same frozen, trapped feeling I'd experienced in Spanish? If so, how would we work together to get past that feeling of helplessness? What else would it take from me—and them—to begin the business of learning to write?

And there was another basic question: how could I use my real experience from the past—coaching approaches that had worked at least some of the time—as I tried to repair the damage of the first few weeks and mend the tattered fabric of self-respect?

Invisible Coaching

And so it was that I inquired into the backgrounds of my students, asked what they wanted at each meeting, and simply *listened* to their responses, both verbal and nonverbal. Listening was not easy, I discovered, because some students had histories of racial anger and suspicion that complicated our conversations, while others were fearful and discouraged, like me. A third group, of course, was avoiding the hard work of the course because of late-night stimulation offered by the university's social scene.

Regardless of their orientation, most basic writers wanted someone to "fix" whatever was wrong with their text and "make it okay." That was why they showed up for tutoring. I tried to meet this need, but I also knew that merely correcting their drafts amounted to a perverse form of academic welfare, one that would not serve them well in the long run. The challenge, I felt, was to give students what they wanted as I helped them acquire strategies that would serve their long-term learning. The trick, in short, was to make my coaching invisible.

My decision to trust my coaching instincts—and to abandon the messianic stance of the syllabus—began to change my relationship with students and the dynamics of our daily encounters. Over time, some wanted to know more about me and what it was like to live among Mormons in Utah. Others wanted advice on how to study and take notes in large lecture classes. A few felt comfortable enough to share a laugh or two. In taking time to listen to students and trying to understand the ways in which they made sentences, I discovered for myself what Mina Shaughnessy would eloquently describe later in *Errors and Expectations*: that basic writers "write the way they do, not because they are slow, or nonverbal, indifferent to or incapable of academic excellence, but because they are beginners and must, like all beginners, learn by making mistakes" (1977, 5). The essence of good coaching, I learned, lies in a relationship that both parties, teacher and learner, regard as "working together."

It was impossible not to think about the Spanish class as I met with writing students individually or in small groups. Experience had taught me how anxiety could completely shut down the processes of language learning. I knew that I had masked my fear so that no one, least of all my instructor, had a clue about my true state of panic. This memory, still fresh and stinging, now prompted a quieter style of working. I wanted students to feel relaxed in their exchanges with me, to know that no question was dumb as far as I was concerned and that I respected their efforts. I applauded anyone with courage enough to show up for tutoring.

Coaching minority students also forced me to get real—to speak in plain, clear terms about matters close at hand. By drawing analogies from their real-life experiences, I tried to help them think about planning—how they might approach a writing task and find a way into it, just as they had found a way from their home neighborhoods to the university campus. We made lists and drew diagrams and did freewriting and used oral dialogues and learned how to appropriate the language of others as support for emerging, half-formed ideas. As the semester progressed, such artifacts gradually began to appear in their journals, which I read and commented on.

Many students had internalized a two-step model of writing from high school classes. First they drafted; then they submitted the text for correction. Typically, they resisted re-writing not only because of the extra work involved but also because they had little sense of what to do beyond recopying or retyping their original material. At first, we practiced adding or developing ideas; then we considered how one might rearrange parts of a text; and finally, we dealt with changing or deleting both sentences and paragraphs. With the latter types of revision, students sometimes got tense and defensive. They wanted me to fix their papers, but they didn't want me "messing" with a text in which they were now psychologically invested. Given the tensions of race and power bristling beneath the surface, it was a tricky situation.

Finally, I tried a two-step response—the first to get their attention, the second to provide scaffolded instruction. When students whined about revising, I nodded and sympathized and then opened a metal file box with a seven hundred-page manuscript, my never-to-be-published novel begun in the halcyon days of high school teaching. I explained how it had traveled close by my side from Utah in a 1950 Dodge van with a rusted-out body and an oil-guzzling engine. I showed them fat folders of scribbled corrections to my second draft, then thumbed through the final copy, done on a manual typewriter.

"You *typed* all that?" they asked.

"Two and three times," I replied. "So how about your revisions?"

My second response was to bring in a book-length manuscript of sentence-combining exercises, ones I had developed over three years of work in middle school, high school, and adult basic education classes in Idaho, Utah, and Colorado. Writing was a kind of game, I explained, and certain skills could be learned through practice. We wouldn't use grammar terms or fill-in-the-blank approaches from the past. Instead, we'd build upon what they already knew. In oral language, they had already learned how to take basic ideas and link them into longer, more complex sentences. Now, we'd explore this same skill in written language. Doing so would help them see and hear many sentence options. With practice in selecting effective sentences, they'd be better equipped to reenter their essays and rework the prose for clarity.

Because some students had athletic backgrounds, I drew analogies to workouts in the weight room. Just as weight training developed flexibility and strength, practice with sentence combining could strengthen their language muscles, I asserted. With practice, they'd surely learn to make sentences that "sounded better" and had fewer mistakes. Why? Because the *content* of the exercise was provided and all they had to worry about was the *form* of written expression. We talked about taking chances with sentences, about not playing it safe. Making mistakes was okay, I emphasized; in fact, usage errors would give us something to talk about and learn from, thereby *speeding up* their learning. They'd practice revising in sentence combining, then apply what they'd learned in the game of real writing. By developing some basic technical skills, they'd also develop an ability to revise.

I tried to communicate the expectations of oral sentence combining in easy warm-up exercises like the following one (Strong 1973, 15)—this to prepare students for more challenging narrative/descriptive or expository/persuasive exercises.

Street Scene

  1. A dude swaggers down the sidewalk.
  2. He clicks his fingers to the beat.

  3. He is tuned in to music.
  4. He is tuned in to verbal hysteria.
  5. These come from his radio.

  6. The sound jerks ahead of him.
  7. It bounces ahead of him.

  8. It announces his arrival to the shoppers.
  9. It announces his arrival to the storekeepers.
 10. It announces his arrival to the girls in the café.

 11. One girl giggles.
 12. She blushes.
 13. She tries to look bored.
 14. She tries to look very cool.

 15. The scene is tense.
 16. The scene is clicking.

                                                                                   ■

The point of sentence combining, I'd emphasize, was to make *good* sentences, not long ones. And as basic writers combined sentences on a first pass through the exercise, the result would sometimes look like the following passage, with heavy use of coordination and some unconventional uses of punctuation and capitalization. Such an effort, relying on a loose linkage of ideas with "and-and-and" syntax, takes few linguistic risks (see, for example, the second cluster, a transformation of sentences 3–5) and then gets into more trouble in the fifth cluster (the transformation of sentences 11–14).

Street Scene 1

A dude swaggers down the Sidewalk, and clicks his fingers to the beat. He is tuned in to music and verbal hysteria, and these come from his radio. The Sound jerks and bounces ahead of him. It announces his arrival to the shoppers, store-keepers and to the girls in the café. One girl giggles and blushes, she tries to look bored and very cool. The scene is tense and clicking.

■

We might transcribe a first effort like this one to serve as a point of reference for further passes and attention to mechanics, but often we'd simply begin to play with syntactic possibilities. What happens if *clicks* becomes *clicking* in cluster 1? And how about the word *swagger*? Can its form be changed to create a new option? Working together in this way, the student and I might generate the following stylistic options for cluster 1:

- A dude swaggers down the sidewalk, clicking his fingers to the beat.
- Swaggering down the sidewalk, a dude clicks his fingers to the beat.
- A dude, swaggering down the sidewalk, clicks his fingers to the beat.

■

"Say the options aloud," I'd advise. "Sure, they're all correct, but listen for the one that seems to sound best in the paragraph context." And if the student were with me, picking up on the challenge to take risks, we might extend the options further:

- As a dude swaggers down the sidewalk, he clicks his fingers to the beat.
- With fingers clicking, a dude swaggers to the beat down the sidewalk.
- Down the sidewalk comes a swaggering, finger-clicking dude.

■

Demonstrations like these—playfully trying out sentences in context—gave students a feel for what was expected in homework assignments. After we'd worked together to create oral sentence options for the various clusters, we'd talk about the idea of listening to language—punctuating by ear—and checking hunches against the patterns in written language. And then we might look back at a problem sentence from the first pass:

- One girl giggles and blushes, she tries to look bored and very cool.

■

Sometimes I'd ask students if anything about this sentence made them uncertain or uneasy. Many would answer my question with one of their own: "Maybe the comma?" Sometimes we'd compare the intonation contour of a problem sentence to ones punctuated conventionally:

- One girl giggles and blushes, trying to look bored and very cool.
- One girl, giggling and blushing, tries to look bored and very cool.

■

And sometimes I'd remind them of previous lessons concerning our old friend, the comma splice. We'd review the idea of stand-alone, but closely related, sentences being connected by a comma, a "weak" punctuation mark, and we'd then discuss how to make the comma "stronger" by converting it into a semicolon, a punctuation mark with the same stopping power as a period but with the ability to link parallel ideas:

- One girl giggles and blushes; she tries to look bored and very cool.

                                                                                                    ∎

After such a minilesson, semicolon usage would often become epidemic, to use Mina Shaughnessy's memorable term. So then we'd explore new ways to embed words and phrases or manage clause subordination. I'd encourage students to think aloud as they did this work and to apply these small lessons to their own writing.

Students who had resisted my field house teaching earlier in the fall were now trying, with varying degrees of success, to revise their prose. I could see how flawed transformations, including what Shaughnessy (1977) would later call "blurred patterns" and various types of "consolidation errors," often emerged from certain habits of oral expression or from losing track of an initial direction and having only a vague sense of parallel structure. Many students appeared to avoid basic transformations, such as relative clauses or adverb clauses, because they were unsure about how to punctuate them; it also seemed clear that their repertoire of literary linguistic moves, such as participial phrases, appositives, and absolutes, had never really been developed, perhaps because of limited reading experience. And finally I saw what students knew about syntax ("Never use *and* to begin a sentence.") as well as what they didn't know about conventions such as punctuation, spelling, and usage.

After plenty of practice—and my occasional coaching to combine the combining and to leave some sentences uncombined for emphasis—small teams of basic writers sometimes achieved texts like the following one, its "chunking" of related ideas signaling linguistic progress:

Street Scene 2

With fingers clicking, the dude is tuned in to the music's beat and to verbal hysteria that come from his radio. He swaggers down the sidewalk. The sound jerks and bounces ahead of him, announcing his arrival to store-keepers, shoppers, and girls in the café. One of them, who tries to look bored and very cool, giggles and blushes. The scene clicks with tension.

                                                                                                    ∎

As students became more adept at producing this kind of text, with appropriate use of relative clause transformations, sentence openers, and parallel structure in predicate and noun phrases, it seemed reasonable to expect that such syntax would begin to emerge in their real essays, the ones so dominated by the conventions of oral language, snarled constructions, and an array of errors in mechanics.

It was all there, vividly enacted as I watched from the sidelines. Eighteen months later, the earlier warm-up exercise would become part of a textbook focused on whole-discourse sentence combining; for now, however, it was fascinating to see how basic writers puzzled their way through clusters of kernel sentences.

The Game of Pattern Recognition

It was during the second semester of my first doctoral year that I signed up for another foreign language class. Having learned my lesson in Spanish, I decided on Introductory French. The instructor was a shuffling, dumpy-looking man with a gravy-stained tie and large crescents of sweat under his short-sleeved shirt. His name was Mr. Baker, and if heaven has a hall of fame for language coaches, his name should be attached to one of the premier seats.

Sitting on the front edge of a desk, with belly hanging over his belt, Mr. Baker explained to the assembled graduate students that he understood our goal—to pass the French reading exam, not to learn French—and that he'd help us do just that.

"We'll take it a step at a time," he said. "You just relax and take it in."

Sure, we'd have assignments, but the thing was, you had to trust yourself, not try too hard. He'd learned that from experience. The key was being relaxed, letting yourself have fun. And looking for the patterns, of course. We'd probably like that part; at least, most students did. And, oh Lord, he'd taught so many students over the years and, yes, they'd been nervous just like us, but most of them had had some fun as they learned—French was a beautiful language, after all—and no way was he going to embarrass anybody in class, so not to worry about that. Not to worry at all. He'd been teaching a long time now, and he knew about how long it took, so if we didn't have any questions, we'd probably better get started. Was that okay?

That is the essence of what Mr. Baker said, along with the footnote, almost an afterthought, that if some of us wanted to challenge the department's competency exam after the first semester's work, we could do that. It would be a very, very long shot, of course—most students took two semesters to pass—but some of us might want to think about that goal. Could we get started now?

Each day Mr. Baker wore the same tie, and each day I felt my veneerlike understanding of written French deepen ever so slightly. I looked for the patterns just as he urged and—lo!—there they were. I made lists of French words and enjoyed the feeling of being able to recognize them in context. And I looked forward to class every bit as much as I had dreaded my Spanish class the semester before.

Was French an easier language than Spanish? Or had I gotten smarter during the past few months? Or was I being coached in a more effective, humane way?

The correct answer seemed self-evident to me. To experience such a dramatic turnaround in feeling—one rooted in how I perceived myself as a language learner—was a lesson never to be forgotten, one that informs my teaching to this day.

Meanwhile, I tried some of the inductive approaches to pattern recognition with the basic writers. Scanning a student text, for example, I might find a transition word or phrase and use this as an exemplar for the concept of signposts. Then the student and I would read paragraphs of expository text or work with a combining exercise to get practice identifying other signposts. Afterward, we'd try to create an organizing structure of transitions within the student's essay.

Increasingly, too, when students wanted me to edit their papers, I'd simply put check marks in the margin, each one signaling an error in spelling, punctuation, or usage. I then used the marks as a basis for coaching. As students read back through their sentences, trying out hypotheses about their errors—"Just take a guess," I'd say—I was able to learn what needed explanation or reinforcement.

In another hands-on approach, either the students or I would select a tangled, overly complicated sentence from a draft in progress, and I'd decombine it into underlying propositions or kernel sentences. The goals of combining, I'd remind them, were clarity and economy, not obfuscation. Then we'd set to work, trying to figure out the intended meaning. Typically, writers would pursue combining in a straightforward way; then come to a point of hesitation, with meanings beginning to break down; and finally there would be silence, somewhere short of the goal.

"So what's the *basic* idea here?" I'd ask. "Let's back up and start there."

The sentences produced through this back-to-the-basics revising were often shorter, clearer, and easier to read than the ones that served as source material. They provided a solid foundation for adding or embedding new ideas. While many students appreciated the clear improvements that followed such hands-on work, others still tried to get me to do such work for them. Certain habits of mind have amazing persistence.

Later, as I helped students make lists of points that they could organize and develop—and as we read back through their essays, looking for ways to strengthen the cohesion ties among sentences—I came to see how sentence combining might prompt students to generate ideas. For example, transformed sentences could be used as a base for expanded pieces of description and narration as shown in the following exercise:

Street Scene 2 (Exercise)

With fingers clicking, the dude is tuned in to the beat of music and to the verbal hysteria that come from his radio.

- What does the dude look like? What kind of music does he hear? What is the verbal hysteria?

He swaggers down the sidewalk.

- What do his head, shoulders, and feet do? How do you picture the sidewalk?

The sound jerks and bounces ahead of him, announcing his arrival to the shoppers, storekeepers, and girls in the café.

- What do people do? What are their expressions?

One of them, trying to look bored and very cool, giggles and blushes.

- How do you picture the girl?

The scene clicks with tension.

- What happens next?

■

Using questions as scaffolds—first my questions, then theirs—students began to see how texts are sometimes framed in terms of general, orienting sentences as well as more specific details that provide interest. And when I created sentence-combining exercises derived from the cumulative sentence models of Francis Christensen (1967), students were encouraged to use patterns such as appositives and participial phrases in exercises like the previous one and in essays they'd brought in for fixing. For example, the Street Scene exercise might become a text like this:

Street Scene 3

With fingers clicking and eyes half-closed, the lanky dude from South Side Chicago is tuned in to the beat of reggae music and DJ patter, the verbal hysteria coming from his radio. He swaggers down the hot sidewalk like a rooster, with head and shoulders bobbing and his pointed patent leather shoes doing little dance steps. The sound, jerking and bouncing ahead of him, announces his arrival to the shoppers, storekeepers, and girls in the café. Some laugh and some frown, and some just shake their heads, pointing to the weird performance. "Is he high?" they wonder. One of the girls, a fox with big hair and looped gold earrings, tries to look bored and very cool as the dude shuffles in her direction. She giggles and blushes.
  "Hey, baby," he says.
  "In your dreams," she replies.
  The scene clicks with tension.

∎

Students liked exercises like this one. But equally important, they came to see how revision might involve a process of layering in relevant details in response to questions. We discussed how pictures in their minds needed to be explicit and detailed for the reader. Although such an exercise would sometimes produce overwriting, the goal of elaboration seemed like a vital one. Later, I discovered support for my intuitions in *Teaching the Universe of Discourse* (Moffett 1968; 1983), a book I came to regard as the Rosetta stone for English education, with James Moffett's assertion that "sentences must grow rank before they can be trimmed" (1983, 72).

Finally, at the end of the semester, I challenged the French reading exam and passed it comfortably. Afterward, I put a note of thanks in Mr. Baker's mailbox, along with a pint of Johnnie Walker Scotch whiskey. I had surmised from his occasionally disheveled appearance that such a gift might not be unwelcome. What my note might truthfully have said is that, thanks to his laconic, plodding manner and his invitation to pay attention to patterns, he had turned out to be just the teacher I needed: an easygoing workhorse, with none of the high-stepping, flashy footwork that had thrown me in Spanish. I welcomed Mr. Baker's exercise routines and practice structures just as some of my basic writers seemed to welcome our little forays into syntax and usage.

When a few of my students dropped by on their way out of town, headed for Chicago and other exotic locations, I told them about passing the language exam.

"All right," they said. "You *did* it."

"So did *you*," I replied. "You're on your way."

The field house seemed like a distant loss. Thanks to the patience of my students—and a little good luck—I had survived the basics of coaching.

Thinking About the Basics

It was several years later, during the summer of 1978 at the Bay Area Writing Project, that I tried to think more seriously about the coaching of writing. Donald Murray came to town, and we had dinner in a Berkeley restaurant with lazy overhead fans, white plastered walls, and blue tile floors. The Man himself was barrel-chested and congenial, with white furrowing eyebrows above intense, listening eyes. He claimed curiosity in the work I'd been doing, then adroitly shifted focus. And what about my personal writing? He nodded, smiled, and asked all the right questions.

In the last week of the institute, a final consultant came to visit, one whose views contrasted sharply with those of earlier luminaries—Donald Graves, Marilyn Hampf Buckley, Arthur Applebee, and Murray himself. A chief reader for the College Board Exams, this consultant had also been my English methods instructor in college. She was poised, authoritative, and supremely articulate about language—in fact, a kind of barracuda in her intimidating advocacy for direct grammar instruction, plenty of error correction, and no-nonsense high standards. Teachers around me fell silent under her challenge, and I myself had little to say. But inside, thinking about what I had learned from my basic writing students, I was furious.

That night, in a bare apartment with a red sleeping bag stretched on the floor, I drafted three pages of notes that I would use in tomorrow's showdown. I contrasted a mechanistic approach, the didactic learning of sentence parts followed by application and correction, with a Zen approach, one in which a relaxed awareness of patterns and details, coupled with practice, might help learners develop a more confident feel for writing. Outcomes of error correction in speech seemed obvious: stuttering, fearful silence, and the gaps in memory I'd experienced in Spanish. Outcomes of correction in writing were more subtle: cramped, illegible handwriting, anxiety, avoidance of risks, unwillingness to say more or to persevere, and the arms-folded sullenness of mental shutdown. The Zen approach, by contrast, was a path of balance, a path of fluency *and* discipline. It meant sustaining the flow of language, but it also meant *meaningful* skill building, the kind that would develop voice, stimulate imagination, add vocabulary, teach conventions, internalize genre, and increase language confidence.

I imagined a continuum for speaking and a parallel one for writing, with both spontaneous (interactive) activities and rehearsed (formalized) activities to develop fluency and craft, respectively. Among the rehearsed speech acts were jokes, campfire stories, and lies. Among the rehearsed writing acts were poems and narratives, profiles and essays, reports and arguments. I imagined a vertical strand of reading/writing tasks to help students internalize the conventions and features of various genres.

The Zen approach, I reasoned, had inner game and outer game dimensions (Gallwey 1976). As Donald Murray had explained, the act of writing often involved a contest of wills between a controlling, critical voice and the expressive voice of the writer. The inner game was a psychological contest. Given its way, Murray said, the nagging, know-it-all voice of the critical self would shut down writing before it ever got started. The defense of the writing self lay in the self-discipline of daily journal writing, timed fluency exercises, a cultivation of language play and surprise, attention to revision and editing *after* drafting, and deliberate tricks to quiet the critical self.

The outer game, it seemed, was the text itself—its ideas, organization, and coherence, as well its voice and surface features. Certainly there were basic principles and strategies for outer game success, such as ways to gain the attention of readers, emphasize and argue a thesis, or connect generalizations to examples. But success in the outer game demanded some level of inner game success.

I thought about the physiology of writing, specifically, the learned sequence of behaviors for transcribing inner voice. Presumably, writers drew upon this voice, held its unfolding syntax in short-term memory, then modified their transcription. What, then, were sentence-combining exercises? Could they perhaps offer another channel to transcription fluency, one useful to students who had shut down mentally or had reached a syntactic plateau? Clearly, the exercises involved speech-into-writing, first voiced, then subvocalized; but they also required writing-into-speech, the work with syntax options. So perhaps they were akin to the dictation activities in my parochial school background. Perhaps they distracted the critical self so that the writing self, the one that did the *work* of writing, could retrain itself naturally. If so, this would mean that the writing self was paying attention to language, the ultimate teacher.

And the showdown in Berkeley? Suffice it to say that kindred spirits joined me on the field of discourse and we held our own. Here, just for the record, are points I *wish* I'd made about writing in general and sentence combining (SC) in particular.

- Some writing difficulties result not from an inability to think and organize but rather from a lack of skill in transcribing the tentative whispers of an inner voice. By working with such skills, we address the play-it-safe syndrome and release students from some of the fear that inhibits their inner game activity.

- Outer game skills are not enhanced via direct grammar instruction but rather through functional SC practice to strengthen the speech-to-writing connection— namely, the echo of inner speech, the imagery of syntax patterns, and the coherence or feel of well-developed paragraphs that students help construct.

- Fluency activities work best when done regularly for brief periods and when students understand reasons for the activities; the aim, always, is to increase skills through scaffolding. As Vygotsky (1978) pointed out, whatever language tasks learners can do collaboratively, they can eventually do on their own.

- Transcribing fluency enables us—literally—to put down words while others are held in memory or arise from verbal consciousness. John Mellon (1981) called this "two-channel thinking." SC builds such fluency and prompts students to write more varied, syntactically mature sentences. Without some degree of fluency, we cannot attend to the meaning-making demands of the inner game.

- Transcribing fluency and automaticity in reading seem essential for distancing ourselves from words on a page and revising them in light of reconsidered ideas or intentions. James Moffett (1968, 1983) called this "decentering." The ability to become deeply and totally absorbed in decentering seems to characterize the psychological state known as "flow" (Csikszentmihalyi 1990).

- Flow experiences in writing, like those in athletics and in the arts, meet certain conditions: clear goals and unambiguous feedback and a balance between opportunities to act and the ability to act (Csikszentmihalyi, Rathunde, and Whalen

1993). "When the conditions of flow are present and individuals engage in these activities, their skill increases and they seek out more and more complex versions of these activities" (Hillocks 1995, 21). *Challenge underlies flow.*

- For perspective, we need to remind ourselves—and our students—of Donald Murray's point that "syntax often breaks down when we approach a new and interesting meaning, something we have thought before or are afraid of thinking, or sabotages what we had thought before" (1984, 39). Having difficulty means that we're probably on the right track, not that something is wrong with us. The point is to learn from the difficulties, not to avoid them.

We will explore these points more fully in the chapters that follow, focusing first on syntax, usage, and style and later on paragraphing, voice, and imagination. And in Chapter 9, "Coaching Genre," we will return to the theme of the inner game of writing, and to Murray's aforementioned point, more directly and personally.

Learning Through Language

1. In Chapter 1, the term *basics* is used in at least three senses, referring to a type of student ("basic writers"), a focus for language arts coaching, and a philosophy of instruction. Jot down key points of your learning about the basics in these three areas. Then circle one of your points for more extended writing. Elaborate through personal examples or reflections—or by challenging the text. Finally, share your writing with others in your group.

2. Find three paragraphs, at different points in the chapter, that especially interest you. Perhaps the description evokes images in your mind, perhaps the sentences seem well-crafted, or perhaps the ideas are provocative. Copy a single sentence from each passage. Then in follow-up writing, explain why you focused on each of these sentences. That is, what was it in this language that reached you? Be prepared to share your work with others.

3. If the chapter was effective, it raised questions in your mind and prompted certain predictions about the rest of the book's content. Write a letter to a partner in class (with a copy to your instructor, if so directed) that first raises the questions you are thinking about and then makes predictions about the chapters to follow. Upon receiving your partner's letter, assume the imagined persona of the author to respond, in writing, to the questions asked and the predictions made.

CHAPTER 2

COACHING SYNTAX

Sentence Combiners Chant

Get the beat! Tap your feet!
There's nothing to it!
Chant this rhyme at any time—
Let your syntax do it!

Sentences! Sentences!
Simple and complex!
Feel so fine as you combine—
Let syntax stand for sex!

A Coaching Flashback

My first experiments with syntax coaching began during the political turbulence of 1968, six months after attending a National Defense Education Act (NDEA) summer institute that provided instruction in archetypal literary criticism, the rhetoric of Kenneth Burke, and the arcane science of transformational grammar. To say that this Olympian curriculum was remote from secondary school realities would be an understated—and generous—assessment.

Like other teachers, I left the institute with lots of questions. The classroom uses for tree diagrams could vary, we had heard, depending on our goals. Given this sage advice, I never imagined that my own discovery of an application for grammar theory would present itself, unexpectedly, in a small Idaho town near Sun Valley, with sunlight glinting off fresh snow and brand-new skis strapped to my VW beetle.

I had deeply mixed feelings about attending another Saturday language arts conference, but finally professional guilt had won out. How could I urge others to get involved in staff development, I asked myself, if I ducked out of meetings like this? Curiously, this small decision became the most far-reaching choice of my career—a point that I hope is not lost upon new teachers in particular. Sometimes, as Shakespeare once put it, "the readiness is all."

In a drafty auditorium stood Dr. Lalia Boone from the University of Idaho, and one of her grammar activities involved a few short sentences for grade school students.

"Yes," I thought. "Of *course*."

The idea of developing whole-discourse exercises for secondary learners—tasks to demonstrate stylistic and rhetorical principles—was immediately clear to me. Such an activity would work, I knew, because it would be interactive, have multiple right answers, and draw upon students' existing knowledge to *extend* their syntax skills. I also knew, with a teacher's sixth sense, that working with sentence options would help bridge the enormous gap between transformational principles and the practical challenges of writing instruction. Such activities might even tease out familiar errors in syntax, with the context offering a nonthreatening way to teach mechanics.

That night, as powder snow fell in the Idaho mountains, I added new paragraphs to my gestating novel and wrote my first exercise using kernel sentences. And the next day I skied the wide-open trails of new terrain until my legs burned.

In the weeks that followed, I field-tested the new exercises in junior high school classrooms. Each exercise was put on a transparency. After a demonstration of what was expected, I'd ask students to combine sentences. They liked working together, so I began to organize them in pairs and small groups. I encouraged students to talk out their sentences before writing them down. Then volunteers would share the sentence options they had produced. At this point, the attention of seventh graders sometimes waned, although we usually had fun with the outrageous sentences they had written.

The problem, I realized, was that spoken sentences immediately evaporated in our sharing sessions. This prompted me to start sending students to the chalkboard so that we could see *and* hear their sentence options. Although working at the board was an improvement, it was still less than ideal because of the time involved and because of management problems—the difficulty of keeping students focused on target sentences rather than ones written by their friends. Finally, I hit upon the idea of having students write on blank transparencies with water-soluble pens. This was fun for them and a management breakthrough as far as I was concerned. I sometimes put two or three transparencies on the overhead projector at once so students could study the options and we could discuss their preferences. They liked this activity.

At about the same time, other teachers and I began assigning the exercises as homework, the task being for students to make the best sentences possible from the given material. We encouraged students to do what they had done in small groups: generate a few sentence options for each cluster of kernel sentences and then make choices based on what sounded good. I'd collect the homework, flip through the papers in the teachers workroom, and underline a single great sentence in each of several papers. Then I'd come back to class and read sentences aloud, pausing dramatically before revealing each author. Spontaneous applause sometimes followed.

It occurred to me that transparencies could become part of the Great Sentence activity. So I took home sets of papers, underlined a great sentence in each one, and came back to class with blank transparencies and pens. The original papers would go out to students, and they'd copy a single underlined sentence onto a transparency. Within five minutes, the teacher would have thirty or more good sentences to put on the overhead projector for praise and discussion. We often extended this activity over a one-week cycle, with a few sentences put in the spotlight each day.

Over time, as students became comfortable with expectations and the idea of writing on transparencies, we focused on problem sentences. The setup was identical. Now, however, the teacher and I flipped through papers to spot errors in mechanics and usage. Again, we underlined a single sentence in each paper, and again, we brought papers back to class so that each student could copy a sentence to the transparency. I emphasized that we'd work together to figure out solutions to problem sentences. It was errors, after all, that enabled us to learn useful new skills for the game of writing. And with coaching practice, I came to establish a final inviolate rule: that no one could laugh at another person's effort.

On the transparencies were anonymous sentences in a natural handwritten state. Typically, the mistakes included punctuation errors as well as problems in subject-verb agreement, misplaced modifiers, awkward constructions, and a rare fragment or two. To a language coach like me, the sentences were game films from the previous day's practice— real sentences done by real seventh graders, not by textbook editors in a New York office. Because content was provided in the exercise, students had no reason to feel defensive about the ideas of the text. Our focus was basic sentence construction, pure and simple.

Coaching like this was great fun. After the third problem sentence went up, some students would grin. They'd never understood the idea of a run-on sentence before, but now they could see and hear the pattern, one emphasized in my oral reading. New hands would edge up at the back of the room.

"Run-on sentence," someone would say.

"You got it." I'd reply. "How did you know?"

"Like the others."

"So how do you fix it? Volunteers?"

More hands would go up. As a class, we'd then focus on the transparency, making changes in punctuation or word order so that the sentence met all of the usual conventions of Standard English. Students would transcribe a corrected version in their grammar notebooks, along with whatever key points had been discussed. With run-on sentences, for example, students could either copy the class solution or come up with another solution that they personally preferred. The notebooks helped personalize and organize what students were learning about language. Finally, of course, we asked students to apply proofreading skills to their own papers.

It was a few months later, at the University of Nebraska NDEA Institute, that I shared this work with a congenial visiting professor, Francis Christensen, whose course was based on principles in *Notes Toward a New Rhetoric* (1967). Christensen wanted students to become "sentence acrobats," to "dazzle by their syntactic dexterity" (15). He focused attention on model sentences written by contemporary writers and showed us how elegantly crafted prose often violated the stylistic prescriptions in handbooks. In class we practiced sentence imitations, which were challenging and fun, and for homework we applied what we had learned in page-length descriptions and narrations. Because this was 1968, before photocopiers had come into widespread use, we submitted our work on purple ditto masters, and these provided the raw material, along with Christensen's marginal notes, for in-class workshops. For me, his research-based ideas and student-friendly methods struck a deeply responsive chord.

And so it was that I showed up in his office.

"Sentence combining," he said.

It was the first time I'd ever heard the term. Christensen told me that Kellogg Hunt had conducted research on such tasks and that John Mellon had just finished a dissertation at Harvard that showed large gains in syntactic maturity for students who learned transformational grammar and practiced sentence combining.

"Interesting," I said.

"You're all on the wrong track," he replied, without a smile.

Christensen then explained his reservations—his hypothesis that aimless practice in sentence combining would ultimately teach bad writing. Such writing would be characterized by bloated noun clauses, passive voice, and endless strings of prepositional phrases. In other words, I was unwittingly teaching a turgid prose style found in social science journals and government documents. Although syntactically mature by Hunt's measures, such writing had to be labeled for what it truly was: a rhetorical disaster, an educational travesty. Surely I was bright enough to see that.

Leaving Christensen's office, with exercises under my arm, I had much to think about. But I also had Kellogg Hunt's address, the title of John Mellon's research report, and a copy of Christensen's essay "The Problem of Defining a Mature Style," which had appeared in the *English Journal* in April 1968, to challenge the premises of sentence combining as well as its effects. My language education had just begun.

Syntax Previsited

Because Chapter 1 and the preceding section offer a narrative introduction to sentence combining, this chapter briefly considers basic theory and then addresses practical matters: how to get students involved in exercises, how to link exercises to real writing, and how to create exercises for different teaching goals. The point of a good language exercise is to help students pay attention to text and assume increasing control over their own planning, drafting, and revising processes.

In other words, work with syntax should always provide support, or scaffolding, for ongoing composition instruction. Think of it this way: real writing offers a context for hands-on exercises, but exercises, in turn, can help students approach composing tasks, such as revision, with fresh strategies. The same principle holds true, in my opinion, for attention to usage and style, paragraphing, and many other language-centered topics considered in later chapters.

As I see it, language learners construct three kinds of knowledge about language. There is *declarative knowledge*, a knowledge about matters like parts of speech or cleft transformations; there is *procedural knowledge*, a knowledge of how to make effective transitions or reduce clauses to phrases; and there is *conditional knowledge*, a knowledge of when to apply the other two types. For example, the sentence you are now reading results from my conditional knowledge that it is time for an illustration to follow the definitions. However, the idea that readers of expository text *need* examples is declarative knowledge, part of our discipline's knowledge base. Finally, procedural knowledge is demonstrated in my transitions—like *for example*, *however*, and *finally*—to signal the three previous illustrations, now mercifully behind us.

During the last century, many English teachers assumed that declarative knowledge about syntax had an instrumental effect on students' use of language. But research on grammar instruction revealed otherwise (Braddock, Lloyd-Jones, and Schoer 1963; Hillocks 1986). So despite heroic efforts to teach students how to do things with syntax—with the same definitions and routines repeated year after year in secondary grades—grammar instruction seemed to have no discernible effects on procedural knowledge. What did seem to work were interventions in which procedural knowledge itself was the focus of instruction, that is, the sentence-combining research.

The utility of sentence combining was confirmed by George Hillocks (1984, 1986) in his landmark metanalysis of seventy-three experimental studies in composition. Five experimental studies on sentence combining met the rigorous criteria that Hillocks established. After statistically converting treatment effects from all studies to "standard scores," Hillocks compared the instructional effects of several approaches, one against the other, in terms of their "effect size," or "practical significance." Figure 2.1 is a summary graph from Hillocks' research (1995).

What is immediately striking is the disparity between the effects of traditional grammar instruction and the effects of the hands-on approach known as sentence combining. Whereas the direct teaching of grammar had *negative* effects on students' writing ability, the SC approach influenced composition in *positive* ways. Moreover, the treatment effects for SC were more positive than freewriting (journal writing alone or in preparation for formal writing), more positive than models (presentation and discussion of text features), and about the same as scales (use of explicit criteria as a guide for revision). Such findings suggest that SC has remarkably powerful effects on student writing, probably because it emphasizes procedural knowledge (how to do things) rather than declarative knowledge (names and functions of things).

When I first field-tested SC exercises in the late 1960s, I put all my eggs in the procedural knowledge basket. What mattered, I thought, was what students could *do* with language. I was fevered and eloquent—and no doubt insufferable—on the essential uselessness of terminology. After all, if kids had no use for such knowledge—and if the research was clear on the futility of such instruction—why beat a dead horse?

But today I am much less certain about such matters. In fact, I now see plenty of reason for students to have at least some declarative knowledge about language as a capstone for the procedural know-how acquired through experience. Why? Because once a certain level of procedural knowledge is attained, it may be enhanced by "knowing what you

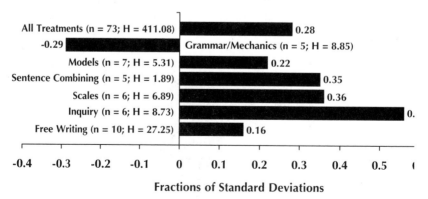

Figure 2.1   *Focus of Instruction: Experimental/Control Effects*
Reprinted by permission from *Teaching Writing as Reflective Practice* by George Hillocks, Jr. (New York: Teachers College Press).

know." Put another way, experiential learning probably remains less than complete unless we have opportunities to make sense of it. The technical term for such knowledge transformation is *metalinguistic awareness*, or what I called pattern recognition in Chapter 1.

My point is this: just as the writing process movement has increased students' procedural and declarative knowledge of writing strategies, certain types of SC activities can bring procedural knowledge about language to a level of conscious awareness. So although my belief in hands-on learning remains as "strong" as ever, I am increasingly interested in helping students know what they know in declarative terms and also in encouraging them to apply such knowledge to texts in which they are deeply invested.

Metalinguistic awareness will be a recurring theme in chapters that follow. If it is true that exercising language is the work of a lifetime, as I asserted in the Introduction, it is hard to imagine how such work can occur without some level of awareness.

Premises, Premises

Early SC research developed from the premise—and implied promise—that increased fluency, or maturity, at the sentence level might result in better writing. Despite the empirical claims, however, some theorists and writing teachers continue to doubt the efficacy of the SC approach. Although SC has become a familiar pedagogy for many, it is sometimes relegated to the dustbin of skills instruction by others.

The concerns of Peter Elbow are typical: "In sentence combining, the student is not engaged in figuring out what she wants to say or saying what is on her mind" (1985, 233). The student is "not saying anything to anyone," Elbow contends, and "the results . . . are more often 'answers' given to the teacher for correction—not 'writing' given to readers for reaction" (233). Although Elbow does see value in SC exercises that "face students with an array of acceptable answers," he worries that "the better and more fruitful the exercise, the worse the danger" (233–35).

To address such concerns, I first want to review the basic premises of SC practice and then urge that we consider the approach within a constructivist, or social language learning, framework. Understanding such premises may help us envision an interactive and collaborative rationale, one that transcends the goal of syntactic skill building, narrowly defined. My aim is to set the stage for advice, demonstrations, and caveats about SC practice in this chapter and later ones.

Syntactic fluency

As background, let me begin with the terms *fluency* and *maturity*. It is well established, of course, that increased elaboration and complexity are hallmarks of language growth in the middle and high school years (Hunt 1965; Scott 1988). It is also known that deliberate, sustained SC practice can enhance syntax development. For example, in Mellon's original research (1969), the growth rate for 250 experimental seventh graders from different schools and ability levels was more than *twice* the rate of control and placebo groups. Mellon called this enhanced growth "fluency" because of his belief that maturity resulted from normal growth in cognition and language. Although Mellon did not suggest that these syntax gains signaled underlying improvements in performance, O'Hare's (1973) follow-up research did link such growth to improvements in writing.

Stated in syllogistic form, then, the teaching premises of the syntactic fluency hypothesis, on which much SC work is based, go something like this (Strong 1986):

- Skilled writers produce quality writing.
- One evidence of writing skill is syntactic fluency.
- Therefore, demonstrable gains in syntactic fluency should lead to demonstrable gains in writing quality.

While not often articulated, these premises build upon the notion of automaticity—the idea that as certain behaviors such as linguistic transformations become habituated or automatic, one frees up cognitive space to attend to discourse-level functions like planning, organizing, and revising in light of one's aims and audience.

How can this be? Think back to the process of learning to drive a car, perhaps one with a clutch. Remember your fierce concentration on starting the car, trying to remember the location of first gear, checking the emergency brake release, pushing in the clutch, feathering the throttle, checking for traffic, and releasing the clutch with a sudden embarrassing lurch. Thankfully, you got better with practice. In fact, over time, whole sequences of skill became completely routine, so that now you welcome the drive to school, one that offers space to plan last-minute details of your day as you absentmindedly sip coffee and listen to *Morning Edition* and notice the quality of light off to the left, a reminder of that little trip to the Andrew Wyeth museum in Rockland, Maine. In driving and writing, so the argument goes, automaticity relieves us of low-level chores so that our attention can focus elsewhere—on dangers in the road ahead, for example, or on achieving the most direct route to our goal. In writing, more specifically, being freed from thinking about how to transcribe, punctuate, or make sentences allows us to think about the larger issues of ideas, organization, and strategy, the matters that make writing interesting and challenging and even fun.

Of course, critics of the syntactic fluency hypothesis are quick to point out that sentence fluency is only one discourse skill among many. Some question why syntax should receive such attention when students also struggle with many other aspects of writing. Joseph Williams (1986), for example, sees elaboration as a dubious blessing, particularly in the absence of informed writing instruction. After all, if students merely master the art of mind-numbing nominalization—and if teachers unwittingly reward bloated prose with high marks—what have we gained? We will return to this question.

Linguistic premises

Modern SC exercises are the no-account offspring of transformational theory. Specifically, the idea that big sentences are built from little ones became part of the standard SC rationale from the late 1960s forward. Although the analytic apparatus of grammar quickly fell by the wayside, many teachers retained the metaphors of *kernel sentence* and *transformations*. After all, these poetic notions invited attention to the slippery, interesting concept of stylistic options.

But if grammatical theory was the parent of SC practice, empirical research was the midwife. For example, when Hunt (1965, 1970) used SC rewriting tasks as a research tool, his aim was to show how increased clause length, depth of modification, and nominalization characterized naturally developing maturity in written syntax. When Mellon

(1969) linked grammar concepts to SC practice, the context was deliberately arhetorical, part of a course in language study. When O'Hare (1973) adapted Mellon's curriculum, albeit without grammatical cues, his effort was to induce target structures. From the beginning, then, the grammar-based premises for SC were coupled with research paradigms that emphasized syntax.

With insight, James Moffett (1968, 1983) challenged such premises. He worried that if a student "learns to coil and embed constructions as an extraneously motivated intellectual feat, he may write his own sentences without regard to the needs of the whole discourse in which they occur and which alone can provide the proper context for them" (1983, 170–71). "This point in no way undermines the essential validity of sentence-combining experience," Moffett added; "it merely argues for situating the experience within another setting" (171). He pointed to problems with the idea that longer, more complex clauses represent more mature writing. For one thing, "the tightness and readability of mature style depends on clause reduction" (173). For another, "sometimes a single well chosen word can replace an entire clause, producing a far simpler and far better sentence" (173).

Moffett's challenge, like that of Joseph Williams (1986) and Francis Christensen (1968), deserves response. After all, it is true that clause reduction—a stage *following* clause expansion—represents the upper end of a continuum for syntax. And it is true that loose, rambling sentences often result from our inability to access exact words for naming, describing, or qualifying the topic. And it is true that our understanding and use of conjunctive adverbs and intersentence connectors—like *however, conversely,* or *in other words*—seem to be a function of cognitive maturation as well as exposure to particular types of texts. At the very least, then, the syntactic fluency hypothesis should probably be amended as follows:

- Skilled writers produce quality writing.
- One evidence of writing skill is syntactic fluency.
- Therefore, syntactic fluency is a necessary *but not sufficient* condition for demonstrable gains in writing quality.

A skill-building rationale

A rationale for whole-discourse SC practice has several premises. First, "the point is to be *able,* not *obliged,* to complicate one's sentences," as Moffett (1983, 171) himself once wrote. Second, students generate sentence options in given-language materials to increase their ease of syntax production, their elaboration of clauses, and their later consolidation of clauses. Third, when such practice is managed in a playful, exploratory way that is linked to students' real writing, it can prompt genuine inquiry into syntax, heightened awareness of writing style, and increased facility in making informed, contextually sensitive choices. Fourth, the context of SC practice offers a hands-on way to teach elements of grammar and mechanics that many people, particularly test makers, see as essential standards. Fifth—and here the automaticity argument comes into play—SC practice can help some students attend to text more fully, so that the mental and physical routines of scanning sentences, rearranging parts, listening to cadence, embedding new details, and tightening for emphasis become absolutely habitual, as natural as breathing in, breathing out.

At the very least, then, SC practice is a humane and practical alternative to conventional grammar instruction. Any activity that engages students in putting-together processes, encourages risk taking and close attention to text, and builds self-confidence has to be preferred over the pedagogically bankrupt approach of naming sentence parts and filling in blanks. In fact, if one contrasts putting-together versus taking-apart approaches—and trusts either research or classroom experience—there's hardly a contest. Why? Because teaching that works is better than teaching that doesn't. And because there is satisfaction in seeing students acquire the know-how and the confidence to write with style—reducing clauses to phrases, perhaps, or revising loosely linked coordinate clauses to more tightly reasoned subordinate ones.

And yet the larger point is this: by limiting the premises for SC practice to syntax skills, we constrain our own thinking. The provocative ideas of Vygotsky (1978), Bruner (1983a), and Smith (1988) offer ways to consider given-language activities, including SC practice, at least as compelling as the revised syntactic fluency hypothesis. For example, Vygotsky hypothesized a "zone of proximal development," suggesting that whatever learners can do with help they can eventually do on their own. Bruner proposed the metaphor of *scaffolding* to explain how mothers routinely assist children in linguistic and cognitive tasks. Smith asserted that much language learning is vicarious, acquired without conscious intent as we engage in an activity that someone else may actually be doing.

In my opinion, it makes sense to think of SC practice in terms of social language learning, an arena where language coaches do some of their most exciting work these days. We will return to this arena in later chapters of the book.

Sentence Combining in Action

Almost any text can serve as the source for given-language activities, including SC exercises. Literature, including poetry, from an anthology, nonfiction pieces about topics or themes under study, clumsy sentences about the "literacy crisis" from a local editorial page, well-crafted prose from student papers—all are easy to use. And, of course, there are textbooks full of SC exercises.

To motivate student engagement, I suggest several ideas. First, point out that the SC approach has worked in many classroom experiments. Second, emphasize that students will profit from exercises to the extent they search for new sentence options and make thoughtful choices. Third, share the idea that SC builds on existing language with the aim of increasing one's ability to create and revise written sentences. Fourth, encourage students to work with partners, trying out sentences orally and checking for quality. Fifth, note that the goal of SC practice is *good* sentences, not long ones, and that students should apply what they have learned when revising their own texts. Sixth, have students work first with given sentences and then, at a later stage, weave their own details and new sentences into the exercises. Seventh, invite students to notice the syntax in well-written prose and ask, "How did the author do that?"

Using puns

One way to sustain daily sentence-level practice is with puns. I use double and triple puns as starters. Each SC cluster is put on the board or on a transparency and serves as a "bell-ringer" activity to get students working as a period opens. Here's an example:

1. Take care in doing this exercise.
2. The exercise is *homespun*.
3. The exercise is in sentence combining.
4. You may end up with *quip-lash*.

■

The assignment is to write three grammatical, well-crafted sentences from the ones provided and to check the preferred sentence. The activity takes three minutes at most, and students hand in their papers to earn points. If students are new to SC practice, model what you mean by "grammatical, well-crafted sentences" as you make the point that there are four basic processes for combining:

- deleting unnecessary (repeated) words
- rearranging words
- adding a variety of connectors (e.g., *or, unless, otherwise,* and *if*)
- changing word form (e.g., *care* changed to *careful* or *carelessly*)

The exercise shows students that options exist beneath the surface. Ask them to practice within the field of given meanings, but acknowledge particularly inventive combining (as in Sentence 10, which introduces a third pun).

1. Take care in doing this homespun exercise in sentence combining, or you may end up with quip-lash.
2. Take care in doing this homespun sentence-combining exercise, or you may end up with quip-lash.
3. You may end up with quip-lash unless you take care in doing this sentence-combining exercise, which is homespun.
4. This sentence-combining exercise is homespun; take care in doing it, or you may end up with quip-lash.
5. This homespun sentence-combining exercise should be done carefully; otherwise, you may end with quip-lash.
6. To prevent quip-lash, take care in doing this homespun exercise in sentence combining.
7. If you don't take care, quip-lash may result from doing this homespun sentence-combining exercise.
8. Doing this homespun exercise in sentence combining carelessly may result in quip-lash.
9. Quip-lash may result from carelessly combining sentences in this homespun exercise.
10. Exercise care with this homespun sentence combining—or you may end up with quip-lash.

■

Occasionally, students share their best sentences aloud. Students earn extra points by bringing in double or triple puns that you can decombine for SC source material. You can test-drive this activity for a week or so with the following starter puns.

A beautician *waived* her chance.
The beautician was a failing student.
The chance for a *makeup* test.

Carpenters were *tough as nails*.
This was in their wage demands.
They *hammered* home their *points*.

"We *furnace* the ashes," said a
    mortician.
"You *urn* your own way," said a
    mortician.
The comment was *grave*.

The dentist's work was *boring*.
She *pulled a fast one* on her patient.
The patient had fallen asleep.

Nick the barber made a reply.
It was "*Hair today*, gone tomorrow."
The reply was *bristling*.

The outlook is *dark* for electric utilities.

The outlook is *current*.

Nuclear plants have *sparked* debate.

■

Using professional sentences

If the preceding activity is too cute for your tastes, try prompting daily SC practice in other ways. For example, select well-crafted sentences from literature—say, Steinbeck's *Of Mice and Men*—decombine them into simple sentences, and invite learners to combine sentences and then verbalize their expectations before follow-up reading.

1. The rabbits hurried for cover.
2. They were noiseless.

3. A heron labored up into the air.
4. The heron was stilted.
5. It pounded down the river.

6. The place was lifeless for a moment.
7. Then two men emerged from the path.
8. They came into the opening.
9. It was by the green pool.

Original Text

The rabbits hurried noiselessly for cover. A stilted heron labored up into the air and pounded down the river. For a moment the place was lifeless, and then two men emerged from the path and came into the opening by a green pool.

■

Professional sentences might also come from a book of quotations such as Donald Murray's *Shoptalk* (1990). Break down one or more target sentences into underlying kernels; invite students to recombine in ways they find satisfying; and, finally, show the original sentence(s) and encourage comments or journal writing. From a section in Murray's book titled "At Play with Language," three sentences by writer Joan Didion make a challenging exercise for high school students.

1. I know about grammar.
2. I know its power.

3. Its power is infinite.
4. One can shift the structure of a sentence.
5. This alters the meaning of that sentence.
6. The altering is definite.
7. The altering is inflexible.
8. It is like a camera's position.
9. The position alters the meaning of the object.
10. The object is photographed.

11. Many people know about camera angles now.
12. Not so many people know about sentences.

Original Text

What I know about grammar is its infinite power. To shift the structure of a sentence alters the meaning of that sentence, as definitely and inflexibly as the position of a camera alters the meaning of the object photographed. Many people know about camera angles now, but not so many know about sentences.

∎

Of course, as students compare their sentences to Didion's originals, they pay close attention to syntax. Language itself becomes their teacher, inviting attention to word order, phrasing, the positioning of old and new information, and punctuation.

Using SC cues

Any SC exercise like the previous one can be scaffolded as you provide oral cues—for example, "Try the word *what* to open the first cluster." But for teachers who prefer more directed SC practice, it's possible to use graphic cues or signals. Such prompts can be engineered into worksheets or put on transparencies to guide combining along predetermined lines. The following example contains basic signals used by O'Hare (1973) as applied to the Didion exercise.

1. I know about grammar. (WHAT . . . IS)
2. I know <u>its power</u>.
3. Its power is <u>infinite</u>.

4. One can <u>shift the structure of a sentence</u>. (TO)
5. This <u>alters the meaning of that sentence</u>.
6. The altering is <u>definite</u>. (-LY) + (AS . . . AS)
7. The altering is <u>inflexible</u>. (-LY)
8. It is like <u>a camera's position</u>.
9. The position <u>alters the meaning of the object</u>.
10. The object is <u>photographed</u>.

11. Many people know about camera angles now.
12. Not so many people know about sentences. (BUT)

∎

Another approach to cuing occurs via closure prompts—cue words plus blank lines to suggest a syntactic pattern (Strong 1984b). It is *essential* for students to write out complete sentences on their own, not merely to fill in the blanks. Shown here are three prompts to stimulate collaborative combining for the Didion exercise:

What _____ power.
To shift _____
as definitely and inflexibly as _____ .
many _____ ,
but _____ .

At middle school and junior high levels, I often use closure prompts for oral and choral SC practice. For choral combining, I like to use three closure prompts of increasing difficulty for each SC cluster so that students *hear* the syntax options.

Using student writing

To stimulate involvement with SC practice in whole-discourse exercises, one strategy is to excerpt a well-written passage from a student text, get permission from the student to use it as an in-class exercise, and then break the passage into kernel sentences. Following is one such passage written by a middle school student and the exercise that followed (Strong 1986):

Original Student Text

My cat was barely breathing at the bottom of the cardboard box. He lifted his head a little and looked up at me. He didn't meow. I wanted to pick him up, but I knew it would hurt him more. I just sat there in the garage and talked to him a little. Then I smoothed his silky fur with my fingers. It was getting cold and starting to rain when my mom called me in for supper. "I have to go now," I said. The cat didn't look up. (9 sentences)

—KRISTIN STRONG

SC Exercise

The cat was barely breathing. He was at the bottom of the box. The box was cardboard. He lifted his head a little. He looked up at me. He didn't meow. I wanted to pick him up. I knew that it would hurt him more. I just sat there. I was in the garage. I talked to him a little. I smoothed his fur. His fur was silky. I used my fingers. It was getting cold. It was starting to rain. My mom called me in for supper. "I have to go now," I said. The cat didn't look up. (19 sentences)

■

Again, the process is to withhold original sentences until students have tried their hand at combining. Then students can share and compare different texts, perhaps writing on the chalkboard, on transparencies, or on networked computer screens. Finally, the student author shares her text and responds to questions about her syntactic choices. If no one notices the power of the single uncombined sentence, "He didn't meow," the teacher should certainly draw attention to it. Afterward, the writer basks in the warm glow of applause, and class members turn to revision tasks with renewed enthusiasm.

Creating student-centered practice

Activities like the previous one help link SC practice to real writing. Another approach to this goal involves students in creating SC exercises. Begin by modeling your expectations in a kind of think-aloud for students. Start with a few main clauses like the following one and then ask questions to generate modifying sentences as shown.

A student approached the teacher's desk.

Who was the student?	He was a 240-pound lineman.
What did he look like?	He had missing teeth.
What was his attitude?	He had a snarling disposition.
What was his purpose?	He wanted to ask about his grade.
What was his grade?	His grade was a D–.
Why was it important?	It would keep him out of tonight's game.
What was the game?	It was for the state football championship.

■

After students try their hand at combining, invite teams to generate similarly formatted exercises. Each exercise has a main clause and modifying sentences, and each is written on a single note card. On the flip side of the note card, students write three well-crafted transformations. This activity is fun for students, especially when you use their exercises as bell ringers over the next several days or when you have groups swap exercises. Equally important, the activity helps students realize that embedded details are a writer's response to the questions of imagined readers.

The generative approach can also be applied to whole-discourse SC exercises, with students creating the modifying sentences for given main clauses:

A student shuffled to the school.

What did he look like?	He was short but muscular-looking.
What was the school?	It was Middleton Middle School.
How did it look?	It was a low brick building with a curved driveway.

He hesitated before going inside.

Where did he hesitate?	He stood on the front steps.
What else did he do?	He bit his lower lip and glanced inside.
How long did he wait?	He hesitated until the halls had cleared.
What was he thinking?	He wondered what the first day would be like.

He felt unsure of himself.

Why was he unsure?	His family had just moved into town from California.
What was he thinking?	He thought about his friends back home.

Finally he made his way to the office.

What did he see?	The hallways were draped with campaign posters.
What did he hear?	He could hear squawks from the music room.

The school principal stood behind a counter.

Who was the principal?	Ms. Howard was the principal.

What did s/he look like?	She was tall and elegant with a swath of gray hair.
What did s/he do?	She welcomed him with a big smile.
What did s/he say?	"Welcome! We've been waiting for you!"

■

Rehearsing key concepts

SC exercises may also serve as unit reviews, as working groups develop fact sheets to rehearse key concepts or as teachers develop minimal activities like the following one, with plenty of room for students to interweave their own language and ideas.

"The Lottery" Essay

Combine sentences below. Use them as part of your analytic essay on Shirley Jackson's "The Lottery." Each cluster contains a key concept that you will need to develop and support with ideas from the text or from your class notes.

1.1 Jackson builds tension.
1.2 Jackson builds a sense of mystery.
1.3 She describes the atmosphere of the lottery.
1.4 The atmosphere is festive.

2.1 The lottery is a practice.
2.2 The practice is rooted in tradition.
2.3 Its meaning is now obscure.
2.4 Only its ritual is remembered.

3.1 The lottery seems to fill a need.
3.2 The need is psychological.
3.3 The lottery has its counterparts.
3.4 The counterparts are modern.

■

Using SC to teach language content

As shown in "The Lottery" exercise, good SC exercises often have a knowledge base. So what about the possibility of using a discipline's content as material for given-language exercises? What key skills and concepts do seventh graders need? Perhaps teachers could develop a list of skills and concepts, divvy up the development work, and devise a range of interesting exercises.

Working from this premise, I developed dozens of word etymology exercises for middle school classrooms. Each exercise centered on the history of a single-word and was accompanied by an array of support activities. Middle school teachers who are interested in field-testing such material may contact me through the Department of Secondary Education at Utah State University (<www.seced.usu.edu>).

The Story of *Maverick*

1.1 Sam Maverick was a lawyer.
1.2 He moved from Massachusetts.
1.3 He moved to Texas.
1.4 He took up cattle ranching.

2.1   Texas rangeland was unfenced.
2.2   This was many years ago.
2.3   Herds grazed together.
2.4   Herds mingled together.

3.1   Ranchers branded their cattle.
3.2   Ranchers branded calves.
3.3   This was to prove ownership.

4.1   But *Maverick* refused to brand stock.
4.2   He trusted his neighbors.
4.3   His neighbors had branded theirs.

5.1   People in Texas heard of his policy.
5.2   *Maverick* soon came to mean a calf.
5.3   The calf was unbranded.

6.1   *Maverick* then referred to any person.
6.2   The person thinks independently.
6.3   The person holds unusual views.
6.4   The person refuses to conform.

■

Developing SC writing prompts

Almost any whole-discourse SC exercise can serve as a writing prompt or a point of departure. Warm-up narratives like Street Scene in Chapter 1 beg to be extended imaginatively. Issue-centered SC exercises can pose thinking tasks that invite follow-up writing. For example, an exercise like the following one, from *Sentence Combining: A Composing Book* (Strong 1994), can stimulate response (see "Invitation") and further research.

Pumped Up

You've seen muscle magazines on the newstands—ones that reach an estimated readership of seven million Americans who want to be "pumped up."

1.1   No one wants to be a 97-pound weakling.
1.2   This is especially true for young American men.
1.3   They have seen *Rambo* and *Terminator* films.
1.4   These present "macho" images of strength.

2.1   Adolescents are inspired by images from TV.
2.2   Adolescents are inspired by muscle magazines.
2.3   Adolescents have created a bodybuilding subculture.
2.4   It often uses steroids to achieve results.

3.1   The black market for steroids is enormous.
3.2   It supplies 1 million users with drugs.
3.3   Half of this number are teenagers.
3.4   It grosses at least $400 million annually.

4.1   Steroids can stunt a person's growth.
4.2   Steroids may lead to liver problems.
4.3   Steroids may lead to kidney problems.
4.4   Most men start using "juice" before age 16.
4.5   Some start as early as age 10.

5.1   Overdoses of growth hormone can cause acromegaly.
5.2   Acromegaly is called Frankenstein's syndrome.
5.3   This condition distorts the face.
5.4   This condition distorts hands and feet.
5.5   This condition eventually leads to death.

6.1   Equally serious are psychological mood swings.
6.2   Cycles of steroid use create the mood swings.

7.1   Steroid users often experience depressions.
7.2   They are not using the drugs.
7.3   This pattern typically leads to increased use.

8.1   "Juicers" may have feelings of euphoria.
8.2   The euphoria is invincible.
8.3   Irritability often accompanies the "pump."
8.4   An urge to fight often accompanies the "pump."

9.1   Such aggression can lead to vandalism.
9.2   Such aggression can lead to assaults.
9.3   Such aggression can lead even to murder.
9.4   It is sometimes fueled by delusions.
9.5   It is sometimes fueled by paranoia.

10.1   Over 80 percent of teenagers believe something.
10.2   Steroids are completely harmless.
10.3   Half this number would continue their use.
10.4   This was even if they were convinced otherwise.

Writing Tip: For sentence variety, try opening cluster 2 with *inspired* and cluster 8 with *while*. Also, be sure to check subject-verb agreement as you combine cluster 8.

Invitation: No federal money has been spent studying the long-term health effects of steroids. How would you convince federal officials that the study of steroids should become a priority?

■

Integrating grammar

Informal lessons in practical grammar result from in-class exchanges—as students work in small groups, write on acetate sheets, or use networked computers. But SC demonstrations can also be engineered so that students are introduced to grammar terms. For example, in *Writer's Toolbox: A Sentence-Combining Workshop* (1996), I created minilessons on both basic and advanced grammar (relative clauses, appositives, participial phrases, transitions, noun substitutes, and absolutes).

As mentioned earlier, procedural knowledge (how to do things with syntax) can provide a foundation for declarative knowledge (grammar terms and syntax functions). I recommend using such minilessons selectively. Have students use them when the SC activities raise questions in their minds, for example, how to embed and punctuate adjectives or how to handle parallelism. After students get comfortable with combining and moving modifiers, they are much more interested in the names and functions of grammatical structures. Harry Noden's *Image Grammar* (2000) is one of the best professional sources for integrating grammar in interesting, practical ways.

To conclude this chapter, I reprint a brief episode from *Creative Approaches to Sentence Combining* (Strong 1986)—this as a reminder that old paradigms do not always serve us well, whatever our good intentions.

A True Story

The young teacher moved toward me, smiling pleasantly. "You're the workshop presenter?" she asked.

"Right," I grinned.

"I use sentence combining already."

"Hey, terrific."

"It doesn't work in *my* class."

"Not so loud," I joked. "Others will hear you."

"I'm serious. My students just don't like it."

I paused. This person *was* serious, so my setup of workshop materials would have to wait.

"Okay, tell me how you use the approach."

"What do you mean?" she asked.

"How do you structure the in-class practice with sentence combining? What do you have kids do?"

She looked at me questioningly. "Well, I assign an exercise—usually toward the end of class. You know, to keep the kids busy? Or maybe on an assembly day if they're getting hyper."

"The same exercise for all students?"

"Yes. But each student works alone."

"What happens with the sentences they've transformed?"

Silence began to grow between us as she wondered about the point of my questions.

"Do you have students compare the results of what they've combined? Do you discuss sentence options and make choices as a group?"

"Uhm, no. Not so far."

"After the students have finished an exercise," I asked, "what do you usually have them do?"

She smiled again. "Oh, I see what you're getting at. We exchange papers—or kids come up to my desk—and I tell them whether their answers are right or wrong."

Learning Through Language

1. In Chapter 2 you read about the theory, research, and applications for a teaching approach known as sentence combining. Write to an imagined close friend who is either traditional in instructional methods (a dyed-in-the-wool grammarian) or progressive in approach (a whole language zealot). Your purpose in writing is to get this person's written response to a summary of the chapter's key points. Exchange letters with a writing partner and then respond to your partner's letter.

2. A key point of the chapter concerns the rationale for SC practice. One type of rationale centers on syntactic fluency, whereas another centers on the idea of social language learning. Which, if either, of these rationales do you find convincing or compelling? What do you find potentially interesting about SC exercises? What is your main area of concern about such materials and teaching approaches? Jot down your responses, and be ready to share.

3. According to the chapter, SC exercises (and related activities) can be drawn from student texts or from quality literature, both prose and poetry. Find either a student text or a piece of literature that you believe has potential as an exercise. What instructional potential do you see? Break the text down into kernel (or near-kernel) sentences and create clear directions for the exercise. Then share your exercise with others in the group and get their feedback on its possibilities.

CHAPTER 3

COACHING USAGE

Reading Them Papers

Reading them papers you done last weak
I seen some usage witch was quiet unique;
Theirs mispelt words, the commas was wrong,
Plus what was wrote, it was WAY to long!

With alot of misteaks I'm taking my stand,
Like NO MORE sentences starting with AND!
And one more thing its incumbent to say—
Your gonna proofread or get grammar today!

Anguished Language

Let me call him Clint. With thinning hair, a crooked grin, and muscled forearms, he would be no more amused by "Reading Them Papers" than he was by terms like *fused* and *fragment* sentences, *dangling* participles, comma *splices*, *shifting* viewpoints, or *misplaced* modifiers—all red flags on the strange playing field called written language, which he had never understood.

Clint was twice the age of typical students hoping to become teachers. He had worked on ranches and in construction and at a steelmaking facility that went through the convulsions of downsizing. He wore cowboy boots and western-style shirts and a massive belt buckle. He had eaten too many cheeseburgers at roadside cafes, and he walked with a slight limp from a rodeo accident in his youth. He had a working wife and school-age kids, and his eyes filled with tears when I gave him the results of the Teacher Education Writing Exam. Again he had failed.

"I'm sorry," I said.

Clint's mouth trembled as he studied the backs of his hands and took a deep breath. Was there anything else he could do? He'd been to the Writing Center, and that was a dead end. He didn't want no handouts.

It was close to lunchtime. "Let me look at your exam," I said.

In terms of its surface features—usage, spelling, punctuation—the paper was pretty much a disaster. And as for its development of ideas, it was roughly what I might have

45

gotten from an average seventh grader. As college coordinator for the writing exam, I had no trouble seeing why Clint had failed. Maybe the exam was serving its purpose, and it was now time to wash him out of the program.

"Tell me about junior high and high school," I said. "You know, way back when. What you learned about writing."

The story had its setting in rural towns of southern Idaho, and Clint told it in the vernacular of the region, one studded with status-marking usage forms like *we was* and *they done* and similar expressions. It was a tale of a roughneck kid who didn't see much point to school and had only vague recollections of workbooks and sentence-diagraming activities. Clint didn't make any excuses. Although one or two teachers had assigned an occasional essay or book report, no one took such work seriously. The kids he knew had other things on their minds, like cars and girls and getting out on their own to earn some money. Only later, as an adult, did he begin to understand "what a tough row to hoe" he'd chosen. And now, in college, he'd finally swallowed his pride and gotten help with vocabulary and study skills. He'd come a long way.

Writing wasn't his thing and never had been. His wife had helped him get through freshman-level writing courses, where he'd finally managed a C, thanks to her editing and proofreading and more. But now, having to write on his own in an exam, without anyone to help with the ideas and the grammar—well, he didn't know where to start or how to do it. Some people had it—a writing talent—and others didn't. Writing wasn't his thing.

"You understand *why* we have the writing exam?" I asked.

"Hey, no problem with that," Clint replied. All he wanted was some way to measure up. Was there something he could read, a book he could study, that would show him the way? He'd do anything.

I nodded. "I can see that."

His eyes were wet again as he explained the helpless feeling of not knowing how to write. To be a teacher that kids respected and liked, you had to communicate with authority and good grammar. He liked kids—no problem there—and his authority came from the school of hard knocks. What he lacked was language skill, mainly in "correct-type speech" and "writing basics, like your prepositions and such."

I didn't tell Clint that I'd long been a sucker for single parents struggling through school or for working-class students who had finally gotten their act together. For me, such situations always presented a coaching challenge. Like how to deal with the student's hope for a quick fix. And how to dismantle self-defeating ideas or redirect a misguided strategy. And how to sustain a commitment when things became one step forward and two steps back. To deal with usage was to deal with habits.

"I'll coach you," I said.

"You?"

"Yeah, me. We'll work on writing all summer. I'll give you a sample prompt from a previous exam, and we'll discuss how to approach it. You can write for an hour, and then I'll go over your paper so that you can see its strengths and weaknesses. We'll do this over and over until you get the hang of planning and organizing, followed by editing and proofreading. We'll keep at it until you *get* it, skills and all. What do you think?"

Clint leaned forward. "So what if I *can't* learn it?"

"No problem," I said, "if you pay attention and do the work."

"But—"

"Look, trust me about this. The exam that didn't pass shows potential."

"Really?"

"And when you're ready, not before, you'll retake the exam. No special treatment, no handouts. Pay attention and you'll learn how to write. That's the deal."

Clint showed me the gold in his dental work. "This is for real?"

"This is for real," I replied. "Right after lunch."

Usage Awareness

Happily, Clint's story had a positive outcome. We met over a two-month period, and he worked his butt off, learning to spell dozens of words, punctuate text with reasonable skill, and spot all kinds of errors. More importantly, he learned to organize and develop brief essays in which he took a position, provided examples and support, and made transitions from point to point. When he finally achieved a solid pass from two anonymous faculty judges, he grinned from ear to ear. Today, he is a good-hearted teacher who has effectively mentored many student teachers.

From the viewpoint of students like Clint, the playing field of written language is a dangerous one. Almost any move can break a rule and bring penalties in the form of teacher correction, deducted points, public embarrassment, low grades, or derailment of a career. Students know that errors matter. And in trying to *avoid* errors, some of them become virtually paralyzed, unable to produce text. Others conclude that usage rules are arcane codes available only to teachers, whose bizarre job is to fix student writing with one hand and grade it with the other. In the game of schooling, "turning in" a paper often means turning over its development—its *correction*—to an adult examiner.

The big issues of usage coaching center on context and motivation: How do we create "active learning environments" (Hillocks 1995) and demystify conventions? How do we recruit students to take on active, self-assessing roles—but not premature or overactive roles—in editing written texts? At what point in the writing process should errors be addressed, and how should we respond? And what about the needs of basic writers? Questions like these compel attention because so many parents, newspaper editors, legislators, and business leaders love to be appalled by declining standards, the "stunning illiteracy" of today's young adults, and the erosion of Western civilization's foundations. Like other teachers, I am often trapped on airplanes or cornered against barbecues, listening to the lubricated angst and self-righteous indictments of such individuals. So far, I have failed miserably in recruiting them as usage coaches.

In this chapter I offer a balanced approach to usage instruction, blending writing process dogma with ideas for in-class demonstrations, miniconferences, daily practice activities, and attention-getting gimmicks. One such gimmick—a simple task designed to heighten awareness of usage as a topic for learning—is shown here. Imagine it as an introductory attention-getting activity, much like the poem that opens this chapter.

Just Suppose

Suppose you read a sentence like this one, and you come upon too wirds with spelling problems—as you just did. Suppose the next sentence; it also has other Error's in mechanics and usage. *Can you feel your uncertainty as a reader grow?*

Reading like this—having to guess at the "hidden message" of the first two sentences—forces you to slow down and work hard. It's a little like trudging through knee-deep sludge. If you're like most readers, you quickly get irritated with such reading. After all, a writer who forces you to slow down and work hard is treating you rudely. On the other hand, a writer who pays attention to usage and proofreading is treating you with respect. How do *you* like to be treated?

Directions: Think of two real-life occasions, once when you were treated with rudeness and once with respect. Maybe these occasions were at school or at home or hanging out with friends. Jot down a few notes about each occasion. Be ready to share them in a small group. Pay attention to the stories you hear. Later on, we'll write about rudeness and respect.

■

The Just Suppose exercise frames usage differently from its usual terms—*right* or *wrong*, *correct* or *incorrect*. Most students can develop connections to the ideas of rudeness and respect. One appeal is to students' growing maturity. Another is to their imagination—putting themselves in a reader's shoes. By asking students to take responsibility for editing and proofreading, we set the stage for ongoing attention to usage—with workshops, peer response, and editing conferences coming midway, and later, in each cycle of text development.

As part of the overall context for workshops, a usage corner can be useful. File folders are stapled to a bulletin board, each forming a pocket for sheets of specific skill-building practices. The same goes for proofreading visors—decorated cardboard eyeshades like those worn in yesteryear by Bartleby the Scrivener types. Literacy club gimmicks? Absolutely. But if we wear costumes for other ritual activities—like parties, ball games, and going to bed—why not use special metalinguistic gear for activities as important as editing? As one middle school teacher said to me, "Whatever *works* to develop proofreading awareness!" And she was right.

The Usage Environment

Let's return to the themes of instructional context and student motivation that provide focus for this chapter. What matters most are the attitudes we betray, the relationships we establish, and the working conditions we set up, monitor, and fine-tune. In general, brief minilessons should address conventions in a practical, ongoing way. Proofreading demonstrations and minilessons—coupled with student-centered examples and follow-up practice—should set the stage for roving conferences. To set up an active learning environment, we can use inventories like those in Chapter 6 and Chapter 8 in addition to the following exercises—what Hillocks (1995) might regard as gateway activities for usage study.

Usage issues

One approach is to present students with language situations involving choices more complex than right or wrong. As described years ago by Neil Postman and Charles Weingartner in *Linguistics: A Revolution in Teaching* (1966, 114–15), the strategy sets up inquiries into many language issues, including usage. What are the effects of one choice versus another? How will communication purposes best be served?

The Situation

You are being interviewed for a part-time job. The job is important to you because you know you will need the money in the weeks to come. At one point in the interview, your prospective employer says to you, "I hope working on Saturdays don't bother you."

Your Language Choices

a. "No, it don't matter to me."
b. "Working on Saturdays *doesn't* bother me."
c. "No, it doesn't."
d. "No, it don't."

∎

Exercises like this one seem as useful as ever. Also interesting for its situational problems is Larry Andrews' *Language Exploration and Awareness: A Resource Book for Teachers* (1993, 107). Here is one of eighty exercises devised by Andrews.

Exploration: Talking "Right"

Directions: Recall the last time someone corrected your use of language. Perhaps a teacher, parent, or friend told you you had misused a word or that something you had written was inaccurate or awkward. Write a paragraph about such an event in which you explain (1) what language was "corrected," and (2) how you felt as a result of the correction.

1. Share your paragraphs in a small group and discuss *why* others have attempted to correct your language.
2. Was the attempt to correct your language successful? What do the others in your group report? Did they change their language?
3. Do you think corrections work? When are corrections successful? Unsuccessful? How do we learn different ways of using language?

∎

As students consider questions like these, they weigh the effects of usage. Doing so helps prime the pump for usage workshops.

Field research

A second strategy for activating the environment involves field research from students. By putting students in the role of researchers who actively construct knowledge, we change classroom dynamics. Creating a survey instrument like the following one and collecting data can become a class project.

Language Survey

Directions: Please mark how you feel about the italicized word or phrase in each sentence below. Also, please answer a few brief questions for us.

Your Age? ____   Occupation? _____
Gender?   M   F   What are your feelings about language study?

Items	Right	Wrong	?
1. *Your* probably wondering about this survey.			
2. Just *between you and I*, English can be fun.			
3. So *me and my friends* are researching usage.			
4. This cool idea *come* from our amazing teacher.			
5. We *was* challenged to become active learners.			
6. I am a *very unique* thinker, so I agreed to do it.			
7. All but one of my friends *has* joined with me.			
8. This friend says that usage study *don't* matter.			
9. There *is* always teachers who will catch errors.			
10. This person's opinions are *different than* mine.			
11. But each person has a right to *their* own views.			
12. To *myself*, usage involves lots of choices.			
13. My *friends* idea is that language controls us.			
14. Usage, he says, is *alot* like conforming to rules.			
15. Being happy and not *to worry* is his philosophy.			
16. *Doing this survey*, my awareness was raised.			
17. *Its* part of growing up to get smart about usage.			
18. Taking risks and making errors *is* essential.			
19. But learning to write *good* is my ultimate goal.			
20. Thanks for your assistance *of us* in our survey.			

■

By developing survey items, students become experts in a domain of usage. Afterward, they might compare their results with those of Maxine Hairston (1981), who studied the errors that business and professional people see as most serious in reports and business letters. See Noguchi (1991) or Weaver (1996) for details of the Hairston study as well as discussions of usage research by Connors and Lunsford (1988).

If working with a multiple-item questionnaire seems too daunting, consider having students, in teams of two, focus on a single usage item in their field research. Each team could become resident experts on some aspect of grammar, usage, or writing conventions. Following, for example, is a type of data-collection tool that students might create to investigate possessive apostrophes. Other minisurveys could be developed with a similar format.

Minisurvey on Usage

Our English class is studying usage in writing, and we invite you to participate. Your name will *not* be used as we gather data and report it. Please read the five sentences below from a business letter. Then mark:

> X = "Does not bother me."
> Y = "Bothers me a little."
> Z = "Bothers me a lot."

1. ___ This years report to stockholders showed increased sales.
2. ___ We were also pleased by our workers improved morale.
3. ___ Our marketing director's effort was especially noteworthy.
4. ___ The companys prospects appear to be solid at this time.
5. ___ We welcome our stockholder's advice on operations.

As you can see, the five-item questionnaire contains four errors in apostrophe usage, with one sentence (the third one) being correct as written. No mention is made of apostrophes in the directions. The point of such research, after all, is to determine what readers actually notice. Students who administer such an inventory might probe with brief questions: "What bothers you about sentence 2?" Their report of research, addressed to others in class and to the teacher, would focus on methodology, results, analysis of findings, and discussion of implications. In actively investigating usage, students may well experience increased openness to language learning.

Usage as Development

My precocious grandson Will was just thirty months old when he glanced up at my son and said, with a characteristic grin, "You're a *bab*, Dad, not a *bad* dad."

His father wore a puzzled expression. "Why did you call me a bab, Will?"

"Because I'm making a joke. I added a *b!*"

For a child of Will's age to engage consciously in humor—let alone *verbal* humor, let alone *phonemic awareness* humor—is hardly typical. On the other hand, it suggests that an awareness of usage conventions can develop very early. Thanks to interactions with his mom and dad and older sister, Will had already learned that usage norms can be violated—and that breaking the rules is interesting, even funny enough to try out on a parent in the form of a joke. Let's hope that teachers build on this awareness.

The developmental ideas in Chapter 2 serve as a backdrop for usage. We considered the idea that syntax involves processes of ongoing language acquisition, long after basic sentence patterns have been internalized through the give-and-take of oral interchange. Of course, the patterns of written language have unique rhythms and structures tied to genre, level of formality, and individual style. Few of us sound like books when we speak, though sometimes at professional meetings we do swell up with self-importance as we share our rehearsed talks. To write well is to draw upon the resources of speech—that is, to "hear" language on the page—but also to draw upon the codes and regular features of text. Written discourse is not just transcribed speech. It has its own grammar and rhetoric, which differ from those of speech. And, obviously, processes of producing written text differ markedly from those of producing speech.

Errors and anxiety

The idea that learners internalize usage conventions by testing and breaking the rules may sound like a dubious proposition to those with conservative sensibilities. But the process of making errors, mistakes, blunders, and goofs does indeed seem to underlie language acquisition at all levels.

Language learning is richly experiential, and we all use different experiences to make sense of usage. How strange it is, then, that we so often constrain and channel the natural predilections of students to experiment, make errors, and learn. We say, in effect, to students: Don't trust the trial-and-error processes you used when learning to walk and talk and balance on a skateboard; instead, pay attention to our rules, the neat prescriptions we've outlined for you to practice. Of course, the effect of our injunction is to make learning an *unnatural* act. And our nasty habit of grading the practice efforts, of making judgments about them, serves mainly to heighten anxiety.

Good coaches know that fear shuts down learning. For me, this lesson was driven home, as I described in Chapter 1, while trying to learn Spanish. The corollary to the lesson was the follow-up one in French—namely, that a more relaxed and risk-taking attitude made learning not only possible but also fun. Both contexts required effort, of course; I had to attend class, do the reading, and practice. However, the strict, finger-snapping demands of my Spanish teacher caused me to grit my teeth, tense my body, and *try* as hard as I could to learn. When I failed to learn Spanish after plenty of no-nonsense trying, I drew conclusions about my language-learning abilities. My self-esteem was in the toilet for weeks.

Because this point is so basic to informed usage instruction, let's consider the views of W. Timothy Gallwey (1976), whose work in athletic training is widely known. Gallwey says that in the inner game of learning—whatever the domain—there is often a struggle between two aspects of self. The executive self, or self 1, gives directions and makes judgments relentlessly; meanwhile, the performing self, or self 2, tries hard to follow directions but often withers under the onslaught of critical judgments. Gallwey's work explores this tension and offers exercises for quieting self 1 and allowing self 2 to reassert its natural "self-coaching" ability. Here is what Gallwey has to say about errors in learning:

> Any kind of learning requires feedback on the results of our actions, and in order to get such feedback it is essential that we let go of our fear of making errors. The contemporary idea in learning theory that trial and error is an outmoded way of learning, because errors give students a sense of failure, is nonsense, in my opinion. Trial and error is the way we learn, like it or not. What we need to eliminate is not occasional mistakes, but our *fear* of mistakes and the sense of failure we attach to them. (40)

There, in one neat paragraph, is the foundation for a philosophy of language instruction. It is a philosophy that values the guesses, the approximations, and the errors of individuals because they are *central* to language learning.

Errors and growth

Constance Weaver (1996) provides a helpful point of departure regarding error in student writing. Instead of seeing errors narrowly, merely as deviations from standards, she often regards errors as "evidence of the writer's thinking and, in some cases, clear indicators of the writer's growth in mastering the structures and conventions of written English" (59). Like Kroll and Schafer (1978), Weaver believes that errors arise naturally during the process of language learning and reflect underlying strategies of "overgeneralization, ignorance of rule restrictions, incomplete rule applications, [or] hypothesizing false concepts" (1996, 62). She agrees with Mina Shaughnessy's observation that "it is not unusual for people acquiring a skill to get 'worse' before they get better and for writers to err more as they venture more" (1977, 119). She convincingly argues that simple errors are often replaced by "more sophisticated" ones. And she welcomes the involvement of students in defining their goals for language learning.

With a psycholinguistic perspective, Weaver concludes, as she did in *Grammar for Teachers* (1979), that there is "little value in marking students' papers with 'corrections,' little value in teaching the conventions of mechanics apart from actual writing, and even less value in teaching grammar to instill these conventions" (1996, 82). Rather, she argues for attending to error in writers workshops and "serving as an advocate, rather than adversary: as editor, rather than as critic or judge" (84). To teach final revision and proofreading, she recommends minilesson demonstrations, brief individual conferences, and peer-group editing, "provided the teacher has guided the students in learning how to do what is expected" (87). And for errors that persist in final drafts, she recommends strategies ranging from "benign neglect" (Rosen 1987), to "targeted" error response, to check marks (generally for careless errors), to actual copyediting (say, for student publication). Weaver sees danger in "behaviorist" approaches that so often stunt student growth as a consequence of trying to "weed out" error. She suggests that "the Error Beast is to be welcomed and tamed, not slain" (1996, 101), a point that we will return to later.

Performance skills

As with syntax, usage conventions require extended periods of learning, with at least three layers of acquisition. John Mellon (1981) notes that students learn surface levels of orthography—spelling and the conventions of capitalization and punctuation—mostly on an incidental basis through reading, although many teachers do point out such features in context or, more likely, provide instruction and drillwork on them. A second level of orthographic mastery, Mellon believes, involves the performance skills of two-channel thinking and decentering:

> In *two-channel thinking*, a person learns to inscribe what is being written at the moment while simultaneously storing in memory what has already arisen in verbal consciousness but is yet to be written down. . . . The skill of *decentering* is also vital, in that it allows the writer to "stand apart" from whatever has been written, whether a sentence or two, or a complete discourse, and to regard it objectively as something totally under one's control, an artifact to be crafted and shaped to conformity with both the dictates of the writer's thought and the needs of the reading audience. Without the skills of two-channel thinking and decentering, it is doubtful that persons could write at all. (50)

Finally, Mellon identifies several more performance skills related to usage, including "knowing which words of the spoken language (especially coterie slang, conversational and juvenile locutions, and expressive intrusions of other sorts) are barred from the registers of formal writing, unless used intentionally for effect" (51).

Reading provides basic knowledge of spelling, capitalization, and punctuation. But because most basic writers have had very low levels of "comprehensible input" (Krashen 1984, 1993), they often have a limited knowledge base. Moreover, because such students have yet to develop the skills of two-channel thinking and decentering, they lack strategies for getting better at writing. Clearly, such problems are not turned around overnight, and just as clearly, attention is required. Whether students choose the old-fashioned route of perseverance or the trendy new route of self-governance makes little difference. What matters is whether they put in the time.

Three Approaches to Instruction

In writing, two key behaviors require coaching: spending sufficient time on early stages of work—background reading, planning, and drafting—and developing "the habit," as Mellon says, "of rehearsing elements of one's sentences repeatedly in mind during and after their inscription, and of stopping frequently to reread and contemplate and reformulate what one has written" (1981, 52). The latter behavior, of course, underlies two-channel thinking and decentering.

Workshop-style instruction

Having primed the pump with regard to usage, some teachers will follow the footsteps of Nancie Atwell (1987, 1998), whose pioneering work with writing conferences helped change teaching across the nation. Today, Atwell asks students to write "as correctly as they can right from the start, . . . to develop the habits of real writers" rather than luxuriating in the mode of "sloppy copies," an "unfortunate legacy of the early days of writing workshop" (1998, 250). Attention to conventions comes late in the process and follows Atwell's one-on-one conferencing, where the focus is on both content and craft. She deals with conventions in three stages that are summarized here:

- First, students edit on their own—and often with a partner—using a pen or a pencil that differs in color from the text. The editing focus comes from each student's proofreading list, a growing list of points developed from teacher feedback. To the papers submitted for teacher editing, students attach an editing checksheet, the specific list of conventions to which they have personally attended.
- Next, the teacher reads the paper, using a third color for complete copyediting. From this copyediting, the teacher identifies no more than two skills to be taught in a brief follow-up conference. Skills for follow-up teaching are put on a student's editing checksheet so that the student can add them to a personal proofreading list. Also, misspelled words are added to a personal spelling list.
- Finally, after the one-on-one editing conference, the student writer prepares a final text from the fully copyedited one that the teacher has returned. The revised and copyedited text is what the student publishes and includes in a writing portfolio. The portfolio includes the unblemished texts of students—the upper reaches of their capabilities, with peer and teacher assistance. (249–61)

Proofreading lists, editing checksheets, personal spelling lists—all of these are kept by students themselves in writing folders. Because these are lists in students' own hand-writing, not generic lists from a textbook, they help learners pay attention to their own usage. What also differentiates workshop-style instruction from traditional teaching is that Atwell works on texts that have already been marked—by the student and often by a peer—and that she follows up in an intelligent, efficient way, restricting her coaching to one or two context-based skills. Finally, it is from the fully copyedited text that a student prepares a final copy, one incorporating a variety of corrections from self, peer, and teacher. In this final stage, as the student attends closely to small but important changes, correct conventions are copied to the new text.

Traditional instruction

Not all teachers are comfortable with the workshop-style model. A more traditional para-digm is for students to develop their texts as fully as possible with peer and teacher sup-port and then to submit them for evaluation and feedback. The assumption is that students should get credit for what they themselves are able to do. The worry of traditionally oriented teachers—sometimes voiced, sometimes not—is that learners in a workshop environment may come to depend upon peer and teacher copyediting, without develop-ing their own skills. Even with its noble intentions, the traditionalists say, workshop-style instruction may devolve into a kind of welfare dependency for students.

In this respect the traditionalists have a point. Almost inevitably, some students will seek to flatter us or invoke our sympathy or professional guilt, thereby conning us into unwitting partnerships in text development. Others will fake their revising and copyediting. In short, it is all too easy for hardworking writing coaches to appropriate student texts in the process of working with students. On the other hand, traditional instruction certainly has its share of problems. Listen.

> I remember writing a theme paper for my English class. Sitting down I wrote the whole paper and immediately handed it in. When I received the assignment back from the teacher, there were so many red marks that the paper looked more red than pencil gray. I was so disap-pointed I threw the paper away.
>
> —C. J. DUNLAP

This small story is endlessly repeated, with students disappointed not so much in their own performance as in a teacher's response. In effect, all interaction occurs *after* the writ-ing process—and the student rejects it. Equally problematic is that traditionally oriented teachers often find themselves, by default, in a critical, judgmental role, not in a coach-ing role. Thus, a traditional paradigm presents a psychological bind for those who care about students but also care about standards.

Balanced instruction

Workshop-style instruction, especially as modified by Atwell (1998) and Rief (1992), should not be dismissed as unworkable by traditionally oriented teachers, either novices or veterans. The coaching structures of minilessons, conferences, and goal setting can motivate and engage students. At the same time, there is something to be said for rubrics that provide an external standard of performance. And there is something to be said for positive experiences of a traditional kind, which challenge students to stand and deliver, depending only on their own resources and skills, rather than the feedback of response partners and teacher. Why shouldn't students have the benefit of both kinds of instruction?

In *Strategies for Struggling Writers*, James Collins (1998) uses miniconferences to create an active—and responsive—learning environment. For example, basic writers describe specific problems they are having and ask what they can do. Although this may seem an obvious strategy to anyone who knows that writers alternate between composing and planning, it is not so obvious to discouraged, skill-deficient students. Pausing to articulate a problem is a first step toward solving it. For Collins, miniconferences result in a four-step paradigm for teaching:

1.   identifying a strategy worth teaching
2.   introducing the strategy by modeling it
3.   helping students try the strategy out with workshop-style teacher guidance
4.   helping students work toward independent mastery of the strategy through repeated practice and reinforcement (65)

For more about miniconferences, see Chapter 10 as well as "Coaching Through Conferences" in this book's concluding chapter.

Based on his extensive work with basic writers, Collins challenges the orthodox view that editing should come last: "Contrary to one of the basic tenets of process instruction," he writes, "our belief is that work on writing mechanics should not always be put off until the end of the writing process" (197). As noted earlier, Collins invites students themselves to help identify areas of need. For students with serious problems in mechanics, he sees work on periods, commas, capitalization, and spelling as a good place to start, with skills often addressed in that order. Helping learners better manage such conventions enables peer readers—and others—to respond more positively to texts in process. Also, breakthroughs on certain surface features can often be achieved straightforwardly, resulting in big payoffs for student self-esteem.

Sharing such views on usage teaching is Pat Cordeiro (1998). Instead of treating punctuation at the end of the writing process—as a "detail" to be "cleaned up"—she urges students to integrate editing into their composing. Cordeiro sees punctuation not as "mechanics" but as "the most intricate symbol system used by literate writers and readers" as well as "the writer's best means of communicating intentions" (53). To teach this idea, she advocates think-aloud demonstrations in which students hear how teachers segment sentences meaningfully, punctuate a text into paragraphs, and express concerns for what the reader needs and how punctuation might convey meaning. She acknowledges that writing process maxims of "content preceding form" and "revision preceding editing" were historically necessary; however, she believes that the idea of "punctuation as an active, meaning-making system was somehow overlooked," making it "one of the lost children of the process" (54):

> If punctuation instruction is to be successful, we must abandon our view of content before
> form and adopt instead a view of integrated symbol systems. As those of us in process writing classrooms have observed, content changes as the writer edits. Teachers must stop punctuating for students in their absence. Editing is part of the writer's process. But in almost all writing instruction, punctuation is usually added on; editing comes last. In the traditional class-

rooms I learned in, most of the editing of what I wrote was done alone by the teacher and handed back to me without comment. Today, some students still learn writing skills in these hands-off, student-proof ways. (54)

For Cordeiro, punctuation includes "endmarks, commas, capital letters, dialogue markings, and apostrophes" but also "paragraphs, chapters, and titles" (55). As such, punctuation establishes a common playing field for writer and readers. But unlike the skills of spelling, handwriting, and capitalization, which can be "routinized and made subliminal," punctuation is an "open capacity"—one that is "forever open to negotiation" as it "hovers on the edge of a writer's awareness, sometimes peripheral and sometimes focal" (59–60). Thus, skill with punctuation has much more to do with intention and judgment than with the application of mechanical rules. Along with Dawkins (1995), Cordeiro likes to have students experimentally "raise" and "lower" punctuation levels by inserting, altering, or deleting marks in good literature, then in their own texts. Through punctuation, she says, "forms of language expression are learned that are not learnable in oral speech"— namely, the sentence (62).

To some teachers, the idea of dealing with editing and punctuation earlier in the process may seem like a step backward. But in the context of basic writing, I certainly agree with Collins and Cordeiro that attention to writing mechanics should not be delayed until late in the game. To do so is to imply that writing has no boundaries that define the game and make it both rational and interesting. Students like Clint, whom we met earlier, and Stephen in Collins' book (1998) simply do not see the problems in their error-filled texts, although they know their writing isn't "good." Yet these same students, seeing a corrected draft alongside their original, may respond as Stephen did: "Oh, that doesn't matter. The ideas are what are important" (198).

Stephen's beliefs that "ideas are what are important" and that usage doesn't matter may well result from overly zealous teaching of writing process coupled with a sharply reduced emphasis on language per se. In my view, the literacy learning of students like Stephen is seriously compromised by such beliefs. To the world at large, usage *does* matter, and the sooner that such students again learn to pay attention to language—to let language be their teacher—the better.

Usage Through Minilessons

A proactive approach to usage instruction includes brief regular minilessons, often no more than five or ten minutes long (Atwell 1998; Calkins 1994; Weaver 1996). Minilessons grow out of a teacher's reading of papers coupled with professional experience. Each lesson focuses on a specific convention, skill, or concept related to usage. In other words, minilessons activate attention, inviting learners to notice some specific feature in the language environment. Interestingly, this is much the same method used by Gallwey (1976) in his work with athletic training.

Early minilessons should deal with class routines and expectations as well as think-aloud demonstrations of text development, revision, or proofreading. Such minilessons— say, on format, paragraphing, or consistent viewpoint—provide a set of positive injunctions for students, ones to get them off on the right foot. Then, in all likelihood, will come the minilessons that deal with predictable problems: end-stop punctuation, key comma rules, dashes, colons, semicolons. To the extent possible, the movement is from more important items to less important ones. A minilesson on punctuating dialogue, for example, will presumably build upon earlier lessons on end-stop punctuation and commas as well as capitalization and paragraphing.

Following a minilesson, a structured activity can prompt a reflective (strategic) habit of mind. For example, one eighth-grade teacher working with Collins asked students to write a paragraph on the top third of a page, then do this:

STOP: *REREAD* what you have written and write two questions about your paragraph.
1.
2.
Now see if your two questions can help you rewrite and improve your paragraph. (1998, 64)

Students used their own questions to revise the paragraph on the bottom third of the page. A repeated activity of this kind does far more than keep students busy.

It is in the context of minilessons that a few grammar terms, when linked to brief practice activities, become useful to students. My own work on minilessons is outlined in *Writer's Toolbox: A Sentence-Combining Workshop* (1996), where twenty-six demo lessons cover basic and advanced grammar as well as the following usage and punctuation topics. While these minilessons are intended for student use, they do offer many ideas for parallel teacher-developed lessons.

Usage	Punctuation
sentence fragments	commas
run-on sentences	dashes
subject-verb agreement	semicolons
misplaced modifiers	colons
dangling modifiers	quotation marks
faulty parallelism	apostrophes
pronoun problems	

Traditionally, teachers have viewed grammar and usage as a logical system, one that begins with high hopes in September and ends, bedraggled and confused, in late May. A more functional approach is to focus first on high-priority items—fragment sentences, run-on sentences, subject-verb agreement, shifts in tense, status-marking usage (e.g., nonstandard verb forms, double negatives, objective pronouns as subject), and so on—before addressing items of lesser importance, such as apostrophes in contractions, punctuation of nonrestrictive modifiers, and *affect* versus *effect*. Weaver (1996) provides a good discussion of priorities that make sense.

Regular proofreading practice offers a second type of minilesson. In Chapter 1, for example, I described how impromptu workshops in usage can follow from sentence-combining exercises, with students transcribing their anonymous problem sentences onto overhead transparencies. A related strategy, equally easy to use, is to have students jot down problem sentences from their papers onto a sheet that circulates through the room; this sheet can then be photocopied for proofreading practice in the class. Sending students to the chalkboard a row at a time to put up problem sentences also creates a workshop atmosphere. Today, with networked computer terminals, a file of problem sentences can be downloaded from a host computer for student practice.

One popular program, Daily Oral Language (Vail and Papenfuss, 1989/1990), provides two error-ridden sentences to be put on the board each day. Students correct these during a five- to ten-minute lesson. The same approach can be adapted for SC exercises, with errors engineered into transformed sentences. As students proofread, they look back at the SC exercise for underlying meanings and use these to rewrite in a better, more effective way. See Unit 5 in *Writer's Toolbox: A Sentence-Combining Workshop* (Strong 1996) for such exercises in whole-discourse contexts.

Here's another exercise for heightening attention to proofreading (Strong 1991a).

A Proofreading Pretest

Directions: Shown below are forty sentences. Each of the first thirty sentences has one error, and each of the last ten sentences has two errors. Put a check mark above each error, and give yourself two points for each correct item. There are fifty errors in the pretest, so you can earn one hundred points. After finishing, be prepared to discuss your ideas in class.

1. As you read this sentence, see if you can spot the mispelling.
2. An error in Capitalization, as shown here, may result from trying to emphasize a word.
3. This sentence, which may prove tricky has an error in omitted punctuation between the subject and verb.
4. If your skillful in proofreading, you'll see a single spelling error here.
5. Here you may find a sentence fragment. Especially if you look closely.
6. A writer may sometimes put in extra words, as you can see here, in in the process of writing.
7. On the other hand, a writer may sometimes leave words when writing quickly.
8. Dropped word endings, as in this sentence, can interrupt a reader concentration.
9. Of course, a dropped verb ending create special problems in subject-verb agreement.
10. If you switch verb tenses, as in this sentence, you confused your readers.
11. The comma splice, as shown here, is a very common error, it should be rewritten or punctuated correctly.
12. Related to the comma splice is the run-on sentence it tries to fuse two closely connected sentences.
13. Although you may sometimes overlook the missing comma after a long introductory clause like this one try to look more closely.
14. A comma is often used to separate two clauses in a compound sentence like this one but a careless writer may overlook it.
15. You may put in unnecessary commas, that interrupt the flow of meaning because you don't read sentences carefully, listening for pauses.
16. A nicely structured sentence can be ruined while a writer uses the wrong subordinating conjunction.
17. A person which is not proofreading may make errors with relative pronouns (e.g., *who, whom, which, that, whose*).

18. Some sentences are rather difficult to read that put modifying clauses in the wrong place.

19. Trying to make more mature sentences, dangling modifiers can leave the reader confused.

20. It is easy to forget that each pronoun should agree with their antecedent.

21. Alot of readers get upset when careless writers blend simple words together.

22. An other kind of spelling error results from splitting one word in two.

23. It's unfortunate when you don't catch simple errors with apostrophe's in your proofreading.

24. To unthinkingly and repeatedly split infinitives is a common, but often unnoticed, error.

25. Although you may take idioms for granite, they can also present problems.

26. Looking at prepositions, you quickly arrive to the conclusion that they can make a real difference.

27. To write well, a writer should not shift your point of view.

28. Slang-type stuff will also require proofreading and editing.

29. Some phrases, however totally awesome they may sound, probably do not belong in careful, edited writing.

30. Errors in parallelism occur when one is thinking about content, not to worry about proofreading.

31. Its sad but true that omitting *two* apostrophes in one sentence is likely to distract a readers concentration.

32. And curtain types of words, which will not be caught by a spell checker, are quiet often misspelled—as this sentence shows.

33. Unfortunately, their are some writers who ignore there proofreading skills on easily confused words.

34. Unintended humor occurs when you here one word but put down another—as illustrated hear.

35. This sentence would be clearer with quotation marks, you may be murmuring to yourself.

36. To catch the two errors here, you should of looked closely at each words meaning.

37. The semicolon; not the comma, can join two closely related sentences, this rule is broken here.

38. There is various kinds of problems related to subject-verb agreement that deserves your attention.

39. The affect of careless proofreading is hard to measure but definitely effects readers' attitudes toward the text.

40. And last but not least, cliches are a real pain in the neck to read.

■

With the Proofreading Pretest, one reads in a special way, paying attention to the content of sentences as a clue to their form. The feeling of tracking sentences to find their self-referencing errors helps communicate what proofreading is about to students who are often eager to abdicate such "scut work" to others, especially teachers. Following are the answers for the Proofreading Pretest:

1. *Misspelling* is misspelled.
2. *Capitalization* should not be capitalized.
3. There is a missing comma after *tricky*.
4. *You're* is misspelled.
5. The sentence fragment begins with *especially*.
6. The sentence has an extra *in*.
7. The word *out* is omitted.
8. The *'s* on *reader's* is missing.
9. The *s* on *creates* is missing.
10. *Confused* should be *confuse*.
11. A comma splice appears after *error*.
12. A run-on sentence occurs after *run-on sentence*.
13. There is a missing comma after the word *one*.
14. Again there is a missing comma after the word *one*.
15. There is an unnecessary comma after *commas*.
16. The conjunction *while* should be replaced with *when* or *if*.
17. The relative pronoun *which* should be replaced with *who*.
18. *That put modifying clauses in the wrong place* should come after *sentence*.
19. The subject of the sentence should be *writers*, not *dangling modifiers*.
20. *Their* should be *its*.
21. *A lot* is misspelled.
22. *Another* is misspelled.
23. There is an unnecessary apostrophe in *apostrophes*.
24. *To split infinitives* should be followed by *unthinkingly* and *repeatedly*.
25. *For granite* should be *for granted*.
26. *Arrive to* should be *arrive at*.
27. *Your* should be *his* or *her*.
28. *Slang-type stuff* is slang.
29. *Totally awesome* is another slang phrase.
30. *Not to worry* should be *not worrying*.
31. *Its* should be *it's*, and *readers* should be *reader's*.
32. *Certain* and *sentence* are misspelled.
33. *Their* should be *there*, and *there* should be *their*.
34. *Here* should be *hear*, and *hear* should be *here*.
35. There are missing quotation marks before *this* and after *marks*.
36. *Should've (should have)* is misspelled, and *words* should be *word's*.
37. The semicolon after *semicolon* should be a comma, and the comma after *sentences* should be a semicolon.
38. *Is* should be *are*, and *deserves* should be *deserve*.

39.   *Affect* should be *effect,* and *effects* should be *affects.*

40.   *Last but not least* and *pain in the neck* are both cliches.

■

Like minilessons on a specific topic or convention, proofreading practice teaches skills *incidentally,* just as they are often acquired in oral language. As mentioned earlier, think-aloud demonstrations will help students know what is expected of them in peer response groups and in editing their own texts. For an effective demonstration, students need to see the text on a transparency, on an LCD monitor, or on individual computer screens or handouts. Rosen (1998) describes the process as working with texts in progress that students wish to volunteer for group edit. The process begins with positive questions such as "What's effective about this paper?" or "What has the writer done well?" Later, the group can be asked for other suggestions. As various errors come up, they are corrected on the transparency or visual display. A running list of errors is kept so that students can check their own texts for such items as they do follow-up proofreading.

Some teachers also ask students to keep grammar notebooks. Such notebooks list priorities for personal editing, like the proofreading list kept by students in the writing workshop. Following is a format for usage items in the grammar notebook.

Usage Item	Correction	Reminder or Rule
my sisters bike	my sister's bike	's (singular); s' (plural) for possessive
english class	English class	Capitalize languages—always!
sent 1, sent 2	sent 1, *and* sent 2	Don't join two sentences with comma.
it's literary tradition	its literary tradition	It's (contraction) = IT IS!
When . . . we	When . . . , we	Use comma after introductory clause.

In addition, the notebooks can provide an ongoing record of minilessons, a place for students to make notes from proofreading practice, list vocabulary words that they find interesting or amusing, and keep track of personal spelling words. A helpful format for spelling words uses Norman Hall's mark-out system (1962). With this approach, the student keeps the misspelled word in a *corrected* fashion so as not to learn the misspelling when doing practice trials. Each student's personal spelling list serves as source material for a once-a-week spelling quiz, with partners administering the items.

Misspelling	Correction	Reminder or Rule
visⁱble	visible	There are two "eyes" (get it?) in *visible.*
me_∧^ant	meant	*Meant* is the past tense of *mean.*
gramm^aer	grammar	Good spelling helps me get straight As in grammar.

The goal of balanced instruction is easy enough to state—helping students self-assess texts as well as revise, edit, and proofread—but maddeningly difficult to achieve. In all likelihood, no single model of instruction will enable us to figure out the black box of student motivation and anticipate the many distractions (and attractions) of adolescence. For more on balanced instruction, see "Collaboration in Response Groups" in Chapter 8, "Crafting Writing Assignments" in Chapter 9, and the advice on assessment and conferences in Chapter 10 and the concluding chapter.

Learning Through Language

1. In Chapter 3 you met Clint, an adult language learner whose middle school and high school experiences with writing and language study did not prepare him for later realities. Now imagine Clint as a real student in your classroom, one who sees little point in school and even less point in what the English curriculum has to offer. Sometimes "surprise" coaching can reach a kid like Clint. Take a few moments to jot him a note, inviting his active involvement in usage study.

2. Take a stand (one that you explain!) on the following ideas: (1) marking student papers for usage; (2) whole-class drill-and-practice; (3) coaching usage through large-group demonstrations; (4) frequent minlessons on usage topics; (5) an editing corner with self-instructional materials; (6) student editing groups; (7) one-on-one editing conferences; and (8) dealing with errors earlier in the writing process than is usually done. Create a provisional statement of philosophy.

3. The chapter suggests that usage inquiry, including field research, can change the traditional dynamics of instruction. Assuming the validity of this idea, think about the kinds of inquiry that might interest typical middle school or high school students, get them to pay attention to their own language, and perhaps modify their oral or written usage. Envision and develop a single usage exercise or activity for classroom trial that you will share and discuss with others.

CHAPTER 4

COACHING STYLE

Lesson in Style

Our lesson today is writing with style:
It's what comes as you practice awhile.
It's hearing a voice between your ears;
It's getting words down, ignoring old fears;
It's playing with text, then reading it back;
It's words reworked so they stay on track.
It's choices you make to create the page:
Writing with style is you on stage.

A Sense of Style

Whatever else it may be, "Lesson in Style" seems to be about the life force of text. On this subject, Donald Murray raises the central mystery: "How can cold, passive type press ink on a page in such a way that a human voice is heard in the ear?" (1990, 127). Content is important, Murray acknowledges, but ideas alone rarely determine whether we stick with a text and are moved to some new thought or feeling or action. Instead, it is the voice of the text, echoing in our ear, that pulls us along.

And textual voice, whatever else it may be, is a thing made from inner resources in response to situational demands—purpose, audience, and genre, to name the obvious. The question of how we help middle school and high school students find, create, and express a sense of style will be this chapter's focus. More immediately, though, let's explore our topic with the careful academic detachment it so richly deserves.

Riding in Style: A Three-Paragraph Demonstration

To think about style, for me, is to think about cars. And as a cultural product of the mid-1950s, I owned three treasures, each bought for under $150: a dark green '38 Chevy, from whose classic body all chrome was removed and under which I lovingly installed dual exhaust pipes to announce my coming-of-age; then a throaty flathead Ford of '41 vintage, black and pristine, at least until the sunny morning of inattention when I laid it over and climbed out through the passenger's side window; and later a sexy '36 Ford pickup, also black, with all original equipment, right down to its mechanical brakes, the laughable equivalent of dragging one's feet in a careening coaster wagon. Today, these classics, with their all-natural air-conditioning, would provide a portable retirement package for someone who never got good at cruising but had all the aspirations.

When you think about it, cars and writing have a lot in common. Both are expressions of identity, not merely technologies to accomplish transportation and communication. As advertisers know so well, we choose cars, ornament them, and inhabit them to say who we are—or who we'd like to be. So cars express our values, just as writing does. For example, in 1967, while working with rural teachers in eastern Idaho, I bought a white '61 Plymouth sedan—vinyl seats, new tires, good AM radio, and seventeen thousand original miles—because I was a practical family man who knew his top priority was dependability for his long road trips. This car, like the three-part theme cribbed from an encyclopedia by a reasonably bright plagiarist, was hard to fault. So I told myself I really didn't mind its whalelike ride, its great slabs of unrelieved sheet metal, or its swooping tail fins. And to prove that the head knew better than the heart, I intoned the mantra of practicality for a full year while thumbing the classified ads and eyeing the inventory of used car lots around town. Each day, as the thrifty slant six engine did its work, I told myself how much I valued the Plymouth's staid introduction, predictable body, and unimaginative conclusion.

It may come as no surprise that an XK150 Jaguar coupe—a '63 model with faded leather interior and chrome wire wheels—did not escape my notice, despite oxidized orange-red paint and sad back-row status. It stood orphaned for months before I made my inquiry and offered twelve hundred dollars to liberate it to the open road. Giving up the Plymouth was a sacrifice, of course; and there would be days when I would miss the wallowing ride, the stiff chair-height seats, the good heater, the cavernous trunk, and the three-paragraph predictability of cheap, available parts. But the Jaguar had its compensations—say, shifting into top gear at eighty, switching on the electric overdrive, and rocketing through unbroken vistas of sagebrush and volcanic hills, with waxed orange-red flanks agleam, the Corvette V-8 engine full and resonant, the radio turned up. This was truly a car of metaphor and possibility, adventure and style. In fact, it was everything the risk-free Plymouth wasn't. What I learned about writing style from the Jaguar is that sometimes getting there is half the fun.

∎

What can we say about the style of the preceding text? First of all, it has an introduction, a body, and a conclusion. Second, it is written in a fairly lively, personal voice. Third, it develops its topic through an extended comparison between cars and writing. Fourth, it uses descriptive and metaphorical language. Fifth, its concluding sentence echoes the title of the essay and seems to express the writer's underlying values.

In contrast, the analytic (or academic) style you are now reading is more reserved in tone. The sentences are shorter, the diction more elevated, the authorial voice more distant. Also, the present style has explicit intersentence connectors of enumeration (*first, second*) and transition (*in contrast, also*). It is the voice of academic discourse—or "transactional writing" (Britton 1970)—with conventions of attribution as shown in this sentence.

It is a style that secondary students probably need to practice on occasion, as balance to the personal style of the three-paragraph demonstration.

This chapter deals with two approaches to style, both of which use SC exercises as vehicles for instruction. The first method, sentence modeling, derives from the tradition of imitation in classical rhetoric, an approach that was nearly two thousand years old when Shakespeare and Milton came under its influence as grammar school lads. The second method, attention to style in context, involves work with key stylistic principles, the aim being to enhance the clarity of written expression.

Basics of Style

To introduce the idea of style in language and the theme of imitation as a mode of learning, consider having a brief fashion show in class. (Of course, if students in your school wear uniforms, ask a few of them to bring in props for extra credit.) How do boys wear their caps to look cool? What is "the look" for girls right now? What clothing brands command top dollar at the mall? Who sets fashion trends for teenagers? How come the kids in old yearbooks all look the same, wearing those retro outfits? How do kids today know what's hot and what's not? How does one choose what to wear to school, or to a Saturday at the beach, or to church or a funeral?

From such an activity, it becomes clear that style in clothing has at least three levels. There is a broad middle style, often defined by school authorities in a dress code; there is a low (or grunge) style, which sometimes sneaks into school to test the rules; and there is a high (or formal) style, one called into nervous service on prom night. After developing a simple taxonomy for the three levels of style in clothing, students can shift their attention to language, using the terms *high*, *middle*, and *low* as descriptive—not moral—categories. One key idea is that language style, like clothing style, must fit the occasion to be right; obviously, too, the three categories of style blend into one another like colors in a spectrum.

Many students have the mistaken notion that good school writing—in reports, in term papers, and in essay exams—should be written in a lofty high style, with long, windy sentences and bloated diction. But when Latinate terms are culled from a thesaurus to dress up ordinary ideas, the effect is often comic, like wearing an elegant formal outfit to third period English. High style may work for solemn or ceremonial occasions, but most school writing—and, for that matter, most clear communication in business, in government, and in the professions—does not require one to ascend the soapbox or to affect the mannered grandiloquence of nineteenth-century oration. In other words, *intelligent* and *obscure* are not synonyms. Later, we will see how exercises can encourage a shift from high style to middle style, with clear expression as the aim.

At the opposite extreme is low style. Whereas high style may use foreign terms, jargon, abstractions, and interminable syntax in an effort to sound profound, low style is colloquial and chatty, with its elbows on the table. Often it is loaded with slang, contractions, cliches, and general evaluative terms—"I mean, it was like this totally *awesome* experience you wouldn't believe"—and its *I* and *you* pronouns help create a tone of chummy intimacy. Low style is what we typically find in learning logs, in e-mail exchanges, and in scribbled notes to trusted friends. Because it is style close to expressive speech, students may try to use it in school writing tasks. However, before such language enters the arena of middle discourse, it generally needs to clean up its act. Low style can shift to middle style as students substitute familiar words for slang, spell out contractions, eliminate cliches and hackneyed expressions, provide support for generalizations, and review the use of *I* and *you* in relation to expected conventions.

A simple chart may help students better understand the basics of style.

Style Levels	Voice	Diction	Syntax	Contexts
High Style	impersonal, aloof, formal, detached, stiff, ceremonial, pretentious	abstract words, Latinate terms, jargon; words draw attention to themselves	long sentences with complex structures and fully developed paragraphs	ceremonial occasions (e.g., awards, funerals) or formal texts
Middle Style	clear, lively, well-structured, articulate, thoughtful, personal	familiar words, precise use of general and specific terms; reader-friendly	long sentences mixed with short ones to create interest for the reader	school-based writing (e.g., essays, term papers, and most reports)
Low Style	chatty and rambling, chummy, very informal, highly opinionated	slang words, contractions, cliches, and broad terms (*stuff*, *things*)	fragments of sentences, nonstandard punctuation; mirrors speech	learning logs, journals, e-mail exchanges, complaints, advice, lists

With a frame of reference like this one, students are better prepared to tackle the topic of imitation in learning. Ask students to think about the social groups in their school and their norms for dress, behavior, and language—the standards one must meet to be accepted by others. Most students understand that the norms are enforced by group leaders—everybody knows who they are—and that wannabe group members deliberately imitate the dress, the behavior, and the language of those in power. In other words, just as fashion trends are largely shaped by the high-level consensus of advertisers, group norms are determined by a kind of local consensus, with group members tacitly agreeing to imitate one another. Clearly, imitation is a powerful force, although we may be unaware of our motivation to dress, behave, and talk like others.

Next, how do we help students increase their awareness of style and registers of language? To set the stage, ask students to bring in passages that move or excite or surprise them. As students put paragraph-length texts on transparencies or on computer screens, invite readings that the author would applaud. Then talk about the contexts in which the texts were found and the features that students notice. These paragraphs can be put on a bulletin board to serve as anchors for future discussions of style.

Finally, there is the question of motivation for sentence-level work. And here we enter the arena of flow experiences—periods of intense engagement that characterize athletic and artistic performances (Csikszentmihalyi 1990). We might ask students about activities they find intrinsically fun or interesting. Why do some kids spend hours with computer games or practicing foul shots or rehearsing drill team steps in front of a mirror? Why is it that when most teenagers fall off their skateboards or surfboards or snowboards, they don't shrug their shoulders and give up? How do we explain a fifteen-year-old spending a morning on a tough musical score or hunched over a potter's wheel? Young adults choose all of these activities. Why? How would students describe the feeling they get from these (or similar) experiences?

Having articulated their own optimal experiences, students may be interested to hear what well-known writers have to say about crafting their style:

I revise, revise and revise so much, that by the time I've finished, I'm fairly secure in what I've done. . . . Doing that is rapture.

—WILLIAM MAXWELL

Because the best part of all, the absolutely most delicious part, is finishing it and doing it over. . . . I try to make it look like I never touched it, and that takes a lot of time and sweat.

—TONI MORRISON

I feel like a surfrider in the language; the luck involved is at least equal to any skill. I find myself being taken for a ride, and the ride always goes further than I thought.

—WILLIAM STAFFORD

What makes me happy is rewriting. . . . [It's] like cleaning house, getting rid of all the junk, getting things in the right order, tightening things up. I like the process of making writing neat.

—ELLEN GOODMAN

The beautiful part of writing is that you don't have to get it right the first time, unlike, say, a brain surgeon. You can always do it better, find the exact word, the apt phrase, the leaping simile.

—ROBERT CORMIER

Nothing is more satisfying than to write a good sentence. It is no fun to write lumpishly, dully, in prose the reader must plod through like wet sand. But it is a pleasure to achieve, if one can, a clear running prose that is simple yet full of surprises.

—BARBARA TUCHMAN

Writing in longhand has a special kind of magic to it for me. You are so engaged in the manual work of fashioning the word which flows out of the end of your hand as though it were a secretion from your own body, and you watch it being spilled on the page in a certain calligraphy, and it has an energy of its own that carries you along.

—RICHARD SELZER

According to Csikszentmihalyi (1990), flow is something we make happen. The best moments of our lives—the optimal experiences—"usually occur when a person's body or mind is stretched to its limits in a voluntary effort to accomplish something difficult or worthwhile" (3). In short, flow results from concentrating on some kind of challenge or constraint that interests us. Csikszentmihalyi believes that all optimal experiences have certain conditions in common: "They have rules that require the learning of skills, they set up goals, they provide feedback, they make control possible" (72). Working with writing style—like yoga, or painting, or training with weights—can be a source of flow, provided that we enter the zone where we are neither bored from lack of challenge nor anxious from being overly challenged.

Flow helps me understand why one of Andrea Lunsford's tasks for basic writers, the twenty-five-word sentence, worked so well. Lunsford would take routine work with thesis statements, for example, and add the constraint of twenty-five words. "Not twenty-four words," she would say, "not twenty-six, but twenty-five." Students liked the challenge of adding and deleting modifiers to achieve a required standard because the activity put *them* in control of the text. Later, we will return to the paradox of enabling constraints, so central to optimal experiences in writing.

Sentence Modeling

The idea of levels of generality is basic to sentence modeling, so let's start there. A helpful analogy for most students is that a general word, phrase, or sentence is like an aerial view (or long shot) in a movie or a photograph. It establishes the big picture or the overview. On the other hand, a specific word, phrase, or sentence is more like a close-up. It provides details—colors, textures, and nitty-gritty realities. I give students sorting exercises like the following ones, asking them to number general items in each pair with a 1 and more specific items with a 2.

Two-Word Sorts

furniture/chair; color/aqua; frog/amphibian; tennis/sports; government/monarchy; spreadsheet/software; etc.

Two-Phrase Sorts

ugly socks/birthday gifts; life decisions/career choice; flat tire/lame excuse; academic cheating/plagiarizing a paper; etc.

■

The difficulty increases as students sort clusters of words and then phrases into numbered hierarchies. Again, the most general level in the hierarchy is labeled 1, with words, phrases, or clauses arranged in successive levels of specificity, as in the first example that follows. All items at the same level of generality receive the same number, as illustrated in the second and third examples that follow:

Cluster

soft drink
beverage
ginger ale

gossiping about others
picking one's nose
nasty personal habits

Hierarchy

1 beverage
  2 soft drink
    3 ginger ale

1 nasty personal habits
  2 gossiping about others
  2 picking one's nose

manages money well	1	signs of increasing maturity
follows through on plans	2	manages money well
avoids risky behaviors	2	follows through on plans
signs of increasing maturity	2	avoids risky behaviors

■

After promising that we will return to long shots and close-ups in sentence modeling, I ask students to pay attention to simple dramatic activities that serve as springboards for writing. I mime an action and then transcribe what I have done in simple sentences. For example:

The teacher grabbed a piece of chalk.
He faced the class with an evil smile.

Although these sentences can be joined by coordinating or subordinating conjunctions, which students will easily supply, they can also be combined in other ways—say, with a verb cluster either before, within, or after the main clause.

- *Grabbing a piece of chalk*, the teacher faced the class with an evil smile.
- The teacher, *grabbing a piece of chalk*, faced the class with an evil smile.
- The teacher grabbed a piece of chalk, *facing the class with an evil smile.*

Next, I ask a student or two to mime a simple action, the sillier the better. The students come up with basic sentences, which we then combine:

Jason sat at his desk.
He flexed his rippling muscles.
He smoothed back his silky hair.
- Jason sat at his desk, *flexing his rippling muscles and smoothing back his silky hair.*
- *Sitting at his desk, smoothing back his silky hair,* Jason flexed his rippling muscles.

During these experiments with style, I encourage students to listen closely to the sentences they construct. How is it, I ask, that the first two of the following sentences work while the third one sounds odd? How could the third sentence be improved?

- Jason, *sitting at his desk*, flexed his rippling muscles and smoothed back his silky hair.
- *Smoothing back his silky hair*, Jason sat at his desk, *flexing his rippling muscles.*
- Jason flexed his rippling muscles and smoothed back his silky hair, *sitting at his desk.*

From this problem-solving exercise, students see that they may need to move certain free modifiers closer to the headwords they modify, since proximity matters in sentence construction, or use a subordinating conjunction such as *while*:

- *Sitting at his desk*, Jason flexed his rippling muscles and smoothed back his silky hair.
- Jason flexed his rippling muscles and smoothed back his silky hair *while sitting at his desk*.

Once students get familiar with free modifiers like these, it is a natural step to apply grammatical labels to such structures, for example, *verb phrase* in the middle grades, *participial phrase* in the upper grades. The terms become useful as students encounter more analytic approaches to sentence modeling.

Next, you can take model sentences and challenge the class to imitate their structure. Transparencies, slides, and dramatic pictures work especially well for this activity—or you can call upon Jason again. After the scaffolded work on modeling, with students sharing and comparing sentences produced from visual prompts, assign them to apply sentence modeling to photographs ripped from magazines or to topics of their choice. Then use Rebekah Caplan's Showing, Not Telling activity (see Chapter 5).

Most students can manage sentence-modeling tasks with success. Using the concepts taught earlier, you can then break down a model sentence into its levels of development. The main clause in the following scaffolding is labeled 1, the additions 2.

2	Smoothing back his silky hair,	(verb phrase)
1	Jason sat at his desk,	(main clause)
2	flexing his rippling muscles.	(verb phrase)

■

To create additional interest in the exercise, try organizing students into groups of three. First each student creates a verb cluster; then papers are passed to the right and each student writes a main clause; finally papers are passed again and each student adds a second verb cluster. The result will be dozens of strange sentences like the following one, which will reinforce the structure of the model.

2	Smiling and humming to myself,	(verb phrase)
1	I stand in front of the bathroom sink,	(main clause)
2	hearing my sister pound the door.	(verb phrase)

■

At this stage, too, you may want students to think outside the box of a model. Ask students how they like the following additions. The first is a prepositional phrase, the second an adjectival phrase (appositive adjectives), the third a noun phrase (appositive noun), the fourth a pair of absolute phrases. Of course, all of these sentences can be analyzed into a main clause (level 1) and free modifiers (level 2).

Jason sat at his desk, *with rippling muscles and silky hair*.	prepositional phrase
Jason sat at his desk, *muscular and silky-haired*.	adjectival phrase
Jason sat at his desk, *a muscular, silky-haired hunk*.	appositive (noun) phrase
Jason sat at his desk—*his muscles rippling, silky hair smoothed back*.	absolute phrases

Exercise Sentences	Original Text
1. They approached the cabin. 2. It was small. 3. It was squat. 4. It was built of logs. 5. It was entirely plain. 6. It was a typical pioneer's cabin.	The cabin they approached was small and squat, built of logs and entirely plain, a typical pioneer's cabin. (from *Across Five Aprils* by Irene Hunt, 1964, Berkley/Pacer, 19)
1. The plane fell into the wide place. 2. It fell like a stone. 3. It was committed now to landing. 4. It was committed now to crashing. 5. Brian eased back on the wheel. 6. He braced himself for the crash.	The plane, committed now to landing, to crashing, fell into the wide place like a stone, and Brian eased back on the wheel and braced himself for the crash. (from *Hatchet* by Gary Paulsen, 1987, Puffin, 28)
1. The old house was the same. 2. It was droopy. 3. It was sick. 4. We stared down the street. 5. We thought we saw a shutter move. 6. The shutter was inside.	The old house was the same, droopy and sick, but as we stared down the street we thought we saw an inside shutter move. (from *To Kill a Mockingbird* by Harper Lee, 1960, Harper & Row, 21)
1. I was still astride the top rail. 2. The bulls crashed through the fence. 3. The bulls were struggling. 4. They splintered the posts and rails. 5. They toppled me to the ground. 6. I was almost under them.	I was still astride the top rail when the struggling bulls crashed through the fence, splintering the posts and rails, and toppling me to the ground almost under them. (from *Old Yeller* by Fred Gipson, 1956 Perennial, 27–28)
1. He's got dark-gold hair. 2. He combs it back. 3. It is long and silky and straight. 4. The sun bleaches it to a wheat-gold. 5. The wheat-gold is shining. 6. The bleaching is in the summer.	He's got dark-gold hair that he combs back—long and silky and straight—and in the summer the sun bleaches it to a shining wheat-gold. (from *The Outsiders* by S. E. Hinton, 1967 Puffin, 7–8)
1. The pony's tracks were plain enough. 2. They dragged through the frostlike dew. 3. The dew was on the young grass. 4. They were tired tracks. 5. They had little lines between them. 6. The hooves had dragged there.	The pony's tracks were plain enough, dragging through the frostlike dew on the young grass, tired tracks with little lines between them where the hoofs had dragged. (from *The Red Pony* by John Steinbeck, 1937, 1993, Penguin, 34)
1. One of the girls was playing the piano. 2. The girl was in yellow. 3. A young lady stood beside her. 4. The lady was tall and had red hair. 5. The lady was from a famous chorus. 6. She was engaged in song.	One of the girls in yellow was playing the piano, and beside her stood a tall, red-haired young lady from a famous chorus, engaged in song. (from *The Great Gatsby* by F. Scott Fitzgerald, Scribner Classic, 1925, 1953, 51)

Students can experiment with the placement of these free modifiers, trying them out before the main clause as well as within it. When such examples get transcribed into grammar notebooks, perhaps with scaffolding, they stick in students' minds. At the very least, we know that Jason is likely to remember them!

You can also pull sentences from the literature being studied in class and use these as hooks to invite prediction and attention to an author's style. I like to withhold the original sentences until students have shared and compared their versions.

The ideas of Francis Christensen (1967) continue to provide a helpful frame of reference for sentence modeling. According to Christensen's scholarship, an essential structure of modern prose style is the cumulative sentence, a main clause plus one or more free modifiers—these often following the main clause to provide elaboration, an increasing specificity of detail. Such a sentence is illustrated here in the analytic layout used by Christensen.

> 2 According to Christensen's scholarship,
> 1 an essential structure of modern prose style is the cumulative sentence,
>   2 a main clause plus one or more free modifiers—
>   3 these often following the main clause to provide elaboration,
>   4 an increasing specificity of detail.
>
> ∎

In the example sentence, the main clause (level 1) is first modified by a participial phrase ("According to . . .") and then by an appositive noun phrase ("a main clause . . ."); the appositive, in turn, is modified by an absolute ("these often following . . ."), and one of its terms is modified by another appositive noun phrase ("an increasing specificity. . .").

As illustrated in the previous example, Christensen invited students to analyze sentences in a hierarchical way, focusing on meaningful semantic chunks (phrases and clauses) within the sentence. His method of analysis—a blend of syntax and semantics—contrasts sharply with the atomistic diagraming of traditional, structural, and transformational grammar. Generally, Christensen's approach captures the way the sentence is actually read; in addition, it helps show the relationship of structure to meaning, particularly as students move parts around and add new levels.

Christensen called his approach a generative rhetoric of the sentence and the paragraph. His premise was that structures in modern prose reflect an essentially additive process, a generative habit of mind. In showing how such sentences often work—by first framing a scene, an action, or an idea in the main clause, then providing a series of close-ups, each semantically related to the levels above—Christensen sought to explain the concept of texture in narrative and informational text. Let's look at another such sentence:

> 2 In showing how such sentences often work—
>   3 by first framing a scene, an action, or an idea in the main clause,
>   3 then providing a series of close-ups,
>   4 each semantically related to the levels above—
> 1 Christensen sought to explain the concept of texture in narrative and informational text.
>
> ∎

Christensen believed that once students see the architecture of well-crafted sentences and paragraphs, they can make these patterns their own through practice, then call upon such schema. In other words, a well-learned pattern can itself prompt learners to extend, generate, or elaborate a basic idea by adding free modifiers. Of course, once these additions have been generated, they can be tightened or moved around for stylistic emphasis. Today, such ideas find much support in cognitive science.

Christensen's scaffolding accounts for the identification of main clauses and free modifiers (or additions), the layout of a direction of modification for these additions (before, within, or after the main clause), and the numbering of levels of generality, with notations on grammatical structure. My adaptations of such ideas are found in *Crafting Cumulative Sentences* (1984a) and in the minilessons on advanced stylistic structures in *Writer's Toolbox* (1996). Harry Noden's *Image Grammar* (2000), which uses sentence-modeling activities, also draws its inspiration from Christensen's pioneering work with style.

Style in Context

What principles of style do you value? If I had to limit myself to three principles for middle school and high school teaching, my list would include the following:

- conciseness
- sentence variety
- parallel structure

With conciseness, I can draw attention to the verbal padding that muffles or obfuscates voice. With sentence variety, I can deal with issues of length and structure as well as with strategies for achieving emphasis, such as openers, interruptions, questions and commands, or unusual patterns. With parallel structure, I can show how helpful it is to have ideas packaged in similar syntax (as in the three sentences you have just read).

The next four exercises follow naturally from sentence modeling. After students read work by a given author—say, Gary Soto—and discuss stylistic features, a brief SC exercise is prepared so that students can become the author, using the moves that they have noticed. Of course, a well-chosen passage reinforces certain structures—verb clusters, appositives, absolutes—that have been the focus of modeling instruction.

Exercise in conciseness

Consider the SC format of the following exercise, one set up in kernel sentences, with problem sentences providing rewriting prompts. This exercise is drawn from the "Riding in Style" demonstration essay that opened the chapter. After students have rewritten the problem sentences, the original text offers useful points of stylistic comparison.

Conciseness Exercise

Directions: We've discussed lean, direct writing—how less is more sometimes. Now, try your hand at rewriting wordy sentences. Compare the word counts in your sentences with the problem sentences. Share your results with a partner.

1.1　You think about it.

1.2　Cars and writing have a lot in common.

Problem 1: With just a moment of thoughtful reflection, it becomes clear that cars and writing have a large number of features of commonality. (22 words)

2.1 Both are expressions of identity.
2.2 They are not merely technologies.
2.3 One of the technologies accomplishes transportation.
2.4 One of the technologies accomplishes communication.

Problem 2: There is no doubt that both of them are expressions of individual identity, which is to say that they are not merely technologies in the areas of transportation and communication, respectively. (30 words)

3.1 Advertisers know something so well.
3.2 We choose cars.
3.3 We ornament cars.
3.4 We inhabit cars.
3.5 This is to say who we are.
3.6 This is to say who we'd like to be.

Problem 3: Among the various kinds of things that advertisers know so well is that our choice of cars, our ornamentation for them, and our habitation of them are all part of the larger effort to say who we are on the one hand, or who we'd like to be on the other hand. (52 words)

4.1 So cars express our values.
4.2 Writing expresses our values.

Problem 4: It is clear, therefore, that there is an expression of our personal values through cars just as there is an expression of our values through writing. (26 words)

Original Text

When you think about it, cars and writing have a lot in common. Both are expressions of identity, not merely technologies to accomplish transportation and communication. As advertisers know so well, we choose cars, ornament them, and inhabit them to say who we are—or who we'd like to be. So cars express our values, just as writing does. (59 words total)

■

Exercise in sentence variety

By focusing on sentence variety, you aim to show students how a mix of short and long sentences can create stylistic interest. The following exercise, drawn from the "Riding in Style" essay, might be approached in stages. Students could work with the six clusters, producing a six-sentence text with parallel structure for clusters 3, 4, and 5.

After students have made a first pass through the exercise, encourage them to focus on their stylistic habits, comparing their work to that of partners in their group. In the sample student text that follows, we see how one student has relied on coordination and relative clause transformations, particularly *that* and *which* pronouns. Instead of labeling such features good or bad, mature or immature, it makes sense simply to notice such characteristics in a context of alternatives. This student is in the developmental stage of clause expansion; with practice and encouragement, perhaps the later stage of clause reduction will be reached.

Finally, you might challenge an able class to combine the combining in clusters 2, 3, 4, and 5, producing one sentence in place of four. Such a move, you might say, is like the grand slam in baseball or the triple lutz in ice-skating—not something one does every day, but certainly fun on special occasions. As students work on this task, they will see that the text becomes a sequence of three sentence lengths: short, long, and medium. Is such variety effective, in their opinion? This exercise invites students to consider the effects of a sophisticated style (for example, infinitive phrases in cluster 1; appositive adjectives in cluster 4) and advanced punctuation (use of the colon to introduce a series; use of semi-colons to separate noun phrases).

Sentence Variety Exercise

Directions: Let's focus on sentence variety—in both length and structure. Write the best sentences you can from the following clusters. After doing the exercise, take a second look at it. Work with partners to see whether you can recombine clusters 2–5 into one well-crafted, easy-to-read sentence.

1.1 I think about style.
1.2 I think about cars.

2.1 And I owned three treasures.
2.2 I was a cultural product of the mid-1950s.
2.3 Each one was bought for under $150.

3.1 There was a '38 Chevy.
3.2 It was dark green.
3.3 I removed all chrome from its body.
3.4 Its body was flawless.
3.5 I installed dual exhaust pipes under it.
3.6 The installation was loving.
3.7 This was to announce my coming-of-age.

4.1 Then there was a flathead Ford.
4.2 It was throaty.
4.3 It was a '41 vintage.
4.4 It was black and pristine.
4.5 This was until a morning of inattention.
4.6 The morning was sunny.
4.7 I laid it over.
4.8 I climbed out through the passenger's side window.

5.1 Finally there was a '36 Ford pickup.
5.2 It was sexy.
5.3 It was also black.
5.4 It had all original equipment.
5.5 The equipment included mechanical brakes.
5.6 They were roughly equivalent to dragging one's feet.

5.7 The dragging was in a coaster wagon.

5.8 The coaster wagon was careening.

6.1 These classics would provide a retirement package today.

6.2 They had air-conditioning.

6.3 The air-conditioning was all natural.

6.4 The retirement package would be portable.

6.5 It would be for someone.

6.6 Someone never got good at cruising.

6.7 Someone had all the aspirations.

Student Text

When I think about style, I think about cars. And I was a cultural product of the 1950s, so I owned some treasures that were bought for under $150 each. There was a dark green '38 Chevy, with a flawless body that I removed all the chrome from, and under it I lovingly installed dual exhaust pipes to announce my coming-of-age. Then there was a '41 vintage throaty flathead Ford that was black and pristine until the sunny morning of inattention that I laid it over, then climbed out through the passenger's side window. Finally there was a sexy '36 Ford pickup that was also black and had all original equipment which included mechanical brakes that were roughly equivalent to dragging one's feet in a careening coaster wagon. These three classics had all natural air-conditioning, and they would provide a portable retirement package today for someone that never got good at cruising but had all the aspirations.

Original Text

To think about style, for me, is to think about cars. And as a cultural product of the mid-1950s, I owned three treasures, each bought for under $150: a dark green '38 Chevy, from whose classic body all chrome was removed and under which I lovingly installed dual exhaust pipes to announce my coming-of-age; then a throaty flathead Ford of '41 vintage, black and pristine, at least until the sunny morning of inattention when I laid it over and climbed out through the passenger's side window; and later a sexy '36 Ford pickup, also black, with all original equipment, right down to its mechanical brakes, the laughable equivalent of dragging one's feet in a careening coaster wagon. Today, these classics, with their all-natural air-conditioning, would provide a portable retirement package for someone who never got good at cruising but had all the aspirations.

■

Exercise in parallel structure

One of my favorite exercises in parallelism is drawn from Mildred Taylor's *Roll of Thunder, Hear My Cry* (1976). I like to emphasize that although parallel structure can create heightened emphasis, it can also result in monotony when overused. I present the exercise to students in unclustered fashion and ask them to figure out what goes with what. After students have worked with the exercise, we examine a sample student text for parallel structure; then students look for parallelism in their own writing.

Parallelism Exercise

1. Revivals were always affairs.
2. The affairs were very serious.
3. The affairs were gay.
4. The affairs were long-planned-for.
5. They brought pots from shelves.
6. They brought pans from shelves.
7. They shelves were out-of-the-way.
8. They brought dresses from chests.
9. They brought pants from chests.
10. The dresses were mothball-packed.
11. The pants were creased.
12. The chests were hidden.
13. They brought all the people.
14. The people were from the community.
15. The people were from neighboring communities.
16. The people came up the school road.
17. The road was winding.
18. The road was red.
19. The people came to the Great Faith Church.
20. The revival ran for seven days.
21. It was an occasion.
22. Everyone looked forward to it.
23. It was more than just church services.
24. It was the year's only event.
25. The event was social.
26. The event was planned.
27. It disrupted the humdrum of everyday life.
28. The life was in the country.

Student Text

(1) Revivals were always serious, but they were also gay and long-planned-for affairs. (2) They brought pots and pans from out-of-the-way shelves. (3) They brought mothball-packed dresses and creased pants from hidden chests. (4) They brought all the people from the community (neighboring ones included) up the red and winding school road to the Great Faith Church. (5) The revival ran for seven days. (6) It was an occasion that everyone looked forward to. (7) It was more than just church services. (8) It was the year's only planned social event. (9) It disrupted the humdrum of everyday life in the country.

Original Text

(1) Revivals were always very serious, yet gay and long-planned-for, affairs which brought pots and pans from out-of-the-way shelves, mothball-packed dresses and creased pants from hidden chests, and all the people from the community and neighboring communities up the winding red school road to the Great Faith

Church. (2) The revival ran for seven days and it was an occasion everyone looked forward to, for it was more than just church services; it was the year's only planned social event, disrupting the humdrum of everyday country life. (233–34)

Afterward, students examine Mildred Taylor's original sentences, sometimes with gasps. Then I ask them to study one of their own texts in progress to see whether they can apply the principles of parallel structure in a sentence or two—and to note this application in the margin. In this way, students are helped to know what they know.

Exercise in de-writing

As students get serious about style, they will probably enjoy de-writing, a type of exercise derived from literature or professional nonfiction. A de-written text consists only of main clauses, with all modifiers removed. The task for students is to work from the bare bones of the exercise text, imagining its visual details, and then to embed these details in interesting ways. Such an activity invites two levels of comparison: first with peers, then with a skilled professional. The following exercise, derived from John McPhee's "Travels in Georgia" (1975), focuses on Zebra, a Georgia rattlesnake.

De-writing Exercise

Directions: Read the passage below and imagine the scene. Then layer the details you imagine into the given sentences, developing and expanding this moment for readers. Make your writing about twice as long as the exercise.

The gerbil began to walk around. Zebra gave no sign that he was aware. The gerbil explored Zebra's domain. The gerbil stepped up onto Zebra's back. Still Zebra did not move. Zebra had been known to refuse a meal. Perhaps that would happen now. The gerbil walked along the snake's back. It stepped down. It continued along the boundary. The strike came. The strike was so fast. The snake lanced across the distance. The gerbil fell dead.

Original Text

The gerbil began to walk around the bottom of the big glass jar. Zebra, whose body was arranged in a loose coil, gave no sign that he was aware of the gerbil's presence. Under a leaf, over a rock, sniffing, the gerbil explored the periphery of Zebra's domain. Eventually, the gerbil stepped up onto Zebra's back. Still, Zebra did not move. Zebra had been known to refuse a meal, and perhaps that would happen now. The gerbil walked along the snake's back, stepped down, and continued along the base of the jar, still exploring. Another leaf, another stone, the strike came when the gerbil was perhaps eight inches from Zebra's head. The strike was so fast, the strike and recovery, that it could not really be followed by the eye. Zebra lanced across the distance, hit the gerbil in the heart, and, all in the same instant, was back where he had started, same loose coil, head resting just where it had been resting before. The gerbil took three steps forward and fell dead, so dead it did not even quiver, tail out straight behind. (81)

An exercise like this one, with taut prose mirroring the action, provides a nice segue into the Showing, Not Telling activities described in Chapter 5, "Coaching Paragraphs."

Academic Style

To some language coaches, attention to style may seem peripheral to the development of an authentic voice or to text features such as organization, coherence, and logical development. But to dismiss issues of style as mere technique is to shortchange students in important ways. In fact, writing instruction will always remain incomplete if not grounded, to some extent, in syntax and style. This is why Donald Murray emphasizes that "as we revise, considering each word, each piece of punctuation, each phrase, sentence, paragraph, page, we make decisions that lead to other decisions" (1995, xiv). His emphasis on craft reminds us that stylistic knowledge—a sense of options—is absolutely basic to growth in written language.

Moreover, the development of an analytic (or academic) style seems basic to school success. Perhaps you can still recall, in your own student days, trying to sound academic and knowledgeable as you responded to some literary text for a teacher. Perhaps you were not quite sure how to play the role of literature student successfully. Perhaps you were admonished to marshal textual support for your interpretation; or perhaps, like me, you had a friend whose old papers demonstrated some expertise in analysis and thereby helped you figure out how to get started, cite examples, and make transitions. Perhaps, as a professional adult, you have looked back at those papers and read sentences so awkward, pompous, and confused that you had to laugh aloud.

If so, you can appreciate the perspective of Mike Rose (1989), who confesses that many of his own sentences "piled up like cars in a serial wreck" as he tried to find his way around the language of the academy:

> Appropriating a style and making it your own is difficult, and you'll miss the mark a thousand times along the way. The botched performances, though, are part of it all, and developing writers will grow through them if they are able to write for people who care about language, people who are willing to sit with them and help them as they struggle to write about difficult things. (54)

Rose is talking about socialization, of course. Students become junior members of the academic club by adopting its language, its conventions, and its rituals. The key, Rose says, is held by coaches "who care about language" and assist students "as they struggle to write about difficult things."

The strategies in this chapter, when linked to academic texts, can help students acquire new registers of language. All of the exercises share the same underlying premise: that whatever students can do with structure and the help of others, they will eventually be able to do on their own (Vygotsky 1978). To develop certain habits of mind—and an awareness of one's own style—is clearly a lifelong pursuit. It is assisted by collaborators who can verbalize what they notice about a text, in terms more specific than *lame, good,* and *awesome*. A common core of stylistic terms can serve students well, particularly when those ideas are anchored in meaningful practice, with frequent opportunities to apply learning to texts in progress. In the next chapter, we consider some structural features of academic style.

Finally, the point needs to be made that there is no virtue in stylistic complexity (or technical terminology) for its own sake. Work with style pays off when students read in new ways, noticing how one author handles punctuation or how another mixes long and short sentences for emphasis, and it reaches its full flowering when learners point with pride to specific stylistic improvements. Good language education helps students understand recurring patterns in their repertoire and apply what they know. Whenever possible, we should allow language itself to do the teaching.

Learning Through Language

1. In Chapter 4 you learned about high, middle, and low styles, a framework for middle school and high school students. Assume that you have introduced such a taxonomy. What next? That is, how do you see such a construct being used? Is it simply a way to classify texts? What good is that? Would it be useful to have students transform texts up and down the taxonomy? What good is that? Would you have students examine their own style? What good is that?

2. The strategy of sentence modeling is central to the chapter. As you did for Chapter 2, write a letter to *another* close friend who is either traditional in instructional methods (a dyed-in-the-wool grammarian) or progressive in approach (a whole language zealot). Your aim in writing is to get this person's written response to your summary of sentence modeling. Exchange letters with a *different* writing partner, and then respond to your partner's letter.

3. Examine your letter and the response of your partner from activity 2. There are two styles of writing before you. Hear the different sentence rhythms. Look at the word choice in each. Pay special attention to features like voice. Now, assuming an academic (or analytic) voice, list the contrasting text features. Put these on an overhead transparency. Finally, present your findings to other group members and your instructor, referring to text examples for support.

CHAPTER 5

COACHING PARAGRAPHS

Instruction

The coach has taught her how to swing,
run bases, slide, how to throw
to second, flip off her mask for fouls.

Now, on her own, she studies
how to knock the dirt out of her cleats,
hitch up her pants, miss her shoulder
with a stream of spit, bump
her fist into her catcher's mitt,
and stare incredulously at the ump.

—**Conrad Hilberry**

Literacy and Civility

For me, the seeds of literacy and civility were sown early. As a five-year-old growing up in southeast Portland, I had begun to roam the streets, much to my mom's dismay. I hung out with some pretty scabby characters—tough, older kids mostly—but on Saturday afternoons I sometimes found myself in a quiet, book-smelling place made of sand-colored bricks, where I'd sit on the floor and a nice lady in a flowered dress would have us gather around. Her stories seemed to be for me personally, and they came to me as smiling speech.

The book lady spoke of worlds beyond a rough-and-tumble street world of junk cars and vacant lots and abandoned house trailers. While I stared at her chunky ankles or her round, bifocaled face, I was captured in a net of words. Time, as we usually think of it, was meaningless. In fact, I worried about going into the library during daylight hours, coming out after dark, and never finding my way home. Maybe it was this sense of danger—living on the edge—that brought me back week after week. Or maybe it was imagery and the cadence of literate language that nudged me toward civility.

After all, aren't literacy and civilization linked?

And isn't one, at least potentially, a *means* to the other?

I'm not saying, of course, that early coaching changed the reality outside the library. The time-honored laws of childhood, like survival of the fittest, still held sway. Vandalism, street fights, and nickel-and-dime extortion remained facts of daily survival for a kid like me. So, story or no story, the bully next door continued to settle disputes in his inimitable tight-lipped way, wielding a chunk of concrete one hot summer afternoon to split open my skull. When bright red blood streaked the white picket fence on Foster Road, I felt no less pain for having heard lovely words the Saturday before.

But what the language did begin to change, I think, was a reality *inside*—an emerging sense of values. Maybe the change began with sitting still and not hitting others. Maybe it was nurtured as I heard themes of courage and loyalty and friendship overcoming darker forces in the world outside. Maybe it was strengthened as I shared my responses to stories and listened to others—in effect, consolidating new values by talking them through. Or maybe it was a combination of things. Literacy and civility have many roots.

When my family moved across town, the nuns at St. Clair's School took up where the librarian had left off. But the discipline I learned was more than sitting still, not talking out, and behaving myself on the playground. It was a discipline of language. I memorized hymns and the answers to catechism questions. I learned not just the words of prayers but their meanings. I practiced reading—and, more important, rereading—my favorite parts in books, saying them aloud until their rhythms became part of me. Dictation practice taught me to hold long stretches of syntax in short-term memory. And in the fourth grade I learned, profoundly and indelibly, that I could write.

In my memory a nun swoops back and forth across the room, a face framed in black and white, her sleeves like bat's wings. Flip-top desks are bolted to long wooden runners, and rain slides down the classroom windows. Radiators along the wall suffuse us with steamy heat, the smell of wet wool. We all stare at a row of pictures above the dusty chalkboard, and I'm choosing the one I want, a picture of a cowboy astride his horse—"Palomino" I'll call it because that is the kind of horse ridden by Roy Rogers. There's a dog at his side. I can see them now, coming down a narrow trail strewn with gray, jagged boulders. It is dangerous country, with deep ravines. Then, as I become the cowboy, I can feel the horse, rounded and solid beneath me, even though I've only ridden a pony at the fairgrounds. "There's a story in your picture," the nun is saying. "Let's write about it."

The room becomes quiet, and pencils begin to scratch. I don't know what to write or how to do it. All I know is that the trees are cottonwoods—cowboys and cottonwoods go together—and there's danger up ahead as we descend the steep, narrow trail. The spaniel moves out ahead of the palomino, picking his way through the rocks. A Texas sun casts harsh shadows on the landscape, and no birds sing. And suddenly, the dog freezes, sniffing the air, his left paw slowly lifting, pointing toward certain death in the trailside shadows. It's ready to strike from the place where the horse will pass in the next few moments—a huge coiled rattlesnake, with its head back and black eyes glittering, tongue flicking in and out, rattles hissing in a devil's dance. In truth, I am afraid of snakes, and I barely manage to rein in the frightened horse—"Easy, boy, easy." The horse's life and my life are saved by a trusty companion, whose steady paw is forever raised in unflinching alarm.

Although my fourth-grade story was just a few paragraphs long, a few days later I found myself trembling in front of a surly seventh-grade class, reading it aloud. What I only vaguely understood was that the seventh-grade teacher was using me as a visual aid to embarrass this grim bunch into better writing. "If a fourth grader can do this," she barked, "what's the matter with you?"

Here I was, shrimp of my class, not to mention the school, and I had secretly wet my pants. I beat a hasty retreat down the echoing wooden hallway past Mother Superior's office and laid low for the next few days. My early lessons in street survival had not been entirely forgotten.

The next thing I knew, however, my cowboy story was published in the school newspaper, a barely legible publication run from purple ditto masters and stapled in the upper left corner. I couldn't believe it, seeing my name typed at the bottom of the page. Success was sweet, even delicious. When Dad came home from working in the Oregon timber and sat at the Formica table with chrome legs as Mom fixed supper, I read it aloud and watched him nod approval.

And then we visited my grandparents' house on a Sunday afternoon. We were all there, my family and grandparents in a room with horsehair furniture, lace doilies, and a huge potted plant in the east window. An old mantle clock ticked in the background. It was after Sunday dinner—fried chicken with mashed potatoes and gravy, no doubt—that Mom dragged the crumpled school paper from her black vinyl purse. "Oh, yes," they said. "Let's hear it." They wanted a good, strong voice.

The room grew silent, and I once again created the scene of the cowboy astride his palomino, the cottonwoods shading the trail. My voice tightened as I shared the paragraphs, every phrase and image now committed to memory. There was something in that small moment, my family gathered around, their faces listening and waiting for what I had to say, that I have never forgotten.

"Why, that's very good," they finally said.

I stood there grinning—and in some ways I still am.

The Paradox of Paragraphs

I begin with this memory for two reasons: first, to focus on its substance, those cowboy paragraphs that, alas, went up in flames when my family's house burned down; and, second, to focus on its form. Although I wrote the cowboy story more than fifty years ago, I still remember the look of those paragraphs in the school newspaper, the typewritten words flowing left to right, all neatly spaced and aligned on the page, just like real writing. To have written all that—and to hear my voice behind the words—stopped me in my tracks.

A case can be made, I think, that by fourth grade I had developed a primitive schema for narrative paragraphs, a way of chunking sentences together. Part of this template was probably created as I listened to adventure stories in the library and tried not to worry about the gathering twilight outside. Part of it probably resulted from the discipline of language—dictation, rereading, and memorization—for which Catholic schools have long been famous and often been criticized. As for expository paragraphs, I was taught to embed given questions into the first (or top) sentences of my written responses. Of course, this injunction prompted me, continually, to transform adult language into superordinate (or topic) sentences, with the development of those first sentences serving as daily writing practice.

My adult narrative "Literacy and Civility" presents several paragraphs stacked atop one another to invite reflection and analysis. In your reading you may have noticed how descriptive and narrative paragraphs tell a story but also serve other ends as well. Specifically, they develop a thesis concerning the civilizing and empowering effects of literate language. The basic argument, developed over two paragraphs, is that literacy can be a means to civility—first, in the social expectations it requires and the underlying values it promotes, then in its processes for bringing the discipline of literate language use under increasing self-control. Unlike my schema for narrative, the schema for developing a thesis probably developed in the secondary grades and in college.

In this section I repeat the argument made earlier for syntax and style—namely, that paragraphs provide a means of working, in miniature, with many of the big issues of composition, including what Jim Burke (1999) calls "the Five Principles of an Essay":

- thesis
- focus
- concreteness
- organization
- mechanics

If you like analogies, you might consider well-crafted paragraphs as bonsai, the lovely miniature landscapes made famous by Japanese gardeners. Although a bonsai may differ in scale from the sculptured Japanese garden that stands as backdrop, both express similar aesthetic principles. In fact, the same patient hands may create both.

Some teachers may sigh and roll their eyes as I broach the subject of teaching the paragraph. Why? Because the writing process revolution grew out of a rejection of such instruction, with its transmission metaphors and emphasis on discrete skills and proficiencies (writing the paragraph among them). It has long been an article of faith for process writing disciples that meaningful, self-sponsored writing—when coupled with rich reading experiences and social support—will enable most students to naturally acquire the structures and technical skills that underlie effective prose. But in recent years serious questions have been raised by researchers and theorists about the basic assumptions of natural process instruction (e.g., Delpit 1986, 1988; Gee 1990; Hillocks 1986), for both mainstream and minority students. In special education, particularly, much work has been done to assist struggling students with strategies (e.g., Collins 1998; Englert 1995; Harris and Graham 1996).

The idea that many struggling learners lack an internal image for paragraphs—or lack motivation to activate what they do know about text structure—is hardly news to veteran coaches. Such students, faced with the task of developing a coherent line of thought, may go strangely silent or draw upon default strategies such as "knowledge telling" (copying) or "telling a story," according to James Collins (1998). As Collins puts the matter, based on his research in secondary schools, struggling writers "seem often to imagine academic writing in a 'minimally acceptable' version of the genre, as 'collections' of words and sentences filling a required amount of space on paper, but not as coherent paragraphs or whole texts and certainly not more space than is required" (117). Collins and his teacher researchers help students build upon existing strategies to coconstruct new imagery for text structure, including the paragraph.

How does imagery assist performance? If you were an intermediate skier, just past the snowplow stage, I would coach you to face downhill and imagine yourself as a waiter on skis, carrying a small tray of food to high-paying customers down the slope. In fact, I might have an actual tray as a prop, and you might grip its two sides. We would visualize the scene together, imagining how you slowly ease forward, keeping the tray level, and over the downhill slope, facing all that breathtaking scenery. And I would show you how the tray stays level in the turns, first one way, then the other. You would see it in reality, and you would see it in your mind, your body erect, knees bent, relaxed hands gently gripping the edges of the tray to maintain its orientation in space, the imaginary coffee cups and pastries riding smooth and level, gliding along, turn after turn. And you would have it, an image to guide your practice on easy terrain and then on steeper, more challenging slopes. I would not talk about ski edges or the dangers of sitting back or the techniques of unweighting in the turns. Your schema for skiing would be based not upon discrete, skill-based rules but upon your visualization of a performance—an exemplar with you in the spotlight.

In a similar way, it may be useful to visualize paragraphs as frames. Within each paragraph frame, a series of images, ideas, or sentences can be arranged and layered for desired effects. Of course, boundaries of frames can also change, for example, when a writer divides a paragraph into parts or when sentences are deleted, reordered, or expanded. To help students see how paragraphs build on one another, many teachers use schematics such as the inverted pyramid (introduction), rectangles (body), and pyramid (conclusion). Often such graphics are linked to model essays. Students are asked to notice how an introductory paragraph narrows to a controlling idea or how the language of enumeration (*first, second, third*) or concession (*It is true that . . . However, . . . Therefore, . . .*) provides direction for a series of body paragraphs.

James Collins (1998) activates such metaphors by asking young writers to box or frame coherent paragraphs with a computer drawing program and then notice text features within a frame—for example, how the first sentence compares with other sentences. Out of this coconstructed understanding of paragraphs, basic writers create flexible templates to visualize paragraphs and activate the knowledge they have begun to internalize about text structure. Later, they use arrows in the computer's drawing program to link supporting sentences and topic sentences, thus highlighting a paragraph's cohesive ties (Halliday and Hasan 1976). I demonstrate a similar approach at the end of this chapter.

The paradox of paragraphs centers on their metaphysical slipperiness. On the one hand, a paragraph can be regarded as a structure, a way of packaging related sentences by means of underlying cognitive processes. A structural view might lead one to teach organizational strategies beneath the surface of text and the signal words or the markers for each pattern: spatial order, time order, numerical order, cause/effect order, compare/contrast order, and general/specific order. On the other hand, one can argue that paragraphs exist only as arbitrary conventions, a way of segmenting the flow of the discourse stream into bite-sized sections for the reader's convenience. Such a view might lead one to treat paragraphing, like punctuation, as strictly a function of social convention, a readability issue linked to purpose, audience, and genre.

With characteristic cowboy diplomacy, I sit on the paradoxical fence. Certainly there are times in my writing—and rewriting—when I use a paragraph template or schema to move the text along. For example, in the paragraph preceding this one, I found myself drawing upon (or generating) a compare/contrast pattern as sentences began to reveal themselves, one after another. In rereading that text—and rearranging it slightly—I could see its underlying architecture, one outlined in the following layout with the levels of generality technique described in Chapter 4:

Levels of Generality for Paradox Paragraph

1. The paradox of paragraphs centers on their metaphysical slipperiness.
  2. On the one hand, a paragraph can be regarded as a structure, a way of packaging related sentences by means of underlying cognitive processes.
    3. A structural view might lead one to teach organizational strategies beneath the surface of text and the signal words or the markers for each pattern: spatial order, time order, numerical order, cause/effect order, compare/contrast order, and general/specific order.
  2. On the other hand, one can argue that paragraphs exist only as arbitrary conventions, a way of segmenting the flow of the discourse stream into bite-sized sections for the reader's convenience.
    3. Such a view might lead one to treat paragraphing, like punctuation, as strictly a function of social convention, a readability issue linked to purpose, audience, and genre.

∎

As noted previously, Christensen's (1967) method of discourse analysis reveals relationships between syntax and semantics. Logically, each downshift elaborates the immediately preceding level.

But did I plan the paragraph as illustrated earlier, then follow my own blueprint? Of course not. My plan consisted of a few words and phrases jotted on a yellow pad. I had a vague idea for the paragraph, partly because I had named this section "The Paradox of Paragraphs" and partly because I knew it would offer a rationale for sections that follow. As I drafted it, the opening phrase of the second sentence (*On the one hand*) immediately suggested an overall structure. At some subliminal level, I no doubt called upon the image (or schema) of elements being contrasted. Later I tinkered with the sentences so that clear parallel syntax contributed to paragraph structure.

Given the discussion here, it probably comes as no surprise that my standing homework assignment, as a greenhorn teacher, was a paragraph a day for all five classes. I reasoned, flawlessly, that by writing 180 paragraphs, students would develop a feel for them and draw upon this knowledge in writing longer papers. Of course, like other messianic coaches, I got the prescription only half right. As students whined in unison, I groaned under the glacierlike weight of spiral-bound notebooks. Although I read only a paragraph a week from each student—and "checked" the others—I soon concluded, "There *has* to be a better way!"

Regrettably, Rebekah Caplan's *Writers in Training* (1984) came along too late to save me from such zealous self-abuse. In the next section, I review Caplan's smart, manageable method for training students to write well-crafted paragraphs. A by-product of such work with composition miniatures is that students construct vivid schema that will serve them well in the future.

Showing, Not Telling

In "Language Competence" (1981), John Mellon remarks that "the performance skills of language are not acquired in a psychological vacuum" but instead require attention and work—"sometimes exhilarating, sometimes drudgery; sometimes boring, sometimes fun" (52). "Also important in language learning," he adds, "is the willingness to accept a teacher's criticism and corrective feedback without letting them lower one's self concept, generate animosity, or kill motivation" (52–53).

The Showing, Not Telling exercises in *Writers in Training* (Caplan 1984) offer a useful way to engage students in meaningful, enjoyable practice as well as in evaluation. Based on her background in dance and other performing arts, Rebekah Caplan contends that certain moves in writing, like leg lifts for the ballet dancer, must be practiced relentlessly if one is to achieve grace and naturalness in spotlight performances, the kind assessed in major assignments and on high-stakes accountability tests. Clearly, a basic move in writing focuses on one's ability to render objects, scenes, actions, and characters in sensory detail, to show in compelling ways so that readers *experience* text. For example, in "Literacy and Civility" at the beginning of this chapter, I tried to create both a classroom scene and the feelings of being a fourth-grade writer.

Through models, Caplan helps learners understand the difference between a *telling* paragraph and a *showing* paragraph, drawing out the contrast between general and specific language. Here is the kind of material that might be used, with a showing paragraph drawn from Mike Rose's compelling narrative *Lives on the Boundary* (1989).

> *Telling Paragraph*: Discipline methods at the school were unpleasant and intimidating. Two of the teachers used corporal punishment. Sometimes, too, they would verbally abuse or insult their students.

> *Showing Paragraph*: My homeroom was supervised by Brother Dill, a troubled and unstable man who also taught freshman English. When his class drifted away from him, which was often, his voice would rise in paranoid accusations, and occasionally he would lose control and shake or smack us. I hadn't been there two months when one of his brisk, face-turning slaps had my glasses sliding down the aisle. Physical education was also pretty harsh. Our teacher was a stubby ex-lineman who had played old-time pro ball in the Midwest. He routinely had us grabbing our ankles to receive his stinging paddle across our butts. He did that, he said, to make men of us. "Rose," he bellowed on our first encounter; me standing geeky in line in my baggy shorts. "'Rose'? What the hell kind of name is that?"
> "Italian, sir," I squeaked.
> "Italian! Ho. Rose, do you know the sound a bag of shit makes when it hits the wall?"
> "No, sir."
> "Wop!" (24–25)

As readers, most of us would say that the second paragraph is better than the first. But what, specifically, makes it better? Well, it describes two weird and frustrated teachers, we might add. But *how* does it show their weirdness and frustration? Finally, of course, we would point to specific details in the text, say, the image of eyeglasses skittering down the aisle or the one of students grabbing their angles. And we would mention specific words or phrases that resonate, like *shake or smack*, *stubby ex-lineman*, *stinging paddles*, and *bellowed*. And we would point to the unforgettable—and to us unimaginable—dialogue.

Caplan's core activity—one to which many other activities are linked—centers on students' daily practice with dozens of discursive telling sentences like the following:

- The pizza was delicious.
- The room was empty.
- The school bus was noisy.
- The teacher looked tired.
- The mall was crowded.
- The beach was sweltering.

Students are asked to show in paragraph-length writing the sentence they are given, but they are admonished not to use the sentence in their paragraphs. A constraint? Absolutely. But once students begin to practice this kind of exercise challenge, most look forward to it and become quite skilled at it.

Notice how Caplan's approach differs from traditional daily writing, the kind that filled my car's trunk with heaping cardboard boxes. First, the given sentences are not just topics—like "pizza" or "school bus" or "mall"—but instead establish a controlling idea, or direction, for thinking and writing. With broad given topics, students spend much of their writing time struggling to find direction in the absence of context. In contrast, the context here is clear—showing, not telling, with teacher and peers as audience—and students have lots of running room to show their creativity and writing prowess. Still, the fact that Caplan does establish a common playing field for practice—and subsequent instruction—is part of the secret of her approach. When students come to class with homework in hand, they wonder whether it will be read aloud for class comment and also how others handled the task. Because they have exercised on parallel playing fields, students are receptive to one another's writing performances.

So, in contrast to traditional exercises, where students typically wait for a tired teacher to pass judgment on their texts, Caplan relies on the context of immediate feedback. Exercises are written to be shared, and students never know whether their piece will be read aloud during the first fifteen minutes of class, the time during which the class engages, relentlessly, in observations and evaluations of one another's work. The evaluation focus is positive, of course—the strengths of the text, the specific details that stick in students' minds. In this work, Caplan compares herself to a drama instructor using improvisation:

> Just as drama students search for ways to express ambition or despair by imagining themselves in real-life situations that would evoke these feelings, and in so doing discover wide ranges of bodily and facial expression, my students arrive at ways of showing "empty rooms" or "difficult puzzles" by experimenting with language expression. For the first six weeks of the course, I instruct the class very little, preferring that they find their own solutions. If they are to learn new or different ways of expressing the same idea, it will come from comparing the results of different interpretations written by fellow students. (1984, 8)

Caplan's rationale directly parallels the themes I have expressed earlier, for work on basic skills (Chapter 1), syntax (Chapter 2), usage (Chapter 3), and style (Chapter 4). The activity of sharing and comparing—with students paying attention, voicing what they notice, and bringing their observations to a level of awareness—is part of a context in which language itself does much of the teaching.

As a practical matter, Caplan evaluates each of the chosen texts on the spot, underlining a phrase or image with a "good showing" notation or jotting down helpful suggestions offered by the class. Then each workshop paper receives an immediate private grade—A, B, or C—as long as the text represents a reasonable effort. Of course, students who do not have a paper ready to share receive no credit (NC) and eventually suffer the consequences. "To secure against numerous no-credits," she writes, "I also give students a chance to turn in weak papers with the special request that they *not* be read and evaluated orally" (11). Students are allowed only four "Do Not Read" (DNR) requests a semester. On the other hand, if students write paragraphs that they know are good ones, they can write "Please Read" at the top of the paper and improve their grades. Finally, students sometimes write helpful comments on one another's papers and volunteer classmates' work for recognition.

Caplan tries to be unpredictable in selecting papers to be read aloud. As a crafty professional, she may call on the same student two or three days in a row, and she sometimes extends the activity so that several students, not just a few, benefit from the workshop process. Of course, the message about being prepared is not lost on classroom-savvy learners. All papers not read in class are returned by the next day at the latest, with a check mark and the instructor's initials. Students earn completion credit, not to mention the benefits derived from writing practice and meaningful, focused discussion. The letter grades are averaged to become one-third of each student's total grade for the course—a powerful incentive for daily preparation.

From a coaching viewpoint, the benefits of daily writing, with an accompanying focus of evaluation, seem self-evident: learners are continually engaged in making an effort, attending to the efforts of others, and incorporating feedback from teacher and peers. They *work* at writing, imagining their peers (as well as their teacher) as audience. They learn, as Caplan puts it, "developmental techniques, even linguistic patterns from one another" as a consequence of "hearing regularly the effective writing of peers" (14). And, last but not least—for those coaches who want to work smarter, not harder—the in-class evaluation approach helps reduce the nightly grind of paper grading, freeing up time for sporting life pursuits described in this book's final chapter.

And what about application to students' own writing? The skills learned in the cycle of daily writing and evaluation—specificity and elaboration—become the focus of response group activities for major writing assignments, those requiring research, planning, drafting, revision, editing, and eventual sharing through publication. Having learned how to identify soft spots in a text, student responders identify general telling sentences, those that seem to need more development. "Instead of the usual daily routine in which everyone has the same sentence to develop," Caplan writes, "students now use sentences from their own writing" (14). In this way, of course, the showing, not telling training becomes a vital part of each student's approach to revision.

Varying the Workout Routine

Beyond the structures described in the previous section, Caplan recommends a number of variations for the routine of daily workouts, offering new challenges for language exploration. Here are some basic ideas, using her categories:

1. Undoing Cliches: Helping students appreciate the deadening effect of cliches has long been a goal of language arts coaches. So with the help of students, why not assemble a long list of cliches—"A chill ran down my spine," "It was on the tip of my tongue," "I was caught between a rock and a hard place"—and use these as telling sentences for imaginative expansion?

2. Encouraging Brevity: To secure peer approval, many students tell stories in the daily workouts, hoping for a laugh or other high compliments, for example, "How gross!" As time moves on, Caplan encourages conciseness, asking students not to belabor the point. Language growth is reflected in the quality of well-chosen words and well-crafted sentences.

3. Developing Vocabulary: Caplan sometimes embeds target vocabulary into daily telling sentences, asking students to show the word. For example, the words *ignoble* and *meretricious* could be embedded in the sentences "She came from an ignoble background" and "Her meretricious manner seized our attention." To lodge such words in long-term memory, students can first use their dictionaries—and then use their imaginations.

4. Developing Reading Comprehension: As part of literature study, Caplan assigns a particular telling sentence to prompt engagement and thinking. For example, for London's *Call of the Wild*, students might be assigned a sentence like "Buck is an intelligent dog." They would use details from the first chapter to support this idea, applying showing, not telling in a new context, one that involves marshaling evidence to support interpretation.

5. Showing Ideas Through Single Sentences: With this activity, Caplan asks students to produce a single well-crafted cumulative sentence in response to a telling sentence prompt. Of course, this sentence uses free modifiers as outlined in Chapter 4. Like the Conciseness Exercise activity, this one challenges students to imitate and internalize sophisticated structures.

6. Modeling Paragraphs: Using whole paragraphs from literature as models, Caplan asks for "close imitations." The activity begins with exact imitations of simple sentences, then progresses to more complex sentences. Finally, students are turned loose on a key paragraph or two from the text being studied.

7. Imitating Other Styles: In a creative (and hilarious!) extension of the method, Caplan invites students to emulate the prose style of a favorite author as they retell a familiar nursery rhyme or fairy tale. With this approach, students integrate not only the showing, not telling strategies but also the insights acquired from single-sentence imitations and paragraph-modeling activities.

8. Making Generalizations: As a kind of capstone for the variations, there is the activity of having students compose a telling sentence—a generalization—from

a given showing paragraph, sometimes in a literary work. Students must create an abstraction that accounts for all the details or facts in the text—a demanding task but one essential to literary interpretation. In those instances where the target text already contains a topic sentence or generalization, Caplan purposely removes it so that students are forced to invent it—or one like it.

With these variations as context, let's now return to a theme I introduced in the previous section: the idea that success with composition miniatures can help learners tackle larger projects with increased skill and confidence. Clearly, there is an enormous gap between the task of writing an amusing narrative paragraph on the one hand and the demands of crafting a carefully reasoned comparison/contrast essay on the other. How do we bridge the gap in our coaching? The answer lies in adapting a now-familiar method, showing, not telling, to new exigencies.

In the comparison/contrast essay, for example, Caplan begins with telling sentences that prompt a basic comparison/contrast structure at the paragraph level, such as "Saturday is different from Sunday," "My mother is different from my father," or "My _____ teacher is different from my _____ teacher." After students try their hands at such tasks, she presents effective student models, in which the contrast is handled through parallel construction. Subsequently, students choose their own telling sentence for comparison/contrast practice. Then students move toward integrated comparison/contrast, drawing upon models from professional writing. During practice writing, references are made to the upcoming comparison/contrast essay in literature, and students think strategically about how it might be approached, with the paragraph models as points of reference. They discuss transition words for comparison/contrast and the conditions under which these methods of development are generally effective.

Another intriguing activity to prepare students for comparison/contrast writing involves pairs of words with similar denotations but contrasting connotations. Students select a pair of appealing words to rehearse the target strategy. Of course, showing techniques learned in daily practice activities are called into service again. The following list contains the types of word pairs that Caplan uses for this particular activity.

pride/conceit	curiosity/nosiness
skinny/trim	rug/carpet
wisdom/knowledge	lady/chick

With all of this coaching, students are technically and mentally prepared to take on the challenge of a major literary essay or a similar assignment.

Although psycholinguist Frank Smith opposes language exercises, I contend that his account of "vicarious language learning" describes the kind of activity recommended here. According to Smith, all of us recruit "unwitting collaborators"—individuals or texts that demonstrate the kind of expertise we are trying to acquire, however unconsciously, to maintain our membership in the literacy club. Our learning is always social and linked to those people we see as being like us or with whom we identify. Indeed, Smith says, "the greatest help to newcomers in the club of readers and writers may be those experienced members who never tire of being approached and interrogated, the authors of the printed page" (1988, 10).

Structuring Paragraphs

As we have seen, expert teachers like James Collins (1998) and Rebekah Caplan (1984) offer hands-on strategies to assist basic and mainstream writers with the demands of paragraph-level writing. This work helps students internalize images of paragraph structure. To support such teaching, particularly for learners who stick with narrative because of its low risks, let me recommend other given-language exercises.

The first exercise type was illustrated in my paradox paragraph—an analysis into levels, using the hierarchical scheme popularized by Francis Christensen (1967). This approach can be understood by most high school students, particularly if they fathom how links work hierarchically on Internet websites and in computer software. According to Christensen, there are two basic types of paragraphs—coordinate sequence and subordinate sequence—but many paragraphs involve a blending of the two paradigms. To illustrate once again how the approach works, here is my analysis of a coordinate sequence paragraph from the "Literacy and Civility" section of this chapter.

1. But what the language did begin to change, I think, was a reality *inside*—an emerging sense of values.
  2. Maybe the change began with sitting still and not hitting others.
  2. Maybe it was nurtured as I heard themes of courage and loyalty and friendship overcoming darker forces in the world outside.
  2. Maybe it was strengthened as I shared my responses to stories and listened to others—in effect, consolidating new values by talking them through.
  2. Or maybe it was a combination of things.
1. Literacy and civility have many roots.

■

For more examples and practice materials that might serve as models for your own exercises, see my textbook *Writing Incisively: Do-It-Yourself Prose Surgery* (1991a). Other given-language materials in this section also come from that book.

A second type of exercise is the old standby of sentence scrambling, which usually works best as a small-group collaborative activity. The idea is to dismember well-constructed paragraphs, sentence by sentence, and then ask students to put the pieces back together in a reasonable order. Using a transparency that has been cut up into sentence strips, one can model the expectations. First trials of the activity should be structured with such strips (an envelope of sentences given to each group) so that students can manipulate sentences in a hands-on manner; afterward, they can move to rank-ordering tasks. After the activity is understood, a little friendly competition among groups may prove useful. Of course, to reorder scrambled sentences requires close reading of semantic and syntactic clues until a negotiated best solution is found by each group. If more than one solution comes up—and this is often the case—these are discussed. Finally, downloaded exercise sentences from a file server offer practice in blocking and moving text, preparing students for revision work on their own texts.

The following is one such exercise (Strong 1991a) that students could rearrange by putting sentences in rank order (1–10):

Memory

A.   Short-term memory (STM) is one system.
B.   Human memory seems to consist of two systems.
C.   The second remembering system is long-term memory.
D.   Within STM there are actually two subsystems.
E.   STM's second system, working memory, is good for about thirty minutes.
F.   LTM involves chemical changes in the brain.
G.   One subsystem of STM, perceptual processing, lasts for a minute or less.
H.   The capacity of LTM is unlimited because it is organized hierarchically—like Chinese boxes.
I.   The capacity of STM is only about seven items.
J.   LTM draws upon STM to create networks of knowledge.

■

This particular exercise can be reordered in two basic ways, and those arrangements might be arrayed in the hierarchical format used by Christensen (1967; Christensen and Christensen 1978). Students can then discuss the merits of each approach in terms of its ease of readability.

A third type of given-language exercise is both taxonomic and generative. After students consider descriptors and examples of six basic paragraph patterns, they can classify exercise paragraphs into various categories, using familiar signal words and phrases as clues (Strong 1991a).

Six Categories of Signal Words

Spatial Order: Above, below, beside, nearby, beyond, inside, outside, across the hall, in the drawer, toward the back, etc.

Time Order: Before, after, next, then, when, finally, while, as, during, earlier, previously, later, thereupon, subsequently, meanwhile, as soon as, etc.

Numerical Order: First, second, one factor, another type, also, finally, furthermore, moreover, in addition, less powerful, equally important, most significant, etc.

Cause/Effect Order: Because, since, for, in that, in order to, so, so that, as a result, therefore, consequently, thus, hence, accordingly, the reason for, the reason that, etc.

Comparison/Contrast Order: Also, additionally, just as, as if, as though, like, similarly, in the same way (for similarities); but, yet, only, though, although, whereas, while, in contrast, conversely, still, however, on the other hand, rather, instead, in spite of, nevertheless, on the contrary (for differences). The comparative and superlative forms of adjectives (-er/-est; less/least; more/most) also signal this pattern.

General/Specific Order: Such as, like, namely, more specifically, for example, for instance, to illustrate, that is, in fact, in other words, indeed, etc.

The work with models, when linked to imitative writing within a pattern, helps create a basic schema in students' minds. Such practice can be followed by textual scavenger hunts, with students searching for paragraphs that exemplify one pattern or another. Again, instructor modeling is important so that students know both where to look and how to look. Textbooks in other curriculum areas make good points of departure.

Although patterns of spatial order and time order will probably require little teaching, many learners will be unfamiliar with other patterns that support exposition and argument—namely, numerical order, with obvious and subtle signaling clues; cause/effect order, so basic to interpretation and analysis; compare/contrast order; and general/specific order, the workhorse pattern. In some classes, you may want to include other patterns of paragraph (or multiparagraph) organization that work in tandem with the basic six, for example, patterns based on a question/answer or problem/solution framework. Asking students to revise a text in progress by applying a paradigm can personalize the learning.

A fourth and final type of exercise invites students to trace the "cohesion ties" (Halliday and Hasan 1976) in coherent text. I first work with samples of coherent and noncoherent text to suggest that skilled writers, as they read to revise, see where sentence threads are weak or missing in the web of meaning. I liken this special seeing to x-ray vision. And I collapse the five categories of cohesion ties identified by Halliday and Hasan into three categories: grammar links, vocabulary links, and transition links. Illustrative arrows in the brief x-rays that follow suggest how words and phrases point to each other in sentences A/B, C/D, and E/F (Strong 1991a).

Grammar Links

A. Grammar links help with cohesion.

    A   B

    grammar links ⟵—— *they*

B. Often they are pronouns that refer to nouns in preceding sentences.

Vocabulary Links

C. Vocabulary links also create cohesion.

    C   D

    vocabulary links ⟵—— *repeated [words]*

    vocabulary links ⟵—— *related words*

    cohesion   ⟵—— *"hang together"*

D. Repeated and related words help sentences "hang together."

Transition Links

E. Finally, transition links help text cohere.

    E ⟵—— *(finally)* ————⟶ F

    E ⟵—— *(for example)* ———⟶ F

F. For example, signal words may be used to connect sentences.

                                                               ∎

After modeling the x-ray process with paragraph-level texts, I put students into groups so that they can work on scaffolded exercises like the following one (Strong 1991a). The basic question is this: What specific links between and among sentences help this paragraph flow or hang together?

Fad Diets (Paragraph Coherence)

Directions: Working with partners, read the sentences below. Then trace the cohesion links by filling in the blanks. Pay attention to specific words and phrases that help the sentences "hang together."

A. Each month a new fad diet hits the bookstores.
B. For all their differences, these diets have one thing in common.
C. They promise a slim body with virtually no effort.
D. Each diet "documents" its claims with testimonials from people who magically transform their waistlines, not to mention their lives, in a week or two.
E. The book jackets advertise a better life on one condition.
F. The individual must make a "Commitment to the Program."
G. That "commitment" begins, of course, with the price of the book.

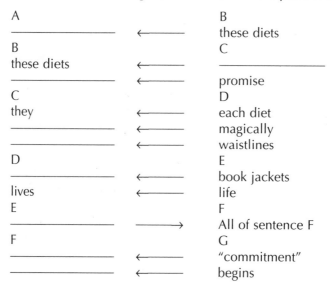

Once students learn from scaffolded cohesion exercises, they can apply the same x-ray vision to their own paragraphs in progress. Here I want to repeat what I said in the context of syntax—namely, that the point of a good language exercise is to help students pay attention to text and assume increasing control over their own planning, drafting, and revising processes. The goal, in short, is for students to enjoy the same obsessive-compulsive pleasures as their coaches—reading, rereading, and tinkering. Constructivist theory suggests that the insights gleaned from scaffolded instruction—in this case, paragraphs—can be applied to larger ongoing projects.

Helping students develop vivid images and strategies for paragraph-level composing supports our teaching of multiparagraph genres such as autobiographical narratives, reports, business letters, critical essays, research papers, and a host of other academic assignments. At the same time, good coaches try to create conditions that lead to satisfying flow experiences (Csikszentmihalyi 1990) in writing. The next chapters deal with such matters. As benediction, let me now invite you to look back at "Instruction," the short poem that opens this chapter.

Learning Through Language

1. In Chapter 5 you read "Literacy and Civility," a brief account of a grade school writing experience. Consider a positive writing experience from your own life, one that occurred in your childhood or adolescence. Perhaps this experience occurred in school, perhaps not. Consider its meaning for you today. Then reread "Literacy and Civility" to see if there are any paragraph-level strategies—description, narration, or reflection—worth borrowing. Write your narrative to share with others.

2. Read your story from activity 1 above in a showing, not telling workshop. Your aim in reading is to solicit feedback from others about the details of your piece. Have someone else take notes as you read your text to the group. Ask your writing partners to name key details of your story that stand out in their minds; then ask them to question you about the situation and characters. Respond orally to questions with showing details. Use these details to revise your text.

3. In the "Structuring Paragraphs" section there are several scaffolding activities for expository or informational writing. Describe, for others in your group and for your instructor, how you would implement one of these activities in a middle school or high school setting. As you think about such a lesson (or a series of lessons), consider the basic question of motivation: how will you get students interested in paying attention to paragraph structure? Can you envision other hands-on approaches?

CHAPTER 6

COACHING VOICE

Gratitude to Old Teachers

When we stroll across the frozen lake,
We place our feet where they have never been.
We walk upon the unwalked. But we are uneasy.
Who is down there but our old teachers?

Water that once could take no human weight—
We were students then—holds up our feet,
And goes on ahead of us for a mile.
Beneath us the teachers, and around us the stillness.

—Robert Bly

Voice Coach

Why do I still remember my high school English teacher? Because once upon a time there lived a man whose many voices invited students to look beyond their blue-collar horizons. Because this teacher took time for a sporting life pursuit, the Zen-like discipline of his own poetry. And because, as Robert Bly so beautifully puts it, "beneath us the teachers, and around us the stillness."

For me, early reports of Lloyd Johnson's teaching came from an older kid in the neighborhood, whose reliability was as solid as his gleaming '48 Chevy, in which I'd sometimes ride with my elbow hooked out the window. The teacher's nickname was Shorty, but because he looked like he had just stepped out of an ad for *Esquire* or *Gentleman's Quarterly*, no one really noticed his height. In class, he had a luminous quality—a relaxed and cocky self-assurance, like Harrison Ford in herringbone tweed. Poised and funny, a little mysterious, he connected with students at the margins.

Opening an anthology on a warm spring afternoon, I learned that anything could happen. Perhaps Wordsworth would be speaking through him. Or Matthew Arnold. Or Emily Dickinson. Whenever Mr. Johnson was in character, it was like attending a seance. He didn't so much read texts as *become* them through electrifying enactments. There he would be as usual—wavy, brown hair and horn-rim glasses, bemused smile, his glance moving toward yellow-green fields and tall fir trees that stretched south of the high school—but his voice would be that of someone else, like Jonathan Swift.

I HAVE been assured by a very knowing *American* of my acquaintance in *London*; that a young healthy Child, well nursed, is, at a Year old, a most delicious, nourishing, and wholesome Food; whether *Stewed*, *Roasted*, *Baked*, or *Boiled*; and, I make no doubt, that it will equally serve in a Fricasie, or Ragoust . . . A Child will make two Dishes at an Entertainment for Friends; and when the Family dines alone, the fore or hind Quarter will make a reasonable Dish; and seasoned with a little Pepper or Salt, will be very good Boiled on the fourth Day, especially in *Winter*. ("A Modest Proposal," 1729, 504.)

Like others in the class, I gasped as the text was delivered with cool and cunning reserve. "What next?" I wondered.

Sometimes, we spoke through our teacher to question the author. And although Mr. Johnson sometimes gave talks and expected note taking—good practice for those thinking about college, he said—his expectations never included the fill-in-the-blank regimen that had led, inexorably, to the downfall of our sophomore English teacher. She quit at midyear, her class in shambles, leaving a hulking principal to redistribute the grammar workbooks.

I was so impressed by Mr. Johnson's different voices, particularly the Oxford-sounding ones with their hints of elegance and erudition, that I sometimes tried to imitate them outside of class, in between hormonal surges. I began to know with the passionate, desperate certainty of adolescence that whatever power Mr. Johnson possessed was worth pursuing. It was more a feeling than a thought. I wanted to visit the worlds he knew, the places he had traveled in his reading or in actual fact.

As my parents' firstborn, I had always been the responsible achiever, the altar boy who was eager to please and anxious to fit in. Now, I had plenty to be anxious about. At home, in the small frame house surrounded by a green laurel hedge, where my father had been flattened by polio thirty months earlier and my mother still suffered the aftereffects of heart surgery, things were tense in the best of times and an emotional minefield in between. We lived on thirty dollars a week and then on the bitter pill of state assistance; I worked after school, summers, and weekends to help out. I knew better than to get my hopes up about going away to college. There was no way.

One day Mr. Johnson pulled me aside. "Try this," he said.

It was a paperback copy of George Orwell's *1984*, the only book that any secondary teacher had ever recommended to me. His gesture had come out of nowhere, like everything else he did. At first I wondered what I had done wrong.

I took the book to my attic bedroom. It was my first pleasure reading since junior high, and I was captured by the chilling detail. Under a thin yellow light, I read some parts over and over. A few days later, when Mr. Johnson asked about my future plans, I hesitated. "Maybe teaching," I said.

He smiled and nodded. "Teaching's a good life."

After graduation, I worked afternoons and weekends as a janitor at the high school. I didn't tell Mr. Johnson about feeling lost in the huge lecture sections and labs or the fact that my do-it-yourself advisement sometimes ignored prerequisite numbers in the math and science sequences. And, finally, I didn't say anything about grades.

"Things are fine," I'd say. "Just fine."

For two years I drifted. Finally, I shifted from science to English education and moved from home to a two-room apartment above a Korean restaurant, splitting the forty-five-dollar monthly rent with two friends. By the time I eventually returned to Mr. Johnson's classroom to ask what he liked about teaching, I had learned to drink beer.

"When students like you come back," he said. "That feels good."

A few months earlier I'd heard him give a commencement talk for my girlfriend's graduating class, a speech so inspired and graceful that it earned him a thunderous standing ovation—and now his generous spirit was acknowledging and including me. It was another unexpected voice from Mr. Johnson, one more color unfolding from the prism of his personality.

Voice Lessons

Now, as I think about Mr. Johnson's teaching, the practical, rational side of me says that he was simply an exceptional reader and public speaker, a man who used his charismatic voice as an instrument to express given texts. But another side of me, a metaphysical side, believes that Mr. Johnson was indeed a variety of personas and voices, whose aim was to coach language from adolescents.

Like Robin Williams or Lily Tomlin, here was a teacher who could capture the imagination. At first, he centered his teaching, with style and good humor, on intriguing or exotic performances of language, mostly his own. Gradually, however, students like me were drawn into the classroom dialogue as participants or as cocreators. Almost everybody paid attention, including a friend who distinguished himself that spring by hijacking a Caterpillar tractor and driving it around the school's construction site. Mr. Johnson's art, as Denny Wolfe (1997) might say, was seductive teaching.

In this chapter I discuss how teachers might help students explore the various voices of past experience. The concept of multiple voices has important practical implications for coaching activities in language arts classrooms. We look first at voice lessons and then consider how a literacy autobiography assignment might build on remembered voices and invite metalinguistic awareness.

Contexts for voice

To think about voice, consider the many worlds of your own experience: schools, backyards, jobs, athletic fields, shopping malls, holiday gatherings, weddings, funerals, vacations, faculty lounges, and so on. It is in such diverse places, each its own social context, that we learn voice lessons.

On the one hand, we learn to interpret the voices of others—such as love, anger, praise, reprimand, apology, gratitude, sympathy, compliment, ridicule, and complaint. Do you remember occasions when these voices came across loud and clear? On the other hand, we also learn to enact such voices. Among other things, we learn to lie, show off, tell jokes, gossip, barter, whine, talk sexy, argue, give sympathy, act smart, play dumb—and the list goes on. It is by paying attention that our repertoire of voices expands and becomes more refined.

Facets of voice include a person's tone and body language. We all learn, for example, that greetings require a certain tone of voice and predictable behaviors. We know that someone is having a bad day not because she didn't say "Good morning" but because her tone of voice or her body language says something else. We learn to read an ironic voice like sarcasm in much the same way. The pragmatics of language use are hardly self-evident, as anyone who has traveled in a foreign country knows; rather, each use is demonstrated—and learned—in context. Language and its conventional uses are simultaneously learned.

Clearly, too, voice also refers to our persona when speaking or writing. Thus, in making a new acquaintance, whether on the phone or in person, we pay attention to subtle cues. And in looking at a text, most of us learn to distinguish a tentative voice from an authoritative one or a jokester voice from an academic one. How? By seeing the voice within a larger frame. In reading letters to the editor, for example, we come to infer the raised eyebrow or the tense, clenched jaw because we know that people talk and write for reasons. Of course, sensitivity to the registers of written language deepens as we try to use those registers and make them our own.

So we learn new voices to function within coherent social worlds. By paying attention to the conventions of new voices, we may figure them out and even master them—provided, of course, they do not conflict with our identity. In recent years, for example, technology-savvy English teachers have learned to use computer jargon in their funding proposals. Now, they blush with pride as they interface with others.

Voice stories

One voice that many students practice, perhaps to our despair, is the highly stylized voice of cool talk, in all its regional variations. Learning to sound cool means learning a voice with a distinctive syntax and cadence, plus its own clipped jargon. The swagger of cool talk provides admission to the club, to use Frank Smith's (1988) metaphor. Like, it's really *nerdy* to talk standard, you know? Pay attention to kids around their lockers or at bus stops—many dressed in identical gear—and you will see the stylized posturing of detachment: lids lowered, a hint of sneer, the slouch that signals a "way-cool" attitude.

A much different voice, one that we as writing coaches may still be working on, is intimate talk. Think back to the first time you said "I love you"—for real—to someone other than a member of your family. We all remember first loves. Moreover, we recall the settings of these coming-of-age triumphs, whether on a dusty path in the woods or at a small café with red and white tablecloths or in a parked car with a radio running down the battery. Remember the surprise of hearing this newborn voice, one trying to sound sure of itself. It was your voice, yes, but it was somehow different. Remember, too, the panicky, excited feeling of entering uncharted territory. You wondered where this voice was leading you. Maybe you still do.

A third kind of voice involves a shift in role—becoming someone else, if only temporarily. For example, I remember how I said good-bye to my mother on a rainy January morning as a young man—and how, later that day, I became a parent to my father for the first time. You may have discovered such a new voice at some transition point in your life. Or you may recall a time when a friend came to you for advice, and you provided help and reassurance in a way that surprised you. In such stories are meanings, both private and public, that we construct in words. For my own part, hearing the parent-of-my-parent voice reminds me of the small kitchen table in the white frame house where my father lived for many years before joining my wife and me. A remembered voice helps me enter another world. It is as simple as that.

Behind each voice lesson, then, is one or more stories. Recall a setting, think about the voice—either your own or someone else's—and the images of another world unfold from memory. It is all there, entwined with the voices you have heard and may now use. With a nudge, you are there again. The voices echo within.

I remember the leafy shade along a gravel driveway, where I thrilled myself by deliberately using a four-letter cussword—"Oh, hell!"—to show my preadolescent bravado. I remember a world of sweaty summer evenings on the freight docks where, as a crew-cut college student, I used an unschooled voice as a survival strategy. I remember my first day in my first classroom and the voice I invented to begin my teaching career. I remember my Santa Claus voice on Christmas Eve and the look of joy and terror in my son's eyes as he sat on Santa's knee and then told me afterward, "Thanta was here! Thanta was here!" And I remember marriage counseling sessions where an angry voice expressed views that my more rational voice denied. There are stories behind all of these voices. And what are our lives if not our stories?

It is through such voices and the personal knowledge they call up that we give shape and meaning to our lives. Stories are a kind of compass, a way of reconstructing the world to ourselves. They educate as well as entertain. That is why certain stories, like the Santa Claus story, are told and retold within families and other close-knit groups, particularly on traditional occasions like Thanksgiving. In Hawaii, those who have elevated talk-story to a cultural art form know that we use story to rediscover who we are and the relationships that matter.

Listen to such stories carefully, and you will often hear them told in present tense. Listen more carefully still and you will hear different voices being enacted. It is as if the memory of a family were a collective treasury, with each family member having a different key. And that, of course, is why severe dementia, with its disordering or loss of stories, is so devastating to families, not to mention those whose minds are set adrift. A mind without stories is a mind awhirl, voiceless and frightened and alone.

Shared Voices

As writing coaches, most of us can recall dozens of voices from the worlds of our past experience. My premise is that a remembered voice—your own or that of someone else—can stimulate memory, with language serving as both the vehicle and the content of instruction. Tracking down an inner voice and sharing its story can be a productive language activity. Take a voice, any voice, off the linguistic shelf. Flattery. Politeness. Bragging. Sympathy. Gossiping.

Everybody gossips at one time or another. Do you remember an occasion when your gossiping voice led to your embarrassment? What was that world like? Can you re-create the scene for listeners or readers to show your gossiping voice in action? Call up this vicious, sneaky voice. Get in the mood for some down-and-dirty, heart-to-heart gossip and allow your voice to tell its story, regardless of whether other voices approve. Result? Gossip will have its day in the language spotlight as you enact a real-life drama of remembered experience. And your students will be fascinated.

In focusing on a specific voice and how you learned its uses and consequences, you emphasize shared voices and shared worlds. Of course, for students to function as a community or a club, they have to connect with one another in more than superficial ways. So, after explaining the purpose of this language practice, you invite them to do what you have done: focus on a specific voice and think about times—*real* times, not make-believe times—when they used such a voice.

You explain your process in creating a story—how you got started and how one thing led to another. And you then turn students loose to make notes and talk with partners about fragments of a voice memory. Partners are encouraged to do what interested partners always do: ask questions to prompt details. Such rehearsal sets the stage for independent writing. And finally, after some coaching about the responsibility of students not to embarrass or hurt anyone else with their stories, you invite them to share their texts with the larger group, all of whom are interested in deepening their understanding of real language.

Sharing and comparing, as described here, provide the inherent interest for each speaker or writer. Equally important, the larger group provides an audience that can help each speaker or writer spin out a story and elaborate its salient details. The experience of storytelling and the memory of having successfully engaged one's listeners or readers on a language topic can become building blocks for literacy.

In other words, students can use their language stories to promote learning *about* language. Sharing this rationale is important because students may wonder, "Why are we doing this?" or "What's the point?" Explain, for example, that after hearing and reading the stories, the class might reflect on the roots of gossip or the effects of gossip or even the need for gossip. Point out that having worked at a metalinguistic level, students now have a chance to understand the dynamics of gossip—or some other voice—with increased maturity and perspective. Each such lesson invites awareness of language development as well as the lifelong potential for language growth.

By focusing on a single voice as scaffolding for narrative, students can deepen their understanding of how language is acquired and how it works in a social context. And it is this deepening understanding that can provoke curiosity, as Mr. Johnson would undoubtedly testify. The more we know in personal terms, the more we want to know.

To illustrate, let's consider two exercises written by high school students. Both focus on persuasive voice, and both involve relationships between daughters and their fathers. Do these texts suggest an increased awareness of language?

Persuading Dad 1

This past summer my friend Kevin and I decided to go to Disneyworld. I was at my dad's house in Florida which is about ten hours away. This was a problem because Kevin's old clunker never would have made the drive down.

On a Tuesday morning we were both standing in the living room of my dad's house. We were in front of the window where the morning sun was flooding through, opposite my dad and stepmother April. She was furious that dad was even considering letting me go. After all, he was a he, and 18; to add to it, we had dared ask to take my dad's brand new Mustang on our little excursion.

"She is 17! He is almost 19! For God's Sakes! Use some common sense here; this will not happen. They are not going down there to share a motel room and gallivant about! Matt, you are wrapped around her little finger so tight that you're blind to it, and I won't have it," she screamed as she stomped down the long corridor to her bedroom. The door she slammed expressed her final thoughts to us, and she did it so hard that all the windows in the house shook.

After the shaking stopped, my dad turned to us, completely ignoring April's outburst. He never paid attention to her fits on parenting, because my dad didn't think she was my parent and wouldn't recognize her as such. "Dannie, I know you and Kevin want to go to Disneyworld and spend some time alone together away from the house. I know you have been planning this together for a while. But do you have to do it now? Can't you just wait for two weeks until April leaves for Virginia?"

I hate it when my dad is so understanding and sensible like that, and I knew he had a valid point to his argument, but I wouldn't hear it. Begging and pleading with him I told him that Kevin, the more experienced driver, would drive, and only he would. I tried to reassure him with the fact we'd call every three hours or so to check in. Finally he gave us his consent, as well as his keys.

So I grabbed my duffle bag that was in the foyer and ran out to the Mustang. Kevin grabbed his bag out of the back of his car, and we piled our junk in the back and got in. We even put our seatbelts on before Kevin started the car. Slowly we pulled out of the drive. Reaching the corner we turned, and drove a block or so where Kevin promptly stopped the car and let me in the driver's seat.

—DANIELLE CASELLA

"Is this a true story?" you might ask. The answer, of course, is yes. Has it perhaps been embellished to make it better than the plain reality it is meant to depict? Probably, but that, after all, is part of what we hope to encourage in our coaching.

Persuading Dad 2

It was 1:00 in the morning on a dark cool night. I was standing on my front porch, with white knuckles, gripping the cold metal doorknob to my front door. I was an hour late. To me it was only minutes, but to my dad it was all night.

Earlier that night I had been out with my friends Allyson, Christy, and Melissa. We were dragging Main in my maroon Pontiac Bonneville. On our way home we spotted these guys that were incredibly HOT, and when they turned around (the complete opposite direction from our homes) we found ourselves following them into the empty mall parking lot.

I got so caught up in the conversation with these good looking guys that when I glanced at my watch I about screamed. It was quarter to one and my curfew was midnight. Too worried to think about what I was doing, I cut them off in mid-sentence and told them, "I just realized it's way past my curfew—we gotta go!" As hard as it was, we said good-bye and left.

I knew what was going to happen even before I stepped through the door. I had my excuse all planned out in my head, simple yet believable. I took a deep breath and quietly opened the door. Almost instantly I heard a rough groggy voice yell, "Jennifer, come here." I walked up the stairs to my parent's bedroom. I could see the flickering of the TV through the dark.

My mother had already fallen asleep, and her back was towards my dad. I walked to where my dad was laying and I saw him half open his eyes trying his best to give me a stern look.

"Yes daddy," I said in a sweet and innocent voice.

"What time is it?" he said, trying to blindly find his watch that had fallen to the floor.

My hands gripping my purse tightly, I glanced at my watch and slightly hesitating said, "It's only 12:45, daddy."

"And what time is your curfew," he replied, attempting to sit up.

Hurriedly I started my excuse. "Let me explain. I was dropping Allyson off and she wanted me to see her new room she had decorated. I didn't know when I would get another chance, and we got caught up talking for a minute when . . ."

"I've heard enough," he abruptly cut me off. "You know what time you're suppose to be home and you're late." I could tell he was trying to make his voice sound as angry as possible without waking my mother up.

"I know and I'm really sorry, it won't happen again I promise," I said in my whiny tone of voice. I could tell he was tired and about to give in. He looked at me with concern in his eyes. He knew as well as I did that if he didn't punish me now it was never going to happen. I flashed him my I'm-your-only-daughter-and-you-can-trust-me-look, just for reassurance.

"You look really tired, daddy. I should let you go back to sleep."

"If you're ever that late again . . ." he started.

"Love you, daddy—good night," I promptly cut him off, trying not to smile. I gave him a quick hug and went downstairs to my room. My mind had wandered to other things by this time and I was wishing I had stayed long enough to give that cute guy my number.

—Jennifer Waller

■

Using the concept of voice to stimulate writing is hardly new, but it remains a very provocative idea, especially for students who may not have considered language from a personal perspective. Language, after all, is our principal means of knowing the world, including the worlds within us. We look back at our experience to name its meaning and explore its significance. This fact helps explain why we sometimes hear our voices echoing in our children—just as our parents' voices speak through us.

Of course, once students have used a voice to enter another world, they are likely to read with deeper intelligence. With cool talk as a foundation, for example, you might read "Your Poem, Man" by Ed Lueders. With intimate talk as a foundation, you might introduce "Picnic" by John Logan. With parent-of-your-parents as a foundation, you might discuss "My Papa's Waltz" by Theodore Roethke. A remembered voice helps us enter another world, including the world called literature.

An easy-to-use strategy for sharing voice stories or other short texts is called the read-around group (Gossard 1996), an orchestrated type of swift, silent reading. To prepare for the activity, students put the last four digits of their phone numbers or Social Security numbers atop their papers. No other identifying information is given. Students are clustered into groups of four (or fewer) students, and groups are organized in clockwise fashion around the room. Within each group, one person (the collector) receives and distributes a set of papers, and a second person (the recorder) notes the group's consensus on the best paper from each read-around set.

At the teacher's signal, all collectors in the room follow the clockwise pattern to give and receive sets of papers. Papers are then distributed to members of the small groups. The teacher orchestrates a quick, holistic reading appropriate to the length of the texts (for short in-class writings, thirty seconds to one minute). At the teacher's pass signal, students hand papers in clockwise fashion and start a new text. After the reading of four (or fewer) papers is finished, the teacher asks all groups to choose the best paper in their read-around set. The recorder notes the four-digit number of the chosen paper. Then the process of collecting and receiving papers is repeated. It is important to note that no group reads or votes on the texts written by its own members.

When the read-around process is finished, the teacher calls for the four-digit numbers from each recorder. These are written on the board or on a transparency. Of course, some numbers recur. "What features make certain papers so successful?" a teacher can ask. "Let's read two or three aloud to see what you liked." Thus, the read-around process prepares students to look at their own texts with an eye toward revision.

The Literacy Autobiography

For years, I have used literacy autobiographies in teacher education courses. Although the scaffolding for this assignment keeps changing, I stick with it because of the interest it generates and because middle school and high school teachers now use parallel versions of it. When students come to me with prior experience in reflecting on literacy, we have real opportunities to deepen and expand their autobiographies.

As language teachers, we sometimes forget the power of incidental learning—the off-hand remark, image, or line that lives on. Yet student literacy autobiographies, as described in this section, reveal that such lessons can be very powerful. And, interestingly, literacy autobiographies can serve as an antidote to the widespread theme of student as victim. Through writing, secondary students can understand the many lessons in their back-grounds and choose responses to those experiences, including laughter.

One possibility for introducing the autobiography is an inventory with several student voices. From such an inventory, adapted and expanded as needed, it's possible to glean different attitudes—useful information for responding to students, either face-to-face or in notes. The inventory asks students to take an active role in defining who they are and how they want to be treated. In other words, it anticipates the possibility of a relationship, one that each student might largely control. A second type of inventory, the Exercise in Self-Assessment in Chapter 8, provides another option.

Getting to Know You

Directions: Consider this fact: Each day your teacher faces 150 (or more) students. Knowing you as an individual is therefore a challenge. You can help by circling (or filling in) responses to the items below.

1. The kind of writing teacher I personally prefer is one who
    1. just gets off my case and leaves me alone.
    2. helps me *survive* since writing really isn't my thing.
    3. lays things out 1-2-3 so I can get a pretty good grade.
    4. expects me to ask questions and solve writing problems.
    5. challenges me to continually stretch myself in writing.
    6. _____
2. When a teacher offers suggestions about my writing, I often feel
    1. angry = "What gives him (or her) the right?"

      2. discouraged = "Oh, what's the use?"
      3. indifferent = "Yeah, so what grade did I get?"
      4. questioning = "I wonder what this comment means?"
      5. hopeful = "What can I learn from this for next time?"
      6. _____

3. As far I'm concerned, all of the talk about writing process
      1. really truly sucks.
      2. seems pretty remote from me.
      3. allows teachers to grade any way they want.
      4. sometimes makes me question how I write.
      5. actually holds a lot of interest for me.
      6. _____

4. All of us have different memories about writing. What memory stands out vividly in your mind? (If you want to refer to a past teacher in your memory writing, please use this person's initials, for example, Mrs. K. or Mr. W.) How is your memory from the past related to your present feelings toward writing?

                                                                  ■

The idea is to create provisional categories (A = angry, D = discouraged, I = indifferent, Q = questioning, H = hopeful) for responding to students and their texts: "Rick, what you said about your background is interesting. Are you ready to get beyond those middle school experiences? Do you see us teaming up—maybe working together?" An inventory can tap students' opinions about a variety of matters.

Of course, from the teacher's viewpoint, the literacy autobiography provides the perfect context for reflecting on—and sharing—one's own experiences, as I have done at various points in this book. If we take a districtwide perspective, imagine the power of the literacy autobiography as a standing assignment in middle school and high school grades, one that students could add to and refine year after year. Imagine, too, the cumulative effect for students of hearing their language arts teachers share their diverse and evocative stories of personal literacy each year—and of then being encouraged to reread and further develop their own literacy autobiographies.

For one thing, the autobiography would provide a running record of each student's literacy experiences as well as an archive of his or her growth in language. For another, it would be a great tool for goal setting, assessment work, and parent conferences. For still another, it would put emphasis where it belongs—on the student's construction of personal knowledge and meaning. And if students move around a lot, why shouldn't an electronic version of the literacy autobiography follow them, providing vital information to the student's next teacher about interests, skills, and experiences? And if students have low ACT or SAT scores, why shouldn't they use autobiographies to seek another route to college admission?

The following are excerpts from typical literacy autobiographies written by two students in teacher education.

Writing Memory 1

Mrs. M, my fifth grade teacher, helped me gain confidence in my abilities as a writer. A poem I had written was entered into a contest and won a prize. The poem was actually published in a collection of amateur poetry. I will never forget reciting the poem in front of my entire elementary school at an assembly. Of course, I was nervous, but I was also very pleased with my accomplishments. My parents were there. My teacher sat next to me on the stage. Everyone was so proud of me.

I was sure that I would be a famous author and thought my first piece of work should be dedicated to my teacher, Mrs. M. After all, she helped fuel my desire to write. Mrs. M returned one of the short stories I'd written for her class and across the top of the paper in her neat penmanship she had commented, "I'll read one of your books someday." To this day, I can picture her comments on my paper and remember the warm, fuzzy feeling I had when I read them. What great motivation for a ten-year-old girl! Then and there I planned to dedicate my first book to Mrs. M, "the teacher who inspired me."

My seventh grade class read the young adult novel *No Way Out* by Ivy Ruckman. We were asked to write our own endings to the story before reading the final three chapters. As I recall, most students in our class were excited about the assignment. It was somehow different, so I guess that made it a little more exciting. We even talked about our stories during lunch and after school. Of course, I thought the ending I made up was better than the real ending. Everything happened just the way I wanted it to.

My short story was returned and across the top my teacher, Mr. J, had written: "You should be a writer. You ARE a writer." Naturally, I was very proud of myself. Maybe I even felt a little bit of pressure to make sure my writing lived up to my new status as "writer." I think the pressure was positive, however, because it caused me to work harder to develop my writing. Somehow it made writing fun for me. Even now, I love editing papers—grammar, spelling, punctuation. I still don't really understand how my teacher made studying grammar rules interesting, but we paid attention. I even enjoyed exercises where we had to diagram sentences on the blackboard and label the parts of speech.

—Jeanne Milligan

Writing Memory 2

My sophomore English class was sort of scary for me, mostly because my teacher, a man about 26 years old, semi-handsome with a biting, sarcastic humor, intimidated me immensely. He seemed sort of leftover from the sixties era of love beads and peace signs. He had a beard, wore chunky leather sandals, and sometimes even a poncho-type shirt, no doubt hand-woven by peasants who had dedicated their lives to a preservative-free diet. I liked him, but his sarcasm scared me.

We had been reading short stories in my English class, and the teacher had asked us to write our own. I sat at my desk, staring at the wooden top, coloring in the initials that someone had carved in its surface years ago, and desperately trying to think of something to write about.

After several days, I finally managed a story about an old uncle Luther I had, and how he let me win at checkers. I rather liked the story, but as I sat at my desk waiting to turn in the assignment, I was terrified. I knew that class would be starting soon, and there was a subdued sort of bedlam going on around me. Kids were talking about their exploits during the weekend, shuffling papers, and banging books on desks. I sat at my desk, dreading the moment when the teacher would ask for our papers. My hands were shaking and cold, and my stomach had a distinctly unsettled feeling, sort of like waiting for my turn to go off the high dive. I admired the nonchalance of the other students.

When the bell rang, I tensed. The teacher walked casually to the front of the room and asked for our papers. I passed my paper forward, trying to act unconcerned, but secretly praying that people in front of me wouldn't try to read my paper as it was being passed up. I felt an incredible sense of doom as I realized that Mr. S., my teacher, now had possession of a story *I* had written. A very part of *me* was now up for public criticism.

That was the last time I can remember writing anything creative, anything that required that I put myself on paper. I had forgotten how frightened I was handing in that paper, and how extremely vulnerable I felt. Until now. So this creative-type writing scares me. I guess because I'm not used to it, and I haven't had a lot of successful experiences with it to help boost my confidence.

—Donna Bernhisel

After students brainstorm, select, and narrate literacy events, I always encourage a reflective turn of mind, one that inquires into the personal meaning and the long-term implications of the experiences. Trust me: there are many good ideas in this book, but the ongoing literacy autobiography is one worthy of your reflection for future use.

Voices in Dialogue

In this chapter, we have seen how the concept of voice can lead to interesting writing and reflection. Like Mr. Johnson, the man of many voices, all of us internalize multiple voices from the worlds of our past and present lives, not to mention the worlds of our reading. Such voices invite exploration.

A romantic tradition claims that teachers help students discover or liberate an authentic voice, the essence of self, buried deep within. We tell students that one's *real* voice is a wellspring of power—and we hold out the promise of transcendence as they shed "phoney" voices. But as Mr. Johnson might note, such marketing presents certain problems. First, the suggestion that students have been voiceless since birth seems either an outright lie or a giant exaggeration. Second, the idea that a single voice has greater power than multiple voices seems a dubious claim at best. In most areas of our experience—but especially in language—multiple resources are an asset, not a liability.

For Mr. Johnson, a single voice would probably be limiting, not liberating. We all use multiple voices, he might point out, because we have lived—and continue to live—in many different worlds. He would probably concede that helping students pursue the voice of their core identity is a worthy quest for reflective journal writing. But I doubt that he would characterize other voices, especially the voices in analytic or academic registers, as somehow unreal—or that he would see personal journal writing as a comprehensive program of language education.

To focus on a single voice makes for limited language education. Although I acknowledge the core voice and understand that its expression is essential to one's sense of centeredness, I also think that other voices can be sources of power. Why? Because they extend our repertoire of language skills. Because they give us access to other worlds. And because reconstructing these worlds helps us understand ourselves as storytelling creatures and as creatures of story.

G. Lynn Nelson neatly articulates the problem in *Writing and Being*: "We have many small selves that are the parts we play, the many people that we are. But beyond these small selves is the Self, the I that lies beyond the 'I's, beyond the roles, beyond our ego, beyond our small seeing" (1994, 80). For Nelson, the paradox is this:

> The more I am centered in my Self, the healthier I am and the better I do in my smaller selves. And conversely: *The more I cling to my smaller selves as my identity, the less effective and healthy I am in those identities.* (81)

In responding to Nelson, let me be clear that I do not favor having students abandon their search for a central core voice through journal writing, nor do I advocate having them "cling" to the "smaller selves" of their identity. What I do favor is helping students think of their smaller selves as facets, or faces, of their identity.

Think about it. Is your voice as a teacher any less—or more—real than your voice as a parent, a gourmet cook, a sailor, or an aficionado of opera? Probably not. Each of our voices exists within a particular social context that makes particular demands. We may practice one voice more than another just as we may prefer one world over other ones, but that hardly makes one voice or world any more real.

The suggested exercises encourage students to track down voices—either their own or the remembered voices of someone else. To begin, students might choose a single voice from each set in the following table or generate their own longer lists of voices.

complaining	exaggerating	whining	prayerful
secretive	kind	humble	naive
friendly	outraged	regretful	patriotic
cautious	argumentative	nasty	coy
deceiving	logical	critical	vain
cool	sincere	manipulative	opinionated
proud	fearful	persuasive	gossiping
sympathetic	guilty	poetic	flattering
honest	bragging	authoritative	polite

Each voice probably has one or more stories—or worlds—behind it. Why not use the memories of language learning as content for speaking and writing practice?

Or, why not imagine meetings between voices? Suppose, for example, that naive voice meets flattering voice, or bragging voice meets sarcastic voice, or logical voice meets seductive voice, or cautious voice meets critical voice, or playful voice meets teacher voice. You get the idea. Each neat meeting sets up a tension for students to enact in role-playing exercises and on paper. Have students read texts focused on an interplay of voices. As good coaches know, shared voices make the game of teaching worthwhile.

"But wait," you may be thinking. "Isn't this merely a language exercise?"

"It certainly exercises language," I reply. "That's the point."

"It's language pulled out of context."

"Yes, so that students can focus on it, learn from it."

"But the idea of an exercise seems so contrived, unnatural."

"Many real-world coaches see exercise and practice as a completely natural part of game preparation—and so do their players."

And so did Jerome Bruner, of course. As one of the twentieth century's most distinguished and influential learning psychologists, Bruner gave serious thought to students' acquisition of literacy in his little essay "Teaching a Native Language" (Bruner 1966). Bruner wondered how one achieves "awareness, mastery, and finesse" in various language functions and then offered this rhetorical response:

> How indeed does one become masterfully adept at the rules for forming appropriate utterances for the consumption of others or for one's own consumption, *save by exercise*? (110)

Bruner advocated skill-building exercises in which students would be encouraged "to write in different styles and in different voices" (110). In his view, to involve students in the "conscious deployment of their native language" offered "the best way" of achieving desired ends in language education (112).

Coaching from the Heart

It was more than twenty years after my high school graduation that I saw Mr. Johnson for the last time. I had come to Portland to present a sentence-combining workshop, and there he was, seated near the wall at the back of the room. His smile was the same as ever— serene, benignly expectant—but he also looked tired. We talked briefly. It had been a long time.

To open the session, I expressed how it felt to have a teacher's teacher, especially one of Mr. Johnson's legendary caliber, show up so unexpectedly. He had long been a model for my teaching, but now he was here—and it was more than a little daunting. Then all the teachers gave Mr. Johnson a small round of applause, and he smiled and said some nice things, and I promised not to hold him responsible for my workshop. I think he liked that touch.

A few weeks later, in May, came the brief obituary—a heart attack, of course. In *The Courage to Teach* (1998), Parker Palmer writes eloquently about teaching "from the heart" as the defining attribute of teachers like Mr. Johnson:

> As good teachers weave the fabric that joins them with students and subjects, the heart is the loom on which the threads are tied, the tension is held, and the fabric is stretched tight. Small wonder, then, that teaching tugs at the heart, opens the heart, even breaks the heart—and the more one loves teaching, the more heartbreaking it can be. (11)

Later, some of Mr. Johnson's students formed an association to publish posthumously a small book of his poems, one that would support a memorial scholarship at the high school. The following is my poem for him.

A Coach Remembered

I knew a teacher once
  With words as soft
As moths on summer screens.
  Brittle bright and
Cruel was not his style.
  As others barked,
His whispers touched the dark
  Inside your soul
And seemed to echo there.
  The way was sure.
He always took the time:
  Refused the rush
Of world report for poems–
  And pushed aside
The weight of dusty tomes
  To scratch his nose
And pass around the mints.
  He seemed alive.

You couldn't put him on.
  He'd take a book
And make it yours and his
  In magic ways
That made your breath come quick.
  His wink was slight.
The eyes were bright and clear,
  A hush of greens.
You'd watch the pause of smile,
  A patient blink
That let the question hang.
  His tease would make
You more than eyes and ears.
  It often made
Your insides twist and think.
  I guess he liked
His work enough to make
  It play for us.

Let me close by saying that Lloyd Johnson's voice has been in harmony with the Oregon landscape for many years, along with that of William Stafford, who coached poetry at Lewis and Clark College, where Johnson took classes. If Johnson were closing this chapter on diverse voices, I think his teasing question might go like this: "When I read a William Stafford poem, how come I sometimes hear a soft Kansas drawl, the print taking on a cadence with a mind of its own?"

As you turn to "What's in My Journal," the Stafford poem that opens the next chapter, may your insides twist and think.

Learning Through Language

1. In Chapter 6 you probably thought about teachers who touched your life personally. What did they do or say to gain your attention and perhaps your affection? From the many teachers of your past, both in and out of school, focus on one who influenced you deeply at some point in your development. Now, think of this teacher as a coach. What was his or her style of coaching? Write up a description (or a profile) of this person from a coaching perspective, including significant details.

2. Exchange papers with someone else. Your task will be to read your partner's paper to others in the group as *effectively* as you can. To do this, you must hear that person's voice in the text and let its rhythms speak through you. If you are unsure about how certain parts should be read, check with the writer and imitate that pattern. Your text will be read by your partner in the workshop. As it is read, study the responses of the group. Afterward, reflect in writing on the voice of your text.

3. This chapter presents the idea of exploring voices from past experience. The activity develops writing fluency and community as students share their voice stories. It is after sharing their stories that students reflect, metalinguistically, on their language learning. To explore this teaching strategy, choose a voice from the ones presented, write your own voice story, share it with your group, and discuss. Finally, evaluate the activity as an exercise for language learning.

CHAPTER 7

Coaching Imagination

What's in My Journal

Odd things, like a button drawer. Mean
things, fishhooks, barbs in your hand.
But marbles too. A genius for being agreeable.
Junkyard crucifixes, voluptuous
discards. Space for knickknacks, and for
Alaska. Evidence to hang me, or to beatify.
Clues that lead nowhere, that never connected
anyway. Deliberate obfuscation, the kind
that takes genius. Chasms in character.
Loud omissions. Mornings that yawn above
a new grave. Pages you know exist
but you can't find them. Someone's terribly
inevitable life story, maybe mine.

—William Stafford

Other Voices, Other Worlds

As you read "What's in My Journal" by William Stafford, you hear the voice of the poem, amused and ironic and maybe a little sad. In your imagination, it is a voice from another world—and you feel its silences toward the end, echoing forward. Perhaps you even glanced back at the juxtapositions to notice how they bristle and rub against one another, creating a kind of static electricity.

The electricity metaphor is useful when discussing imaginative language. To develop an analogy for imaginative language, you might give students a hands-on experience in midwinter by having them cross a carpet in stocking feet to shock one another—a tingling snap between extended fingertips. However, if your school is not blessed with low humidity, you can ask a colleague in science teaching to help you collect and use the simple and completely safe materials for inducing static charges. With such a demonstration as background, compare imagination in good writing to the stimulating sizzle of static electricity. Imagination, you might say, helps make writing interesting—and *memorable*.

And the same goes for imaginative teaching. Of the many enactments and demonstrations of imagination I've seen during my career, one of the most vivid and memorable was a compelling lesson given by Teresa Robinson. As a shy undergraduate, Teresa had trusted my advice about paying attention to her instincts and not listening to self-doubts. Later, when she took center stage in a Utah Writing Project invitational institute, she convincingly demonstrated for others what she had learned from working as the one-person English department in a rural Utah school. Her focus was description and imagination, and she knocked our socks off.

Teresa believed in hands-on learning, with low-tech materials. Seeing students who were numb to details around them, she had learned how to awaken awareness and encourage language. It was from basic exercises in observing and listing, she reasoned, that she could prompt students to sort and select details, then use them to construct worlds of real and imagined experience. As a strong writer herself, she understood that particularity was the key to universality, or as Ralph Fletcher puts it, quoting his writing mentor, Richard Price, "the bigger the issue, the smaller you write" (1993, 49). Illumination, according to Teresa, was the result of "striking details"—the kind, say, in a William Stafford poem.

She began with a series of pictures and slides, gradually increasing the level of challenge. We noticed and jotted details, then compared our lists with a second look at the stimuli. We tried to freeze visual details in mind. After studying a face, we were challenged to jot down details about the background of the picture. We began to use similes and metaphors with our first impressions and details.

Finally, after several minutes of relaxed preparation, Teresa turned to a table that had been mysteriously covered with a cloth to hide its contents from view. She had already explained, using items from her purse, how a person's identity might be inferred from personal possessions. Now she said that we would divide into four small groups, each of which would study a set of personal items that belonged to someone. Our job was to pay attention to the items—in fact, to study the details of the items—and make inferences about their owner and imagine why these things might have been kept in a dresser drawer or a trunk or another safe place. Did we have any questions?

Then she removed the cloth, and there stood the four clusters of several objects, patiently waiting, inviting interpretation. As writing teams approached the table to look over the items in their set and take down notes, the room went quiet. I handled an old brass key, a wine bottle, a shopping list, eyeglasses, a brief obituary clipped from a newspaper, two theatre tickets, a scuffed baseball. I took my time like others in my group. Teresa told us that we could add details to the items in our set but that we couldn't leave anything out: that all items were somehow important to the identity of someone and part of his or her story. I am a veteran teacher, and a teacher of teachers, but I was completely taken in by Teresa's "mystery items" exercise. To me, the items she had juxtaposed were vivid evidence of someone's "terribly inevitable life story." I could hardly wait to write or to hear what others had written.

Teresa Robinson's exercise, like the seashell exercise made famous by George Hillocks (1995), illustrates what Hillocks calls a "gateway activity" for writing, one that builds skills for subsequent, more complex tasks in an active learning environment. Hillocks' exercise uses thirty or so seashells as a prompt. In one version of the activity, four or five students receive two shells that are similar in size, color, and shape, but are of different species. The students are asked to write about one of the shells with such detail that another group will be able to pick it out from the pair of shells, or (for even more challenge) from all shells used by all student groups. Readers provide response to one another about the details or features of texts that assisted and hindered their comprehension. In another version of the game, students write about a single shell on their own, receive someone else's text, try to pick out the writer's shell from thirty or so on the table, and again give each other feedback. Hillocks also uses a large shell to elicit figurative language from students. Such language is virtually absent before instruction, Hillocks says; however, "the shell activity prompts about 70% to use metaphor, and that level of use is sustained through the final writing sample" (181).

Another such activity, used by both Robinson and Hillocks, involves the use of audio prompts as the stimuli for naming details, then describing them, and finally integrating them into sound stories. Robinson created her sounds on the spot, using a variety of homemade materials, as students squeezed their eyes shut and later tried to re-create what they had heard and imagined. Hillocks used homemade audiotapes and then got students interested in producing tapes of their own, which could be used in class as writing prompts for imaginative writing.

The activities of Teresa Robinson and George Hillocks are more than gimmicks. They develop skills for more complex tasks. Toward the end of Chapter 6, we heard from Jerome Bruner (1966) that surely "one right path" in coaching students was to have them "write in different styles and in different voices." In arguing for the utility of exercises, Bruner said that involving students in the "conscious deployment of their native language" offered "the best way" of achieving the goals we desire: "awareness, mastery, and finesse in the various functions to which language is devoted" (110, 112). Writer Diane Ackerman echoes Bruner's wisdom. Here, in a *Writer's Digest* interview with Barbara Adams (1997), she shares practical secrets to her success:

> Go to your study, close the door, invent your confidence.
>   And if ideas don't flood through your mind naturally, you can always open up a copy of a magazine at random, let your finger drop onto the page, and write about whatever is there. It's fun, and it's good practice. I've always told writing students that if they don't feel particularly inspired, they should choose one from a long series of exercises to do: Write a love poem without using any "dirty" words or euphemisms—that's tough. Write a poem that is a single sentence and a single narrative. Write a dramatic monologue. Describe in prose a conversation between two people whom you can't hear—just their faces, gestures. And if you're creative, you know that these exercises are never mechanical; they always lead to something interesting. (30)

In this chapter we direct our attention to matters of imagination—and to the conscious deployment of language—by considering an especially creative approach to coaching developed by Judith Summerfield and the late Geoffrey Summerfield. First, I briefly outline key assumptions of their method gleaned from workshops and *Frames of Mind* (1986). Then I explain how the Summerfields have used newspaper stories, among many other artifacts, to prompt students to develop participant texts and spectator texts in a range of voices. It is through such exercises that students can use text to imaginatively enter other voices and other worlds.

Roles of the Game

The coaching framework offered by the Summerfields presents an array of intriguing, accessible texts and invites students to speculate on the contexts that might have led people to write such letters, historical artifacts, notes to self, or literary pieces. They help students focus on the uses of text—self-regulation, reflection, representation, sharing—and the roles being enacted. They prompt responses and coach parallel texts. And they cunningly enrich students' understanding of language, with topics on diction (particularization versus abstraction), audience proximity (close versus distant), and sentence structure (left-branching versus right-branching).

The Summerfields begin with a radical, even startling, premise: that we generate our most extraordinary texts when we are *not* ourselves, strictly speaking, but rather somebody else. How can this be? The answer, they claim, lies in impersonation, role-playing, and fantasy. To escape into role gives us access to language that we do not ordinarily use in our daily lives. Or as Norman Mailer once put it: "The psychological heft of role has more existential presence than real life."

But what does this really mean, you may ask—the idea that we become, psychologically speaking, through acts of impersonation? Here is an exercise.

Just for a moment, reflect on the people you impersonated during your teacher education work, whether in a clinical (apprenticeship) experience, student teaching, or your first year on the job. Recall the twilight zone feeling of your teaching "uniform" and the terms of address that accompanied your new role. At first, you may have felt like a fraud with your grade book and lesson planner and other tools of the trade. But remember how the firmness in your voice, the I-mean-business tone, began to feel less forced, more natural, with just a few months practice and some coaching from battle-scarred veterans down the hall. Perhaps there were mentors or models of quality teaching who heard your frustrations and inspired you. Or perhaps your impersonations were more unconscious, deriving from your observations of "how things are done here." Eventually, of course, you became the role—as we all do.

Now, let's switch from the game of teaching to the game of life. Picture yourself in other popular first-time roles, for example, as newlywed, new parent, newly divorced parent, or newly remarried parent. Few of us feel fully prepared for such major shifts in role, yet sometimes our on-the-spot impersonations of competence lead us to surprise ourselves with the discovery of new voices. Over time, the role in each of these situations becomes part of our identity as does the voice. Over time, too, we may *imagine* how things might be from another's perspective, say, through the eyes of our spouse, child, ex-spouse, or new partner. As we step back from our own situation and put ourselves in another's shoes—"All the world's a stage," Shakespeare once said—role-playing may help us see ourselves and others in context.

For me, this exercise has meant reflecting on several roles in my career. Early on, I impersonated the persona of Mr. Johnson, a respected teacher, and then I came to internalize the role of teacher for myself. Years later, I took a long afternoon run on the Swedish seacoast with one of my heroes, Donald Graves, and then tried to impersonate his approach to presentations after learning the secrets he so generously shared. Now, as I massage these words on a rainy Sunday afternoon, I impersonate the educational writers I admire, passionate and articulate craftsmen like Donald Murray and Tom Romano, whose texts I have always read with care.

So far, we have considered impersonation and role-playing in the external worlds in which we teach and live. But what about the inner world of private thoughts, dreams, and memories? Let's label it for what it is—a fantasy world of our own construction. In this inner world, we strongly identify with characters in movies or in literature, feeling their joy or self-doubt or excitement or regret. With this identification, we impersonate their emotions and even their actions. Thus, as the earnest young lawyer stands before the court to argue for acquittal of the unjustly accused, it is our mouth that goes dry and our sphincter that tightens.

In much the same way, of course, we fantasize idealized future scenarios in which we play starring roles. Sometimes we even act on them. I still remember standing next to a paperback rack at a neighborhood store, thumbing through a short story anthology, and thinking, "I can read these and learn how they're made." And later that summer, working swing shift on the freight docks, I brought home a gnarled piece of ginger root from a broken crate because it had stirred my imagination as a starting point for science fiction. From that primitive first effort, working on a clunky manual typewriter, I learned that fiction writing is harder than it looks. Still, I liked staring at the concrete wall on the neighboring building and listening to language in my head and on the page.

Fantasies are often psychological preparation for major decisions, such as what to study in college, or whom to marry, or how to deal with an aging parent, or where to retire. On an everyday level, we use our imaginations to rehearse solutions to dozens of real-world problems. The daydreams show us as witty, eloquent, poised—never at a loss for words. In our school-based fantasies, we move with self-confident ease to squelch the smart aleck or encourage the lonely transfer student or garner increased funding from a tightfisted superintendent. Sometimes we feel a little blush of pride with our own world-class performance.

To sum up, then, the Summerfields believe that as we enter into a compelling role, one that interests us, we *become* another voice—and this becoming is what enables us to create text. To me, this idea has deep resonance.

Participant Text, Spectator Text

It is through working with impersonation that middle school and high school students come to understand the roles of participant and spectator. Derived from the seminal thinking of James Britton (1970), the terms are used somewhat differently by the Summerfields. In general, participant text refers to any text that presents action, including a narrator's stream of consciousness or inner speech, as if it were actually happening. Spectator text, on the other hand, refers to text in which the speaker is commenting upon an action or an event, either physical or mental. Of course, every text is an illusion of reality. A writer can either be in a present-tense world or be looking back at that world from various viewpoints as spectator. The roles of participant and spectator define our relation to a textual world that we intentionally construct.

Texts can also be broadly classified as either practical or reflective. Practical texts are those that regulate our own behavior and get the world's work done. Reflective texts, by contrast, are used mainly for expressive or poetic purposes—to share our experience or to create states of mind that others enter for edification or for entertainment. Poems, fiction, autobiography, journals—all are reflective texts to one degree or another. To all of this,

Jerome Bruner (1986, 11) would add that these are "complementary" but "irreducible" modes of thought with different types of causality:

> The term *then* functions differently in the logical proposition "if x, then y" and in the narrative *recit* "The king died, and then the queen died." One leads to a search for universal truth conditions, the other for likely particular connections between the two events—mortal grief, suicide, foul play. (11–12)

What is especially interesting here is this point: Reflective texts are those that require us to enter a role and become someone else. But reflective texts, by their very nature, can be impersonations of practical texts. This point has important implications for helping students exercise voices in different registers, including the register of Standard English. Why? Because as language coaches, we can create imaginary contexts that invite students to generate practical texts—such as letters, memos, reports, brochures, editorials, arguments—from a rich variety of real-world roles. This point will be further explored in Chapter 9, "Coaching Genre."

The key, of course, lies in the inherent attractions of impersonation, role-playing, and fantasy. Once students experience the feeling of entering a bizarre but interesting textual world and having fun, they are often inclined to try it again. As Diane Ackerman has suggested, it is through deliberate exercises—easy and playful at first, then more challenging—that "something interesting" always happens in the game of language.

As mentioned earlier, the Summerfields typically begin by inviting students to enter existing texts imaginatively. So imagine reading the following text to your class, say, as part of a district-mandated unit on career education. You might ask: "What do you make of the following written request from a workman to his employer?"

Dear Sir:
By the time I arrived at the house where you sent me to make repairs, the storm had torn a good fifty bricks from the roof. So I set up on the roof of the building a beam and a pulley and I hoisted up a couple of baskets of bricks. When I had finished repairing the building there were a lot of bricks left over since I had brought up more than I needed and also because there were some bad, reject bricks that I still had left to bring down. I hoisted the basket back up again and hitched up the line at the bottom. Then I climbed back up again and filled up the basket with extra bricks. Then I went down to the bottom and untied the line. Unfortunately, the basket of bricks was much heavier than I was and before I knew what was happening, the basket started to plunge down, lifting me suddenly off the ground. I decided to keep my grip and hang on, realizing that to let go would end in disaster—but halfway up I ran into the basket coming down and received a severe blow to my shoulder. I then continued to the top, banging my head against the beam and getting my fingers jammed in the pulley. When the basket hit the ground, it burst its bottom, allowing all the bricks to spill out. Since I was now heavier than the basket I started back down at high speed. Halfway down, I met the basket coming up, and received several severe injuries on my shins. When I hit the ground, I landed on the bricks, getting several more painful cuts and bruises from the sharp edges.
    At this moment I must have lost my presence of mind, because I let go of the line. The basket came down again, giving me another heavy blow on the head, and putting me in the hospital. I respectfully request sick leave.

—JEAN L'ANSELME,
The Ring Around the World

Within the imagined world of this text, the Summerfields invite students to respond by writing one of the following letters, all in spectator roles (like the L'Anselme text itself):

1. The bricklayer's employer replies to the letter.
2. The bricklayer's wife visits him in the hospital, and then writes a letter to her sister.
3. The employer writes a circular, which is sent out to all bricklayers in his employment.
4. A pedestrian who happened to be passing and who was shaken by what she or he saw later writes to the local newspaper about it.

Of course, with just a moment's reflection, you can imagine how you and your students might also become the emergency room doctor whose task is to treat the workman and write up a brief report for medical records, or the insurance claims adjuster whose task is to approve or deny requests for payment in memo form, or the building inspector whose job is to ensure that all building regulations are observed and that workers are appropriately licensed.

All of these impersonations are ones that students are likely to enjoy. As the class shares its spectator texts, a writing coach might ask questions of students: What details in each text seem especially convincing? How does one achieve an official tone and style? What if you wanted to make your text an authentic forgery, one that unsuspecting readers might think was the real thing? Would this be possible? How does one achieve the illusion of authenticity without actually becoming an ER doctor, or a claims adjuster, or a building inspector?

Such questions are hardly trivial. By really paying attention to real-world texts, students notice features of format, structure, and style. To initiate such study, you might try sharing comic texts that result from deliberate impersonations. I am thinking, for example, of Don Novello's classic put-on, *The Lazlo Letters*, Volumes 1 and 2 (1977, 1992). Students will enjoy the persona of Lazlo Toth, a red-blooded American who writes to politicians, business leaders, celebrities, and the customer service departments of major corporations with his outrageous schemes, suggestions, and requests. The responses, rendered in the careful, diplomatic language of customer relations, are often every bit as funny as the pieces crafted by Novello. Share a sample interchange and invite students to make inferences about Toth's politics and education. They will discover that their image of the writer is shaped not only by the content of his remarks and prose style but also by subtle cues such as word choice, punctuation, and the cunning violation of certain conventions for business letters. And how about those response letters? What features do we notice in them?

But back to the L'Anselme exercise. Of course, another kind of challenge for students is to imagine the textual world from the viewpoint of the bricklayer participant—not after the fact, but in process. The events presented in the "Dear Sir" letter unfold quite swiftly. So what would that experience be like from the inside out? Is it possible to create a participant text that renders the quick unfolding of catastrophe from within the workman's mind? Let's give it a try.

Bricklayer (Participant Text)

Ah, let's see—extra bricks. Can't have that, not at their price. Got to make a good clean job of it like the boss keeps saying. So let's see—load 'em up here in the basket, good ones and bad, and do the sortin' later, after lunch. Wonder if it's the tunafish again today. Lord knows I'd like a change—maybe deviled egg and ham, pastrami, something with a little zip. A good woman she is, but why the tuna three times a week? Nice bricks these—maybe from the Ogden kiln down by the river. Too bad they closed her down—good folks there like old Sully, rest his soul. Ah, a drinker he was—and storyteller too, red nose and all. Let's see—finish up here, just a few more—ah, that should do it. Tools in the belt, job looks good, and tunafish time. Now down the ladder—oh, how these bones do ache—oops, easy now, don't want to fall from this high up. Take your time, take your time. One foot, then the other. And now it's ground level, everybody out. Ah, let's see, tools in the box—good—and now to deal with these bricks. Quite a pile of 'em up there, but now there's old man gravity workin' for us, not like this morning, hoistin' 'em up. Good job clean job I done. Just undo this knot and ease back the line, wind her around my fist, good tight grip, and down comes the—what the—Oh, Oh, Oh no, basket heavy, comin'—got to let go!—can't!—Ow! Shoulder, white pain, blue sky comin', up, up, and hold on tight! The beam! Ow! My head! The pulley! Fingers! Ow! And down, down, can't let go—basket comin'—Ow! My shins! Oh, no—bricks hard—comin' fast—no, no—Oomph! Oh, Lord in heaven—what happen—sky, clouds, basket comin' fast—can't move—Oomph!

■

Doing this exercise was great fun for me. After the first several words, I was able to hear a voice—not clearly perhaps, but it was there, like a distant radio signal. I wrote a little further and the voice strengthened. Then, in an odd sort of way, I became the ruddy-faced workman in blue overalls who had left his black lunch bucket at the foot of the ladder. My voice was working class—"maybe just a touch of the Irish in me, don't you know"—and my wife was at home, a plain little row house in the south of English—"and my children, well they be long gone, out of the nest." It was a chilly day, a raw March wind gusting out of the east, and as I glanced up "there was patches of blue between the red brick buildings." Working in my shadow, I picked up the bricks and stacked them in the stout wicker basket—neatly, of course, "that being my way." And the rest was easy: the tunafish sandwich always too moist for the thinly sliced bread; my memories of Old Sully from the brickyard knocking down a couple of pints in the pub; the tools in my leather belt; and a descent down the ladder—"oops, easy now—take your time." The challenge came in the final third of the piece. A video camera would have shown me doing an odd dance—sometimes gesturing, sometimes mouthing the words of the fast-forward action, and sometimes typing. Trying to capture what I saw in my mind's eye was difficult but satisfying.

Feel free to use my participant text in any way that seems useful—as a contrast with spectator texts, as a model of what students might like to try in future exercises, or as an example of poorly rendered stream of consciousness. However you use the text, I still enjoyed writing it—and I feel I profited from the exercise, just as I did from this morning's four-mile run to the top of Pacific Heights Road in Honolulu, where the air is clear and the view is long. What matters sometimes is not the judgment of others but how we ourselves assign value.

Rules of the Game

As coaches using an exercise in language, we first challenge students to stretch themselves, to draw upon knowledge they have gleaned from part-time jobs, TV and movie viewing, books and magazines, their parents and friends, the Internet, and their own fantasy lives. Then we ask them to impersonate a person of their choice, someone proficient in the game of language, though not necessarily a Standard English speaker.

At first, role-playing will probably focus on familiar voices such as parents, teachers, school officials, cops in the community, sports heroes, well-known politicians, entertainers, TV announcers, and so on. Over time, as students experience some level of success with text construction, we can encourage them to take on more difficult challenges of impersonation—for example, the role of ER doctor, or insurance claims adjuster, or building inspector mentioned in connection with the L'Anselme exercise.

The rules of the game are pretty straightforward: "Don't be yourself," we say. "Become somebody else and use his or her voice to play the game. Relax. Have fun." Think back to Diane Ackerman's comment earlier in this chapter that exercises in language "always lead to something interesting."

Exercise source materials are everywhere around us once we try such an approach to coaching. For example, the fillers in newspapers—those little pieces that editors use to fill up a page—provide an endless supply of real-world stories that students can enter imaginatively. Such condensed stories offer students an enabling constraint for writing in either participant or spectator roles. Creating and sustaining the illusion of these voices provides interest and challenge for students. It is the "conscious deployment of their native language," to use Jerome Bruner's (1966) phrase, that helps students develop increased competence and confidence in language use.

To illustrate how all of this translates into real classroom work, I first want to share a brief newspaper filler. Then we'll hear how middle school students used their imaginations to enter the world of this text.

Snake Hunt Goes up in Smoke at House

Omaha, Neb. (UPI)—Herman Ferguson said he intended to smoke out the snake hiding under his house when he started the fire.

The snake, at last report, was still at large, but Ferguson's attempt to force the snake from a hole beneath the back of his house ended up causing $5,500 in damage to the structure and about $500 damage to its contents.

The plywood near the newspaper caught fire and spread up the back of the house to the roof, he said.

"I don't recall anything similar to this," said Assistant Fire Chief Robert Warsocki, a 29-year veteran of the fire department.

Ferguson told investigators he took the drastic action because he was unable to rid his property of the snake by other means and had become frustrated.

To enter the world of Herman Ferguson, eighth graders had to first decide upon a role. Most chose to be Herman, but others chose to be either Mrs. Ferguson or the fire chief or the snake. Here is a text that shows evidence of real attention to language and craftsmanship, thanks to the effective coaching of teacher Denice Turner:

Snake's Viewpoint (Spectator Text)

The fire burned closer and closer, the heat searing the scales off the snake's tender back, jolting him awake. The snake coughed and his eyes darted back and forth as his body cringed against the back of the hole. *Oh no!* the snake thought. *I'm too young to die!* The snake hissed his anger aloud to the yellow flames that were moving steadily closer.

Suddenly the flames stopped moving, but the heat grew stronger. The snake, hoping against hope, scrunched his tiny body up and flung it forward, out into the smoke-filled air. Looking around at the destruction around him, the snake's mouth gaped open in astonishment. The plywood blazed merrily next to the hole that had once been his home, while more tendrils of fire snaked their way up to the roof of the house that he had frequently visited for snacks. The house was soon engulfed in flame, the smoke rising to meet the clear air higher above it.

The snake sighed and shook his head at the foolishness of humans. To think that one would burn his own house down! He then turned and slithered off down the road, away from the burning house. He would find a new better home, where he could live in peace, without fear of fire. Maybe a lake, or even river. The snake chuckled to himself. That would do just fine.

—JULIA MOORE

■

In other classes, students experimented with other forms of spectator text. How did Herman explain the event to his wife, to his neighbors, or to his insurance company? What did Mrs. Ferguson say about the incident in her annual Christmas newsletter? How did the fire chief present what happened in his report? What about the editorial that followed in a local newspaper? Each of these situations requires a different voice. Here is an editorial on fire safety done as an in-class demonstration at the overhead projector, with middle school students volunteering their ideas.

Editorial (Spectator Text)

This is Fire Prevention Week in our schools and therefore a good time to discuss safety around the house. There are a few simple rules that you should discuss with your children.

First and foremost, let's explain that fire is a servant of man. When it is used to burn off weeds, it can be a great benefit to our local farmers. But carelessness with fire can lead to tragic results similar to what happened last week in the Ferguson fire on Elm Street in downtown Omaha.

Accidents do happen, but this fire could have been prevented with a few simple precautions. Never start a fire close to your own house or close to other materials that may easily be ignited. Always have a garden hose and tools handy when burning outdoors. Make sure to keep your fires small and under control.

Finally, let's remember to keep matches and other flammable items out of the hands of those who cannot handle them with care. Fire is a big responsibility, and there is a lesson to be learned from the Ferguson fire. It is not something to be taken "lightly."

■

Sometimes, too, students will enjoy tackling the demands of a participant text—that is, a present-tense narrative from one character's point of view. Here is a short text written from Herman Ferguson's viewpoint.

Herman's Viewpoint (Participant Text)

That darn snake! I'll get him yet! Where is he? Oh, there he goes—into that hole! What to do? Hmmm, a gun? No, impractical. Electricity? No, too complicated. Smoke? Yeah, that's it—I'll burn that sucker out! Uhmm—lighter fluid. That's it—I'll dump lighter fluid down the hole. But where? Gotta be somewhere here in the garage. Oh, good—this can's full! I could probably drown the varmint in it—but I'll burn him to make sure! Okay, sucker, take a bath! Wait! Better save some until I find my matches. Okay, matches, matches. Darn it! That match broke! Alright, good, this one's going. Yeah! Take that, sucker! Yeah! Look at those flames go! That'll get him! Getting hot down there. Yeah, that'll get—Wait! Oh, no! The fire's running up the—Oh, no! Gotta get help! Oh, no!

—ERIC STRONG

Finally, here is my own text, one that I like to use when doing in-class workshops. I invite students to imagine the scene just after the fire.

Narrative (Spectator Text)

The last fire truck had just rolled down the street. A few people from the neighborhood still stood in tight little circles out near the sidewalk, asking each other what happened.

It was just then that Mildred pulled into the driveway. She was a chunky woman who bought her dresses out of the Sears catalogue. She ran to the back of the house and found Herman sitting at their picnic table, his head in his hands.

"That fire truck," she wailed. "These people! What's going on, Herman?"

Herman's face was pinched, and smudges of soot were on his forehead and cheek. He was a small, shy man with big ears and a balding head.

"It's a long story," Herman said.

"Neighbor kids been playing with matches again," Mrs. Ferguson barked.

"Not exactly," Herman said.

"What then?"

"I took care of the snake problem, Mildred."

"You *what*?"

"Don't see any snake, do you?"

"Our *house*, Herman! Just *look* what you've done!"

Herman looked at the blistered white paint and charred back door to his house, where flames had run up the wall, and just beyond that to the scorched lawn. "Guess that'll teach him a lesson," Herman said.

You will notice, no doubt, the differences among these illustrative texts. Each has its own voice, its own purpose, and a distinctive form. Notice, too, how each voice defines a different facet of the world outlined by the news story. Each has emerged from the enabling constraint of the given material, a strange landscape of the imagination.

Here is a second snake story. Try to picture the setting and the people involved. And try to imagine the text you might write in doing a playful language exercise.

Man Gets Even with Rattlesnake

Lake City, Fla. (AP)—When a rattlesnake bit Arlie Waldron on the arm, he decided to get even. He bit the snake's head off, but not before the rattler nipped him six more times, including once on the tongue.

A canebrake rattlesnake bit the 42-year-old Waldron as he started to teach his son about handling snakes as they stood in Waldron's backyard in the pine woods of North Florida.

Enraged, Waldron said he set out to bite off the reptile's head, but the fatal chomp didn't come before Waldron had been bitten seven times.

He was rushed from his home near Lake City to a local hospital that night, July 16, and two hours later was transferred to Shands Teaching Hospital in Gainesville. He spent four days there before returning home.

His head and neck "swelled up like a balloon" Waldron recalled in a recent interview with the Lake City Reporter.

You will agree, no doubt, that the story provides a glimpse into a pretty unusual world. Just imagine how much fun even the most reluctant learners might have in assuming the voice of a character in the story. Some students might try on Arlie's voice while others would become his son. But there are also other voices in this world. How about the voice of Arlie's wife? Or the official voice of the hospital report? Or the editorial voice of the Lake City newspaper? Or the voice of the local humane society? How about writing from the snake's point of view, as this eighth grader did?

Dialogue in Hell—Snake's Viewpoint (Spectator Text)

"Wilber!"

"Clancy! How are you? Never thought you would end up here!"

"I hate it down here in hell! All of us snakes are put in a big pit, and real evil humans are tossed on us poor souls. And they don't die, no matter how much you bite them. But I guess we deserved it. How did you die, Wilber?"

"It's a long story."

"We've got a whole eternity full of excruciating pain and misery, and we have nothing better to do. Go for it."

"Well, I was in the prime of my life, and I was a pretty good snake. I never played with my food (before I killed it), and I'd never bitten a human before. These savages are generally scared of us, but, if provoked, can be deadly. So, I was sunning myself on a nice warm rock one day when a couple of these foul creatures came up to me. One of them was really ugly, I mean uglier than most humans. He was big and round and had a thin line of hair right below his grotesque nose. He had a very, well, let's say *interesting* smell. It was utterly repulsive. The other one was smaller, and slightly resembled the first one, except no hair below his nose. Instead, he had hair on top of his head which was sticking up like spines, most likely to ward off predators. He had a little bit of metal attached to his ear, most likely a charm to mark his social stature. Anyway, they had no shovel so I assumed I was safe. I wasn't aware of the danger until it was too late!" Wilber sobbed onto Clancy's back. "I was so young! I'd hardly lived!"

"It's all right." Clancy tried his best to be comforting.

"No it's not!"

"What happened?"

"Well, the big one walked right up to me, while the younger one approached me cautiously. I had a very bad feeling about this. Suddenly, the big one grabbed me around the neck and held me up for his son to see. He had both hands around my neck, and he was suffocating me! Air! I need air! I struggled as hard as I could, but his hands only tightened like a vice around my throbbing neck. My lungs were burning, I was going to pass out. . . . It was only my instinct that saved me. I twisted and wriggled until I had enough leverage, then . . . CHOMP! I sank my fangs deep into his arm, released my venom, and removed them as the creature howled with rage and pain and dropped me back on the grass."

"Wow! Good for you!"

"Yeah, I was pretty proud of myself. I was lying there on the grass, adrenaline still coursing through me. I was exhilarated, thrilled, thinking *that was the best moment of my life*. But my little moment also proved to be fatal."

"But you'd bitten him! Why didn't he die?"

"Well, humans can be pretty resilient. They don't die that easy. He just picked me right up again and I managed to bite him seven more times. He *still* didn't die. Instead, he did something that I'd have never thought a human was capable of. He lunged toward me, and with all his might, chomped down on my head and bit it off. There was no pain, and it all happened so fast that there was no time to think. And next thing I knew, I was down here with you, Clancy. I shouldn't have ended up in hell though. Maybe there was some kind of mistake. Maybe it had something to do with you."

"I'm only here because I was friends with you."

"Wanna bet?"

"Oh yeah? Well, I'll bite your head like that human did!"

"Not if I can get to you first!"

"Attention all current residents! No slacking off! Get back to your roasting!"

—Kate Rouse

■

Let's now hear another dialogue, this one from a high school student. Notice once again how the student invests herself fully in the world she imagines.

Dialogue/Phone Call—Son's Viewpoint (Spectator Text)

That's right, Kevin. My dad's in the hospital. You'll never believe how he got there! Yesterday, I was looking for my baseball in the weeds when one of those weeds started to rattle. I ran in and called Dad. He's the snake expert in the family. Even though I interrupted his baseball game, he was glad to help out.

"Watch this, Buzz," Dad said. "You just bring your hand behind the snake's head and hold on real tight! Damn! He bit me! I'll teach that sucker a lesson!" Then Dad bit the snake!

And the snake bit Dad!

And Dad bit the snake!

And the snake bit Dad!
And Dad bit the snake!
And the snake bit Dad!

The more the snake bit Dad, the madder he got! Finally, with a roar, Dad shoved the snake's head in his mouth and bit it right off! The nurse at the hospital said that the snake got in at least seven bites, including the one on Dad's tongue. I know Dad got in at least ten!

My dad is just totally awesome!

—Kris Boretsky

■

As we've seen, some students like the challenge of creating a distinctive voice. Here is another example of voice being enacted at the high school level.

Narrative—Wife's Viewpoint (Spectator Text)

"Arlie, are you tryin' to spoil your supper? What do you have a mouthful of now? Spit it out! Spit it out!"

Arlie stumbled through the screen door, sweating as usual, but blood was running down his Metallica T-shirt onto the dirty yellow linoleum. He seemed to be gasping.

"Have you and little Arlie had Big Rocky out of his cage, playing with him in the backyard again?"

Arlie opened his mouth, grabbed his throat.

"What the hell are you doing with a snake head in your mouth? My word! If you're gonna eat him, you could at least *cook* him first!"

—Mike Stoddart

■

Finally, of course, it's important for the coach to get out on the playing field. By doing our own exercises we can sometimes surprise ourselves. Here is my effort.

Monologue—Arlie's Viewpoint (Spectator/Participant Text)

"My kid, he's twelve year old, and I keep tellin' him, these snakes, they's nothing to be 'fraid of. I tell him over and over, 'You're bigger than any ol' snake, and if you gonna be a man, you gotta show him who's boss.' So I went out to the field and brung this ornery snake back home in a gunny sack. I been drinkin' a little, but the way I figure, ain't no time like right now to teach that kid that sometimes you gotta do what you gotta do.

"Now this snake, he's a big 'un. And he's mad. I mean, he's thrashin' round in that gunny sack. I get him home and find a cold beer and tell my boy to get hisself out from in front of that damn TV and out here to the back porch. My boy, he's standin' there, wondering what the hell is going on when I take this gunny sack by the ears and give her a good quick shake. Then this snake, it's a slitherin' out on the floor, and Billy, he's screamin' and jumpin' up on the washer. Made me so damn mad to see a kid of mine behavin' like a pukin' coward! I tell him, 'You dummy, get down here and learn how!'

"This rattler, he's all coiled up now and hissin'. I grab him all right, but bam! just like that, he ups and bites me. Well, that made me *real* mad, what with Billy watchin,' so I figure I'm gonna show this snake what it means to mess with Arlie Waldron."

■

Roles and Rules in Perspective

While the impersonations we've looked at are fun for students to write and share, you may be wondering what they teach. A key lesson, I think, has to do with entering another world imaginatively—seeing the screen door and the Metallica T-shirt and the dirty yellow linoleum, then making those details explicit. Another lesson has to do with strategic surprises—structuring the text so that its final line ("My dad is just totally awesome") can do its work on the reader. And a third lesson has to do with consistency of voice—maintaining the illusion of character in a distinctive dialect.

None of these lessons is simple, of course, and none can be taught in the abstract. Students learn how to frame their writing by paying attention to writing that works, both in their writing groups and in well-crafted literature, both fiction and nonfiction. They learn about setting up the surprises by rearranging sentences and by presenting—or withholding—certain information. They learn about sustaining a voice by writing with both eye and ear, then trying it aloud on other readers. All of these are generic writing skills, ones that students can practice over and over.

Are nonstandard dialects modeled in such activities, perhaps with negative consequences? This concern is unjustified, in my opinion. First of all, for students to write *artfully* in nonstandard dialect is no small achievement. Second, dialect study demands very high levels of language awareness, the kind of awareness that students need if they are to internalize the registers of Standard English. William Stafford was not practicing nonstandard language as he constructed "What's in My Journal" from a series of noun phrases, nor was I risking my command of the prestige dialect by writing in the imagined persona of Arlie Waldron. And even if there were a risk—my use of the subjunctive is intentional—it would be one worth taking.

So, contrary to what the behaviorists would have us believe, language is not learned through simple drill-and-practice or blind, mindless imitation. It is probably learned as we make sense of distinctive contrasts, the many different features and voices of a language. And it is also learned through acts of impersonation, role-playing, and fantasy. Exercises drawn from brilliant expository materials like Don Novello's *The Lazlo Letters*, Volumes 1 and 2 (1977, 1992), seem worth trying.

The idea that exercises offer an enabling constraint was introduced earlier and will come up again in relation to genre teaching (Chapter 9). Veteran teachers know that the "write whatever you want" type of assignment can be problematic for many students. Recognizing this fact, the narrator/teacher in Robert Pirsig's *Zen and the Art of Motorcycle Maintenance* (1974) recalls asking a blocked student writer to focus on a single brick in the Opera House in Bozeman, Montana—an incredible constraint—and thereby freeing the writer to produce thousands of words.

He [the teacher] experimented further. In one class he had everyone write all hour about the back of his thumb. Everyone gave him funny looks at the beginning of the hour, but everyone did it, and there wasn't a single complaint about "nothing to say."

In another class he changed the subject from the thumb to a coin, and got a full hour's writing from every student. In other classes it was the same. Some asked, "Do you have to write about both sides?" Once they got the idea of seeing directly for themselves they also saw there was no limit to the amount they could say. It was a confidence-building assignment too, because what they wrote, even though seemingly trivial, was nevertheless their own thing, not a mimicking of someone else's. Classes where he used the coin exercise were always less balky and more interested.

As a result of his experiments he concluded that imitation was a real evil that had to be broken before real rhetoric teaching could begin. This imitation seemed to be an external compulsion. Little children didn't have it. It seemed to come later on, possibly as a result of school itself. (192)

For now, then, suppose that your students discovered real interest in exploring a range of new voices through acts of imagination. Suppose, too, that measures of their linguistic savvy focused less on identifying parts of speech and more on sustaining and developing the voices they had created. Suppose also that the standards for text quality, negotiated with their involvement, related mainly to the effectiveness of the illusion created. Suppose that students did many practice writings, for which they got credit but which did *not* require teacher comment or correction, and then selected from practice efforts the pieces they wanted to revise, edit, and submit for a grade. Suppose, in addition, that the framework for this program emphasized all types of writing—including reports, analytic essays, and argumentative papers—not just narratives. Suppose, finally, that all language coaches saw their jobs as creating contexts for language production—first, by tapping and extending the real-world knowledge of students and, second, by providing information and feedback about texts themselves.

What you would have is an active learning environment as envisioned by the Summerfields (1986) and researched by George Hillocks (1995). Underlying it would be the idea, as discussed in Chapter 6, that all of us claim many voices in addition to the core voice at the center of our being. If you accept this assertion, then its corollary seems to follow—namely, that a comprehensive program of language arts education should explore a wide range of voices, including the voice of Standard English. Other voices give us access to other worlds.

Learning Through Language

1. In Chapter 7 you considered the idea that "the psychological heft of role has more existential presence than real life." In other words, by playing a role—impersonating somebody else—we can sometimes enter another dimension of experience. After reading the chapter, what do you see as the function or purpose of imagination? How does imagination relate to language learning in your opinion? Now, write about your dream of teaching, and share this with others.

2. Imagine yourself as a middle school or high school English teacher. It is Back to School Night, and several parents have shown up. After you describe your program, a parent raises a hand. "I say English is a practical subject and your *main* job is preparing students for the world of work. Don't teach imagination! Teach *skills*! Focus on the basics!" Jot down notes on how you might respond to this parent. Deliver a brief oral response to your group, then discuss.

3. The concept of enabling constraints is basic to exercises in the chapter. Look for one or more newspaper fillers like those presented. After reading and clipping a filler, create either a participant or a spectator text, using role-playing strategies in the chapter. Afterward, in writing, reflect on this imaginative activity. Was it fun? Did you get into the writing? What, if anything, did you learn? Share your clipping, your imaginative writing, and your reflection with others.

CHAPTER 8

COACHING COLLABORATION

The Voice of Experience

Once upon a time we did group work—
There was so much talk it drove me berserk.
Kids had questions they asked to explore,
But chatter and chaos were hard to ignore.

Losing control is a teacher's worst fear—
Which explains why my teaching is so austere.
They talk about teams in the August Inservice,
But I'll just say that groups make me nervous.

Cross-Age Coauthoring

Picture a typical high school class of juniors—your run-of-the-mill mix of abilities—beginning a new literature unit. Patricia Stoddart and I begin by asking kids to do learning log entries about their early memories of reading as described in the Literacy Autobiography activity in Chapter 6. As students share their informal writing, one story leads to another. We can feel the energy of the class, like popcorn exploding in a pan.

Pat settles things down and asks, "How about a story?" Approval is unanimous. After all, this isn't English, this is *fun.* And so it is that Pat and I read a few children's picture books aloud. The juniors lean back and relax, with smiles on their faces. And before they know it, they're talking about the stories, comparing this one to that one. To open class the next day, we read three more, and discussion continues. And finally we reveal our invitation, a letter from a second-grade teacher across town.

The teacher writes that she wants to involve her second graders in reading and writing, but that some kids, particularly the boys, are reluctant. If the high school students would consider writing stories—and then reading them aloud—some of the second graders might get interested. There's a need here, a real human need, and maybe this class of high school students would like to address it.

We put the letter aside. "So what do you think?" we ask.

The juniors soon agree, for a variety of reasons, to take on the project. Some see it as social work; others see it as time out from *real* English.

And so it is that we bring in lots of children's books for the students to read and analyze in small collaborative groups. Our aim, we say, is to understand how such books are written. We look at characters and story problems and themes, and we even begin to brainstorm possible story ideas. But conflicts among the juniors soon arise. Do second graders like space stories or not? Real-life situations? What about their vocabulary level? Because of our many questions, we finally decide that we need to visit the second-grade class to find out from the consumers themselves the kinds of stories they like to hear.

The project is moving now, with big kids and little ones paired up. The little ones are showing the older ones their favorite books and reading aloud to them. And the older ones are asking questions, trying to learn more about second graders and what their interests are. They take notes and pay attention. A few kids start dictating the stories they want, ones with monsters, for example. They have ideas for characters, plots, funny things that might happen. The high school students begin to realize that they must write for a highly discerning audience, and the second graders sense their own power, the way their ideas are being listened to and valued. We've established the human context for writing and reading aloud.

Over ten days, the high school students, some of whom are low-level readers, read dozens of children's books, both silently and aloud. They develop drafts of stories, which they try out on their peer-group partners for response. We even do minilessons on oral reading so that the high school students will better understand how to engage the second graders. Then we visit the elementary school again to see whether our stories are on track. The second graders make suggestions. They talk about the parts they like and the parts they don't understand. The juniors offer illustration ideas to the little ones. A design for each book is negotiated.

In the final stages of this project, the high school students put the text in final form, and the second graders do the illustrations. That's the lesson plan. What happens in reality is that the juniors and second graders make and color the pictures together. There's a page for biographical information on author and illustrator. And of course everybody reads—first, to each other from the coauthored text; then to other teams in the room; and finally to parents at a special PTA event.

Shown here—without pictures, regrettably, because of space limitations—is one of the books from this project.

The Large and Growly Bear

1. Once there was a large and growly bear. One spring morning, he woke up with nothing to do.
2. "I know!" said the large and growly bear. "I will find someone to frighten! That is just what a large and growly bear needs." So the large and prowly bear went growling and prowling and scowling, looking for someone to frighten. And what did he see?
3. He saw the bluebirds. The bluebirds were busy, for it was spring. They were flying here and pulling up a worm there and hurrying home to their babies.

4. "I can frighten bluebirds," said the large and growly bear. So he took a deep breath, and it came out, "GRRRR!"

5. "Ssssh!" said the bluebirds. "You will wake up the babies!"

6. "But I mean it," said the large and growly bear. "I am frightening you."

7. "Not now," said the bluebirds. "We are too busy flying here and pulling up a worm there and hurrying home to our babies. Find someone else to frighten."

8. "Well, I never!" said the large and growly bear to himself. "There must be someone I can frighten!" So the large and growly bear went growling and prowling and scowling, looking for someone to frighten. And what did he see?

9. He saw the rabbits. The rabbits were happy, for it was spring. They were jumping here and hopping there and bouncing like balls with pink ears.

10. "I can frighten rabbits," said the large and growly bear. So he took a big, deep breath, and it came out, "GRRRRRRR!"

11. "Ssssh!" said the rabbits. "You will mix us up. We are counting our bounces."

12. "But I mean it," said the large and growly bear. "I am frightening you!"

13. "Not now," said the rabbits. "We are too busy jumping here and hopping there and bouncing like balls with pink ears. Find someone else to frighten."

14. "Well, I really, really never!" said the large and growly bear. A large and growly bear was tired and cross and very growly, but all at once he had an idea.

15. The large and growly bear walked softly, softly. No one could hear. The large and growly bear walked slowly, slowly. He held his breath for an enormous GRRRRRRRRRRRRRR!

16. "Fish are never too busy to be frightened," said the large and growly bear. "I will find some little fish, and I will frighten them half to death."

17. At last the large and growly bear came to the shining, silver river. The large and growly bear still held his breath for an enormous GRRRRRRRRRRRRRRR! Then the large and growly bear looked into the shining, silver river. He did not see any little fish. He saw A VERY LARGE AND GROWLY BEAR.

18. "Oh, my paws and claws!" cried the large and growly bear. Suddenly he felt very small. He didn't feel growly but he did feel like hurrying. "Hurry away from the large and growly bear! Fly!" he shouted to the bluebirds. "Hop!" he shouted to the rabbits.

19. The bluebirds and the rabbits laughed. They knew the shining, silver river and the tricks it played. "Did you find someone to frighten?" they called.

20. "Yes!" said the large and growly bear. "Who?" cried the bluebirds and rabbits. The large and growly bear poked his nose out of his door. He cried in a small, not very growly voice, "ME."

—JODY HORLACHER

■

Are high school students feeling good about cross-age collaboration? Are second graders thrilled to be working beside varsity linebackers and other young adult mentors? Does Utah have the greatest snow on earth?

Instructional Scaffolding

"First we shape our institutions," Winston Churchill once remarked, "and then they shape us." In the case of education, metaphors have been especially important, often becoming the lenses through which we view the world. Classroom practice results from perceptions—in other words, from the imagery and language we use to understand and act upon our roles.

For the first two-thirds of the twentieth century, industrial metaphors dominated schooling in America, including language arts instruction. Such metaphors were linked to the needs of business and to a national preoccupation with rational, "cost-effective" solutions to human issues. The factory model of schooling governed building design, staffing practices, classroom organization, materials, and behaviorally based models for managing and motivating students. The teacher's role was to transmit knowledge and skill through "common sense" steps (Mayher 1990), such as diagnosis (or needs assessment), direct instruction, evaluation, and reteaching. According to this paradigm, master teachers engaged passive learners through motivational strategies—clever gimmicks, attention-getting media, and reinforcers. Teachers looked to standardized tests and to taxonomies of knowledge and skill for their curriculum frameworks.

Despite the resilience of industrial metaphors—and their repackaging in the standards movement—the metaphor of instructional scaffolding (Langer and Applebee 1987) has made surprising headway in challenging traditional views. Langer and Applebee trace the scaffolding metaphor to the seminal work of Vygotsky and Bruner, then assert that constructivist thinking offers an alternative model to industrial teaching. James Collins (1998) also makes a compelling case for scaffolded instruction to address basic literacy needs. Similarly, George Hillocks (1995) invokes the metaphor of structural support to argue, persuasively, for an "environmental mode" of teaching and for gateway activities that help secondary students work at higher cognitive levels, at first with peer help and later on their own. Clearly, important changes are afoot in the way we define our work to ourselves.

Simply put, scaffolds support language learners by helping them accomplish tasks that would otherwise be out of reach. In other words, a scaffold entails a shared understanding of the goals for instruction as well as some form of collaborative activity. Langer and Applebee (1987) emphasize that the learning must have purpose from the student's viewpoint and be within what Vygotsky called the zone of proximal development—too difficult to be completed independently yet able to be completed with assistance; in addition, the learning tasks must be clear to the learner, with routines and procedures "embedded in the contexts they serve, rather than being presented as isolated components" (143). Another key feature of successful scaffolding is collaboration, with either teacher or peers providing direction, modeling, feedback, and encouragement in language-learning tasks.

Scaffolds come in many different forms. The following is an interactive fiction scaffold I have field-tested with reluctant middle school students. In this exercise for descriptive and narrative writing, students are organized into writing teams. Each of ten "chapters" in the exercise offers another step in an adventure story called "The Fire." Working together, students combine sentences, then weave their own ideas and details into the fabric of the narrative. Structured work of this kind (focused on adverb clauses, in this case), can help prepare basic students for more complex collaborative tasks.

Chapter 4: The Problem

1.1 Lisa returned to the campsite. (WHEN)

1.2 Her bucket was half empty.
Why was the bucket half empty?
Water had splashed . . .
Lisa had tripped . . .
A thin stream of water . . .

2.1 Lisa backed toward the ravine.

2.2 Bits of flame licked at her shoes.   (WHILE)
Describe what else Lisa did.
She blinked . . .
Coughing from . . .
As she tried to help . . .

3.1 "We're in trouble!" Tony shouted.

3.2 "We can get control!" Tony shouted.   (UNLESS)
What was Lisa's reply?
"Maybe I should . . ."
"I wonder if . . ."
"That fisherman . . ."

4.1 Some of the fire was out.   (ALTHOUGH)

4.2 Other places were flaring up.
What plan did Tony have?
"Let's try to . . ."
"Help me to . . ."
"If we can just . . ."

5.1 Lisa screamed.

5.2 Tony stumbled and fell.   (AS)
Tell how and where Tony fell.
He tumbled . . .
One knee went down . . .
Rolling to one side . . .

6.1 The wind had shifted again.   (BECAUSE)

6.2 Fire leaped toward him.
How did Lisa use the bucket?
Lisa quickly . . .
Lisa grabbed the bucket . . .
Without hesitation, Lisa . . .

Finishing Chapter 4: Reread the chapter so far. Then start a prewriting map to generate ideas. Use "teamwork" as your focus.

Step 1. Think about these questions: What action did Lisa and Tony take? What animals are spotted trying to escape the fire?

Step 2. Imagine Lisa and Tony's progress in trying to fight the fire. To help show the action, use dialogue between Tony and Lisa.

Step 3. Create a sentence such as this one to end Chapter 4: "Oh, no!" Lisa pointed. "Look at the camp stove!"

■

Such scaffolding is intended as preparation for the "handover phase" of learning (Bruner 1986), not as merely an activity for keeping students busy. Middle school teachers interested in field-testing such material may contact me through the Department of Secondary Education at Utah State University (<www.seced.usu.edu>).

In this chapter, we first examine processes for working with response groups, a key collaborative activity in an active learning environment (Hillocks 1995). Then we examine a rationale for coauthoring as well its research base. In the third section, two illustrative exercises are described, followed by ideas for managing student groups. Taken together, these sections may help you coach collaboration and develop scaffolds for language learning.

Along with Langer and Applebee (1987), let me emphasize how important it is that scaffolds come down once students have internalized new language structures and routines.

Collaboration in Response Groups

For veteran teachers, the phrase *socially constructed text* may evoke memories of mind-numbing work on committees—and the fierce negotiations to achieve the pale, bloodless perfection of true committeespeak. In a response group context, however, the phrase has more positive connotations. It is in the give-and-take of trying out ideas on each other that young writers can begin to construct text socially. Effective response groups can serve as human scaffolds for many students, helping them consider their writing from a decentered perspective.

Because of adolescents' interest in their classmates, Moffett saw peers as a "natural audience," the teacher's role being "to teach the students to teach each other" (1983, 196). Moffett was hardly laissez-faire in his approach. He recommended teacher-directed workshops, or what we might now call "craft lessons" (Fletcher and Portalupi 1998), as well as student-run response groups. He wanted papers projected to model informed feedback and called for intensive work in groups while planning, drafting, revising, and publishing. He advocated occasional conferences and minimal teacher comments. He urged that no grades be put on individual papers but recommended that the accumulation of work stand for evaluation purposes.

Novice teachers—and those working in challenging environments—often feel uneasy about response groups. After all, it takes only a little imagination to foresee the kinds of mischief that adolescents, left to their own devices, may perpetrate. So how does one begin to manage students who may have had little experience in responding to each other's work—or who may have had negative past experiences? And how can one use response groups as a foundation for coauthoring activities?

Items drawn from the following self-assessment exercise can prompt discussion about collaboration, helping to set the stage for response groups. At the end of a semester or a school year, students can reassess their attitudes to compare results.

Exercise in Self-Assessment

Directions: Reflect on your attitudes toward writing and the approaches you usually take. Doing so will help you understand yourself as a learner and communicate goals to your teacher. Please keep this assessment on the inside cover of your working portfolio. Respond using this code: 1 = strongly agree; 2 = agree; 3 = disagree; 4 = strongly disagree.

1. ____ I know I can write when I set my mind to it.
2. ____ Figuring things out in writing is interesting to me.
3. ____ Good planning is a key to good writing.
4. ____ I have positive feelings about writing from past experiences.
5. ____ I like to brainstorm lots of ideas before I write.
6. ____ Writing well comes more from *doing* it than from inspiration.
7. ____ I enjoy the feeling of sharing my writing with others.
8. ____ I sometimes surprise myself with insights while writing.
9. ____ Learning to write is more important than the grade I get.
10. ____ I am willing to work hard at learning to write well.
11. ____ Working with others helps me do my best writing.
12. ____ I almost always know whether writing is good or not.
13. ____ Having a quick conference with a teacher helps me write.
14. ____ I generally know how to make my own writing better.
15. ____ Rereading what I write is the way I improve my writing.
16. ____ I whisper my writing to myself to check how it sounds.
17. ____ Even the best writers sometimes struggle with writing.
18. ____ I look forward to others' comments about my writing.
19. ____ It's fun to proofread and edit my own writing.
20. ____ Good writing skills are very important to my future.

■

To communicate the purpose for response groups, it is often useful to have students imagine how they would learn anything—talking, soccer moves, computer programming—in the absence of feedback. Point out that feedback is a key condition for learning and that small groups can offer feedback about writing. The idea, you might say, is that several heads are generally smarter than one. Early on, peers may focus on helping one another find and organize ideas, but later in the writing process, groups may focus on usage and mechanics.

Of course, successful response groups require mutual respect and hard work. The group's aim is to assist each writer in the development of his or her text. It is by really listening to ideas from peers and by asking questions that students can learn much about how to develop, revise, and edit their writing. Groups may be as small as two people or as large an entire class. Generally, however, response groups will involve three to five students. Guidelines like the following ones (Strong 1996) can help to orient students' expectations.

Giving Feedback on Writing

- Listen for the overall effect during the first reading.
- Make notes or comments during the second reading.
- Tell what you liked best about the writing.
- Later, identify a place in the text that may need work.
- Comment on content/organization first, mechanics later.
- Ask questions; point to places on the page as you comment.

Response group training can start with the modeling activities described in the "Showing, Not Telling" section of Chapter 5. After students have repeatedly participated in a large-group modeling of effective response, they can practice in parallel ways using the fishbowl strategy: A small group is set up in the center of the room to offer showing, not telling feedback to a writer; meanwhile, the rest of the class observes the feedback process and later comments on it. Over several days, all students have the opportunity to be in the fishbowl and to hear from their peers how well they provided feedback to a classmate.

Response Group Training

Directions: Observe students in the fishbowl as they offer workshop response. Pay attention to *what* is said and *how* it is said (tone of voice, body language). Evaluate each person's feedback: 3 = very helpful; 2 = helpful; 1 = not so helpful.

Criteria for Effective Response	Jim	Sue	Joy	Ted
Faces the writer and seems interested.				
Makes positive comments to support writer.				
Points to specific places in text with ideas.				
Is friendly but businesslike with suggestions.				
Asks questions and listens to the response.				
Stays on task and doesn't get distracted.				
Uses descriptive, nonjudgmental language.				
Other:				

Of course, student writers must understand that feedback will sometimes confirm their hunches about their text and sometimes challenge them to rethink their content, organization, or writing style. A nondefensive listening attitude may be difficult for some. After listening to the comments of others, the writer's task is to decide what's best for the paper. The following guidelines (Strong 1996) have helped some learners.

Getting Feedback on Writing

- Never apologize for the piece you're going to read.
- Read your work aloud twice unless it's quite long.
- Listen carefully and take notes on what others tell you.

- Don't defend or explain your work as you get feedback.
- Ask questions to clarify what others say or suggest.
- Thank your writing partners for their comments.

In working with others in response groups, it helps to have a shared common code for commenting on papers. Here are four shorthand symbols that students often find useful. Students can use these symbols to mark words, sentences, or paragraphs; afterward, of course, they can explain their responses more fully as they give feedback in their groups (Strong 1996).

Symbol	Meaning
+	I like this.
∗	Say more here.
?	This puzzled me.
✓	Check for an error.

Students can put symbols above individual words or sentences. They can also bracket paragraphs and use the symbols in the margin. Another way of "pointing" to writing features is to use the following simple marking system (Strong 1996):

- Underline striking images, strong verbs, vivid details, or memorable phrases.
- Put a wavy line under pompous language, or stale, empty, repeated phrases.
- Put brackets [ ] around choppy sentences—ones that might be combined.
- Use parentheses ( ) to mark any sentences that seem overloaded or garbled.

In-class demonstrations of these methods of response will help ensure that students understand them and use them in their groups. Direct feedback of this kind can be very helpful to student writers as they search for direction in their revisions.

Effective coaching involves more than admonition. Students need to be involved in practice activities to develop enhanced language skills. In addition to the fishbowl strategy described earlier, you may want to prepare role cards for mock groups so that students see and feel, firsthand, the effects of positive roles (for example, facilitator, organizer, clarifier, fence mender) and negative roles (for example, sniper, clown, monopolizer, mushmouth). Have students keep learning logs focused on group process, in which they voice their feelings and try to understand the dynamics of team interactions (see the Exercise in Self-Assessment). Work with response groups can set the stage for other activities in collaborative writing.

As students learn to trust each other and revise in light of peer feedback, they develop prerequisite skills for coauthoring, with its brave new ways of working. The goal for such coaching is for students to eventually negotiate their differences about work schedule, approach, and individual responsibilities in coauthoring tasks.

Collaborative Writing in Perspective

Some teachers have reservations about having students share resources and work together, especially when their own training has emphasized competition for grades. Others wonder if collaboration is just another fad. So although the method grows more fashionable each year, certain background questions seem reasonable: What is the educational rationale for coauthoring? Does research support it?

Rationale for collaboration

Helen Dale (1997) offers clear, accessible responses to such questions in *Co-Authoring in the Classroom*. Her solid rationale for collaborative writing is grounded in a thorough literature review, extensive practical experience in secondary and college teaching, and inquiry into the dynamics of such instruction. In short, she offers articulate advocacy for the far-reaching benefits of language coaching—in this case, in a collaborative context.

Part of the rationale for coauthoring centers on its potential for helping students prompt one another for ideas—thus bridging oral and written language—and also for developing a clearer sense of audience. Part of it involves a shift in role, where students must teach one another and use each other's ideas to solve problems. And part of it is preparation for life, since collaboration is a workplace expectation for many employees in business, government, and the professions (Ede and Lunsford 1990).

As mentioned earlier, the seminal ideas of Vygotsky (1978) provide theoretical support for coauthoring activities. Learning, according to Vygotsky, is an inherently social activity, one that stimulates development and the internalization of abstract thought. Of course, collaborative writing follows exactly this developmental line, with students verbalizing their thoughts and processes in order to manage them effectively. Contrast this approach with the more traditional image of students stewing in individual juices, often unable to generate ideas, organize or sustain a line of reasoning, or take the viewpoints of an intended audience.

Vygotsky (1978) also believed that learning leads development. As far as coauthoring groups are concerned, the odds are that most students will have individual insights, opinions, knowledge, or technical skills that will enable them to lead others (Dale 1997). Finally, Vygotsky (1986) contended that writing required learners both to elaborate their inner speech and to develop sophisticated conceptions of audience. Collaborative writing would seem to provide a bridging function since groups act simultaneously as authors and as audience. Because such language practice occurs in a social context, it should help students internalize many types of knowledge and skill.

A second underpinning for coauthoring, according to Dale (1997), comes from the work of Bakhtin (1981). Whereas Vygotsky's ideas support the cognitive aspects of collaboration, Bakhtin's theory of "dialogism" emphasizes that language growth results from our efforts to incorporate the speech and the ideas of others into our own evolving constructs. The Bakhtinian view is that because our thoughts and words give voice to our social and cultural contexts, we never write alone. As discussed in Chapters 6 and 7, we internalize multiple voices. In a very real sense, the sum of what we are is nothing less than our reading, our conversations, our reflections, and our life experience.

Finally, collaborative groups inevitably produce competing ideas and language. As students work to resolve differences, they are challenged to broaden their views and to expand their strategic knowledge of discourse. Often, a rich mix of voices can lead to surprising synergies—unexpected insights or breakthroughs from the interplay of ideas.

Research on collaboration

Hundreds of studies in cooperative learning support the claim that collaborative groups produce the results that teachers hope for—namely, higher achievement, reasoning at higher levels, active production of new ideas, and knowledge transfer (Bossert 1988; Johnson and Johnson 1994). Coauthoring tasks greatly increase the amount of time that students spend verbalizing their ideas. According to Cohen, "students who verbalize about what they're learning comprehend more fully than those who don't, and the more explaining a student does, the more benefit that student receives" (1994, 7).

"This is all well and good," you may be thinking. "But do secondary students in coauthoring situations learn to *write* better?"

This question cannot be answered with assurance because so little research has been done on collaborative writing in secondary schools. However, a coauthoring study by Hillebrand (1994, 71) found that collaborative essays were "far superior"—"better developed, [with] more thoughtful analysis"—than ones written by individuals on the same assignment. Also, in a coauthoring study of ninth graders, Dale (1994) found that "14 percent of all coauthoring discourse was spent representing the writing task, and another 25 percent on strategic talk about planning" (Dale 1997, 11). Most secondary teachers would be thrilled to find students engaged in such extensive planning prior to writing.

In addition, coauthoring tasks apparently help novice writers revise. Experienced writers continually revise because of the recursiveness of their processes (Flower and Hayes 1981; Sommers 1980); with novice writers, on the other hand, the revision is far more superficial and frequently serves only to cut off the flow of their ideas (Sommers 1980; Perl 1979). In her research with novice ninth graders, Dale (1994) found that planning and revising behaviors were closely linked, mirroring the processes that seem to be used by experienced writers. Such results would seem to auger well for scaffolded tasks in collaborative writing.

Collaboration Exercises

In this section I describe two coauthoring tasks that can create positive learning experiences for secondary language learners. Each activity suggests a very different approach to collaboration. While I cannot offer double-your-money-back guarantees, I can offer the hope that each exercise may trigger alternative—and better—ideas.

Coauthored poetry

Because I have long scavenged the coaching approaches used by others, I cannot say what prompted me to begin experimenting with coauthored poetry. All I know is that the structures of collaboration work as well today as they did thirty-five years ago and that simple algorithms have triggered dozens of spin-off lessons, coauthored booklets by middle school and high school students, and individually written poems.

As a kind of archetypal introduction—so simple that you may think it's a put-on—I recommend the paper strips strategy. It works like this: First, find yourself a cultural holiday (Halloween, Thanksgiving, Christmas, Kwanzaa, Hanukkah, and so on) or focus on other rituals with special meaning for students (beginning of school, homecoming, spring break, end of school). Begin by sharing what you're looking forward to—your Thanksgiving plans, for example—and say a few words about the rituals in your home, the ones linked to memories of past holidays. Encourage a few students to voice their plans or what they remember of the holiday from years past.

Then, as you feel the gathering of student interest, explain what you want to accomplish in terms of language learning: an exploration of the holiday's meaning from multiple viewpoints. The activity, you explain, involves brainstorming, which you model briefly, using your own memories. Afterward, you direct students to take out two or three sheets of blank paper. And, finally, you work through a series of memory prompts, asking students to jot down phrases or images that burble to the surface of their minds. Students are also asked to skip a space between each of their images, phrases, or lines for reasons that will later become clear.

The prompts, each with two or three minutes of quiet focus, might be like these:

- Recall some of the images and colors of Thanksgiving.
- Recall some of the tastes and smells of Thanksgiving.
- Recall some of the sounds and voices of Thanksgiving.
- Recall some of the textures and feelings of Thanksgiving.
- Recall some of the happy or sad memories of Thanksgiving.
- Recall some of the events or rituals of Thanksgiving.

What your students will produce, in response to guided brainstorming, are random images, the raw material for coauthored poetry. Here, for example, are images from my own Thanksgiving memories:

- the sharp sweet taste of cranberries mixed with grated orange peel
- egg noodles hanging over the backs of chairs to dry
- my mother up alone in the early morning hours
- steam on the kitchen windows and kids drawing pictures
- the Italian sisters huddled in the kitchen, sneaking sips of red wine
- the leathery feel of my grandfather's hand and a quiet, steady gaze
- Kristin and Eric with black olives on their fingers
- the loud groans and after-dinner farts of Uncle Bob
- plump ravioli simmering in red tomato sauce
- men stretched out like royalty, with football in the background
- the high-pitched whirr of an electric carving knife
- turkey gravy oozing over mashed potatoes and into the yams
- no place for Jell-O salad on the plate
- wondering who will say grace
- a moment of quiet for those not with us
- thin flickering light above a small crowded table
- bumping down the bedroom stairs on our butts
- twilight walk through rustling leaves
- mincemeat pie topped with cheap vanilla ice cream
- old cars in the driveway and parked in the tall wet grass
- food-encrusted pans and casserole dishes

Once students have composed their lists of images, ask them to tear their papers into strips—with a single phrase or image on each strip—and they will do so with ripping enthusiasm. Afterward, have students collect the paper strips and put them in a large pile at the front of the room. Mix them up with ceremonial flair or have a show-off student assist with this important work. Now, figure out the number of groups you want to have work with these materials. My advice, like that of Dale (1997), is to divide the class size by three to determine the number of groups, understanding that one or two groups may have four students. Divide the large pile of paper strips into smaller clumps, one clump for each group.

What next? Students count off by the total number of groups so that each collaborative group is randomly assigned. Have students get into groups. Direct the groups to divvy up the strips in their clump, read them quietly, and begin to sort them. Some strips will be interesting or funny or well expressed; others may be less so. Tell students that they may work either together or alone at first but that a good approach is to develop three categories of strips for a poem they will eventually construct from these raw materials: interesting images, "maybe" images, and "probably not" images. Almost immediately, students will begin to read aloud from the strips arrayed before them, and they will soon discover how one image triggers or leads to another. Without explicit instruction, students discover how to arrange the strips in different ways on their desktops or on the floor. Students usually enjoy the process—and of course, everybody secretly waits to see how groups will use (or not use) the images they have created.

Arrangement takes time. Move around and don't rush it. Instead, notice how students develop thematic clusters as they arrange the strips. Notice, too, how these clusters sometimes get organized into larger schema or frameworks. "Let's make the poem start in the morning and end at night," someone suggests. "How about organizing around women's work and men's work," another architect offers. "Look, we have inside images and outside images," another student observes. "That's cool."

Eventually, students are asked to tape their strips to larger sheets of paper and to perform their texts aloud for other groups. Generally, students like this activity. The performance expectation increases interest, and groups sometimes discover exciting ways to share the text orally. Students may invent a choral reading framework or use a refrain to tie sections of the text into a coherent whole. Of course, the more experience students have with poetry, the more likely they are to use such rhetorical and structural devices. An enterprising teacher can always prime the pump by introducing students to such devices in advance of a coauthoring lesson.

With all of this reading, discussing, arranging, negotiating, and problem solving, the students in coauthoring poetry groups learn many important lessons. Clearly, such an exercise can introduce later instruction—for example, when students and coach step back to learn from the experience—but the exercise can also provide the basis for a parallel writing task that students do independently. "Through shared language," as Dale (1997) puts it, "we create ourselves" (5).

Coauthored triptychs

The term *triptych* entered my vocabulary thanks to the work of Kenneth Brewer, a fine poet and gifted teacher of creative writing at Utah State University. You may be familiar with triptychs in the visual arts—three pictures or panels, each independent from the other two but visually related to form a larger scene. In ancient times the triptych was a hinged writing tablet consisting of three leaves, each leaf a part of the composition.

For years, Brewer taught advanced courses in memoir, and the triptych emerged as an important subgenre for his students. Because of his background in personal essay and my interest in collaborative writing, we decided to team teach a special Utah Writing Project seminar on the triptych form and to use collaborative writing as the vehicle for scaffolded instruction. Three such seminars have now been offered, and all have been wonderfully successful from the viewpoint of the writers. In fact, some middle school and high school teachers now use similar collaborative strategies in their own classes, introducing students to three-part personal essays.

Because of space constraints for this chapter, let me now share a poem that will provide you with a good sense of what a literary triptych feels like, albeit in abbreviated form. Please take a few moments to study the following three-part poem. Then ask yourself: How does this text work?

Three Uses of Chopsticks

I.
She drops her head between her knees.
Her long black hair flows over.
She gathers the strands,
flips up her head
and twists her hair
into a silken bun.
She takes a pair of chopsticks,
sticks them into her hair
to hold it up; together with an orchid,
chopsticks make a practical decoration.
The nape of her neck is exposed
tempting him to touch it.
At the right moment tonight
she will pull out the chopsticks
like a knife
and drop her hair
for the kill.

II.
Teeth-chipped red laquer chopsticks
with wood exposed like flesh.
She saves the old ones for him.
He uses the chopsticks to prop
orchid plants heavy with flowers.
From her window, she watches
him stab into the cinder
at the base of the plants.
He is careful of the aerial roots—
blue-green veins more familiar now
than veins on her breasts
that he once tracked
after parting her long, graying hair
fallen across her chest.

She notices he binds chopsticks
and stalks with soft wire
in an unlikely embrace,
preventing winds from toppling
and crushing the plants.

III.
She walks down the path
like a bride—white orchids
fluttering like butterflies in her hands—
to where he waits for her.
She loops white hair
straggling from her bun
over an ear as she walks.
Fronting the small stoop
near gas burners, she bows,
draws a pair of long steel chopsticks
from their case. She picks up
the char-free bones
left among the ashes:
fragments of hip bones, pieces of skull,
parts of teeth.
She drops them into an urn.
She then ties a black cloth
around the copper box,
sticks flowers into the square knot,
and folds her arms around him
and orchids.

—JULIET S. KONO

Before our weeklong seminar, writers read about collaborative writing and develop a sense of the triptych as a literary form. On the first day, we organize into coauthoring teams of three and get acquainted. Then we discuss the week's work, review characteristics of the triptych, and discuss why the form lends itself to collaborative writing. Writers understand that over three days they will be involved in three instructor-led workshops and will repeatedly share what they've drafted with team members.

Each team knows that at the end of the three days they will have collectively generated and discussed nine individual pieces of text. From these nine possible pieces, they will negotiate a three-part collaborative triptych on the fourth day, weaving their voices together so that the composition reflects each team member's work. On the fifth day of celebration, each group's coauthored triptych is shared orally and published in final form. Later, on an individual basis, each teacher writes his or her own triptych, drawing upon the lessons learned from collaborative writing.

The three workshops that provide impetus for teacher writing are designed to elicit sensory and descriptive text, a narrative incident, and personal reflection related to family. We use familiar writing process strategies to prompt drafts—brainstorming, sketching, and role-playing, among others. In the large-group discussions that follow, we pay attention to issues of craft such as voice or concrete detail. We sometimes highlight, for example, how one writer uses a song title to establish setting or how another writer uses dialogue and gesture to establish character.

We have noticed that the triptych provides common ground for collaboration yet leaves room for a wide range of responses. Early in the week, as coauthoring team members share drafts, they begin to see potential links between and among their texts, connections of theme, mood, image, or chronology. It is these up-close-and-personal conversations—within the safety of a small group—that serve as scaffolding for insights about textual possibilities. As team members voice the connections they see, great energy is achieved. The talk in small groups provides what George Hillocks (1995) calls a "gateway" activity for independent writing.

By the fourth day of the seminar, writers are deeply involved in selecting their piece for the group composition and shaping this text to fit within the emerging triptych structure. Typically, certain parts of each writer's work are expanded while others are diminished in emphasis. Individual voices remain distinct as textual links are revisited and revised in oral readings. Collaboratively, each team creates a unique, coherent text composed of three independent but interwoven voices. By negotiating meanings and interpreting links among texts, everyone learns how authentic collaboration can develop and modulate individual voices. Later, as writers present their coauthored triptychs—and as they hear and read the triptychs written by other teams—they achieve even deeper insights into the possibilities of the genre.

It is the sum of these experiences that provides inspiration and support for individually composed triptychs. Afterward, most writers are eager (and able!) to explore the form on their own, using their group members as response collaborators. I recommend this process of coauthoring for teachers with a sense of adventure. Teachers interested in getting a sample triptych or two may contact me through the Department of Secondary Education at Utah State University (<www.seced.usu.edu>).

Working Smarter, Not Harder

The theme of working smarter, not harder was part of this book's introduction, and I return to it here. We've already considered a rationale for coauthoring work grounded in the developmental theories of Vygotsky and Bakhtin as well as in research studies. Now I want to advance a more pragmatic argument for coaching teamwork.

Coauthoring is important, I think, because it reduces the workload of teacher response. In traditional instruction, typical writing coaches face 150 (or more) papers for each assignment. With coauthored tasks, teachers deal with a less daunting number, perhaps 50 (or more) papers per assignment. This number may still be large, but at least it is within the bounds of reason. Most of us know that by dealing conscientiously with a few papers each day, we can probably manage such a load without driving ourselves to distraction. The wisdom of James Moffett is worth recalling in this regard. Moffett's view was that feedback and response are crucial to learning and that "the *quality* of the feedback is the key" (1983, 193).

So coauthoring is a smart strategy not just because it has a solid rationale and gives students lots of practice in writing and responding but also because it gives their coaches a little breathing room. Clearly, if the amount students write is limited by what teachers have time to read, students will never receive the level of practice necessary to develop fluency, voice, mechanical proficiency, or rhetorical competence. By coaching students to coach each other, we advance our mutual interests and leave room for our own sporting life pursuits as described in this book's conclusion.

But collaboration doesn't happen by itself. Planning and teaching make it happen. First, students will need a rationale for coauthoring work, with reasons linked to workplace expectations in the Information Age. Next, they will need coaching in the dynamics of group process to understand why such language learning is important, both now and in the future. In the business world, as Dale (1997, 19) notes, "teamwork is essential to the success of an organization" and these characteristics of the team members have been carefully studied by analysts:

- They have a purpose and a plan.
- They communicate effectively, i.e., they listen to each other and allow everyone to participate.
- They arrive at decisions by taking into account all views, and when they disagree, they do so in a pleasant way.
- They share leadership and value the diverse abilities of the group members.
- They self-assess.

As a practical matter, Dale (1997) recommends that each coauthoring group designate a primary writer for each collaborative assignment. This person has the responsibility for taking notes, integrating revisions and corrections into a fresh draft, and making copies for the collaborative team—a responsibility that rotates during the semester. Dale also urges that "students not break the writing task into parts and parcel it out" (45). Instead, the most productive groups are those that do the writing together, sharing in the decisions about large issues of organization and structure as well as the smaller ones of phrasing and punctuation.

Dale suggests that the quality of the final coauthored product should represent about 50 percent of the individual student's grade. The other 50 percent has to do with three kinds of assessment: (1) moving among the groups and thereby monitoring the contributions of individuals; (2) reading students' learning logs and self-assessment forms; and (3) reading peer assessment forms. Copies of such forms, as well as fourteen coauthoring tasks, are found in her monograph.

Some teachers worry about the loss of individual initiative and responsibility in coauthoring work. They point out that some students are highly adept at faking it in groups—hanging back, for example, and letting others do the work. They note that aimless, frivolous collaboration can be used by cynical teachers as a substitute for honest teaching. And they contend that competitive standards can build character, motivate achievement, and serve as preparation for life.

The critics have a point. After all, some kids do disengage in classes where collaboration is emphasized, and some teachers do use group work as a substitute for careful planning. And most of us do know of schools with demoralized faculties that seem to have given up on academic standards. And, finally, who among us can deny that our nation's success now depends on our ability to compete—as individuals and as groups—in an increasingly global environment?

What is also true, however, is that our traditional emphasis on competition as a means to develop individual talents has given way to the new realities of networking. Increasingly, individual success is linked to one's ability to work well with others, to cooperate and collaborate in multiple ways. This is no less true in business and in industry than in schools. Truly successful faculties are those who team up to coach students.

Learning Through Language

1. In Chapter 8 you visited a cross-age project in coauthoring, one that teamed high school students with elementary school children. With the Internet and the widespread availability of word processing, opportunities for coauthoring have greatly expanded. Collaborate with others to brainstorm the possibilities. Also, discuss the applications of coauthoring for those so often marginalized, for example, second language learners and special education students.

2. Your superintendent has received complaints from a conservative political group that questions collaborative learning activities in writing. You and other members of the language arts team have been asked to develop a clear, jargon-free rationale for coauthoring. Team up with members of your group to list, on an overhead transparency, the key points that will be presented in a school board meeting. Role-play your part of the presentation with members of your group.

3. When response groups work, so does instruction; however, when groups lack motivation and skills, instruction often falls apart. Imagine that you have been asked to develop a training process for secondary students who have no experience in commenting on each other's writing. Write up the sequence of activities you would use to help these learners understand your expectations. Share your writing with others. Based on the feedback you get, revise your text.

CHAPTER 9

Coaching Genre

The Writing Game

Reviews and memos, clever ads—
These are more than passing fads.
Legends, letters, dreams, and lies—
These are forms of exercise.

Stories, essays, poems, and plays—
Games like these can fill our days.
Daily practice hones our skill—
Smooth text moves are acts of will.

Inner Game, Outer Game

Any linguistic act is two games at once—an inner game of intention and strategy and an outer game of actual performance. Much of the writing process movement has shown us how increased attention to the inner game can result in better outer game performance. In a way, this is hardly surprising. Since writing is thinking, more planning should lead to better writing. Yet it is equally and paradoxically true, as many writers will testify, that the act of writing can stimulate inner planning as well as discovery.

The metaphors used here are borrowed from the work of W. Timothy Gallwey, whose books have explored tennis, skiing, golf, music, and the modern workplace. Gallwey maintains that in any complex endeavor—and writing must surely qualify as that—two aspects of self are at work. For many of us, self 1 (or the executive self) speaks to self 2 (or the doer self) with an unrelenting stream of advice, commands, and criticisms about what should be done. And the second self? It listens, tightens its muscles, and strains ever so hard to master a backhand volley, or a downhill run through knee-deep powder, or a tough chip shot onto the green—or, perhaps more to the point here, a written language task. Time after time, the second self makes its attempt, and time after time, the internal stream of self-talk comes between the doer and the activity, resulting in the muffed shot, the headlong fall, or self 1 = self 2 prose that is plodding and perfunctory.

This is not to say, of course, that the self 1-self 2 relationship is always negative. For example, while writing this book, I often made regular runs to the bottom of Pacific Heights Road in Honolulu, knowing full well what faced me next: a two-mile return, all uphill.

It was a long, tough pull, and there were times when self 1 resorted to a four-count chant: "One . . . foot . . . in front . . . of other." In much the same way, self 1 sometimes coached self 2 on ways of getting back on track while writing. Rereading text, thinking aloud in my journal, spending a quiet Saturday in the library on background work—all of these strategies were suggested by self 1, and some even worked.

Clearly, though, the real expertise of self 1 is barbed and personal criticism, the kind that hooks under the skin, draws blood, and leaves a trace of venom. Lying in ambush, self 1 takes sniper's aim after any long, empty stretch in front of the computer screen—but also whenever some strategic effort (one suggested by self 1) does not work as it should. From its know-it-all vantage point, the critical self rarely, if ever, takes responsibility for actions it initiates. Thus, a wasted day in the library results from the ineptitude of self 2, not from any problem in the executive direction of self 1.

For our students, minidramas between self 1 and self 2 are enacted countless times each day as they procrastinate, voice self-doubts, or wear holes in their notebook paper from repeated erasures. And for coaches, too, the inner drama is often alive and well, despite our backgrounds of language experience and despite our knowing better. For me, there is one especially well-etched memory: being lead speaker for the 1997 NCTE Spring Conference session honoring Donald Murray, an assignment that nearly paralyzed me into silence.

To prepare, I had reread Murray until I was awash in his language, then read what others had said about him. Such reading was not easy because I was distracted by problems related to my department head job, most notably a $24 million lawsuit. Although I knew that the basis for the suit was groundless, I had no way of knowing that it would finally be dismissed as such. It was during my struggle to focus on background reading that self 1 gripped me by the throat and whispered in icy tones that I really had nothing to say that would be fresh or different or remotely interesting to the hundreds of people, respected colleagues all, who would gather in Charlotte, North Carolina. So although I had internalized my purpose, audience, and situation, the fact remained that I had not written a single word by the time I left home in Utah, and I was terrified.

On the airplane, I tried to clear my mind and get down to writing. I made one false start after another—and in the hotel room, it was the same story. Nothing was good enough. It was trite, or chummy, or too academic, or sentimental, or simply boring. Finally, in a last-ditch effort to silence the incessant criticism of self 1—to "lower my standards," as William Stafford once put it—I went for a very long run, took a hot shower, and sat down to stare at the notepad in front of me. "What's going on here?" I asked myself. The response came through loud and clear: "You're doing it to yourself."

So I took a deep breath, hoping to quiet the critical voice with sustained attention to the act of writing itself, and then let my hand move across the page, following the deep grooves of syntax. It was slow going at first, just getting a grip and gathering the momentum. And it was tough keeping the inner critic quiet. But this is what my hand finally wrote with a mind of its own.

Donald M. Murray: The Outsider in Perspective

1. Imagine for a moment it is early April, 1997, in Charlotte, North Carolina—late afternoon, say—and you are weary, but still alert, after two days of presentations, corridor conversations, and unread papers in your briefcase. You are

meeting with other English teachers, brethren and sistern from across the land, to consider the burning issues of your profession—curriculum, approaches to assessment, good restaurants. Imagine that Donald Murray is not here—in fact, never *has* been here as a voice to be reckoned with, a writer bearing witness in essays and admonitions, poems and polemics, to the recursiveness of process, the joys of surprise, the demands of craft. Imagine, in the silence of his absence, the enormous yawning hole in the knowledge base of your profession. Imagine your bookshelf empty of Murray's books and journal articles—and imagine that shelf without the work of those who have derived intellectual or spiritual capital from Murray. In other words, imagine hitting the *delete* key for most of the Heinemann list—and a good part of the NCTE booklist as well.

2. My task today is to say a few words about Donald Murray's contributions in a historical context. It's no exaggeration, I think, to say that Murray is one of the High Priests of Process for our Tribe—but one who has always maintained an Outsider's perspective, challenging orthodoxy, authority, and conventional wisdom. His book of thirty years ago, *A Writer Teaches Writing*, challenged a tradition that relied heavily on analysis of prose models. Murray's authority did not derive from the study of classical rhetoric, from literary criticism, from educational theory and research, or even from years of classroom experience. It derived instead from putting his butt in a desk chair each morning and writing readable, engaging, salable prose.

3. Murray's basic assertion, based on years of solid experience as a journalist and free-lancer, was that textbook prescriptions for five-paragraph themes had little to do with the exciting, mucking-about processes of real writers. He challenged the Republican virtues of unity, coherence, and emphasis—first, because he saw them as irrelevant to meaningful instruction and, second, because they contradicted his instincts as a writer. His was a rhetoric of dialectic, not unity—a rhetoric of tension, not taxonomy. Tradition valued certainty, predictability; Murray valued surprise. Tradition valued rules and prescribed forms; Murray valued form following meaning. Tradition valued an objective, impersonal tone; Murray valued voice.

4. But Murray did more than challenge the content and formalism of traditional rhetoric. He also questioned writing instruction grounded in the drill-and-practice of traditional grammar—instruction that emphasized correctness as a precondition for effective writing. As a dropout and flunkout from North Quincy High School—and a winner of a Pulitzer Prize—Murray clearly had the credentials to raise such questions. In his essays, conference presentations, and workshops, he invited teachers to consider a different framework for instruction, one emphasizing the development of fluency at early stages, with considerations of mechanics and usage postponed until later. Obviously, this formulation is firmly in place among informed teachers of today. In addition, he invited those of us who presume to teach writing to do it ourselves—to confront the whiteness of the blank page, to share our drafts and doubts with students, and to think aloud, making our processes both visible and audible. He invited us, in short, to give up the security of old forms—to demonstrate our own learning in authentic, personal ways, from the inside out.

5. Scary? You bet. But well over 1.5 million teachers in the National Writing Project have taken the Murray Challenge and are willing to testify about the tonic effects of the teacher-as-writer movement. And more than a few of those teachers are working with kids at the margins—bright, lonely, sulky kids like Donald Murray of North Quincy fame—kids with different accents, different skin colors, different ways of thinking. Whether he knows it or not, Murray has helped to make literacy education in this country far more inclusive and democratic than it once was.

6. Simply put, then, Don Murray has challenged us to set aside the security of what we know—the preplanned units and lessons with their neat hierarchies of goals—and to work in a new studio environment, side by side with students. For Murray, "silence, emptiness, the essential terror of not knowing" are the primal and visceral conditions for writing. He worries about classrooms in which chatter about writing takes up writing time—or where "writing strategies," devoid of context, become the focus of instruction. As the Apostle of Writing Workshop, Murray has always remained skeptical of the traditional teacher's role—as sole audience and judge of student writing. He has worked to shift authority—authorship—back to students by enlarging the audience and by setting up one-on-one conferences that invite reflection and "re-vision." He is therefore suspicious of cute gimmicks and paint-by-numbers routines that masquerade as "process writing" in most language arts textbooks.

7. His is a writing process complicated by self-discipline and the excitement of questions and deadlines; and his is a fierce commitment to craft, with the text leading the way. In place of step-by-step models, Murray celebrates individual ways of knowing, values receptivity and openness, and preaches the gospel of recursiveness. For him, language itself is always the teacher.

8. Historically speaking, it is clear that Donald Murray is a giant of our profession. From one perspective, he is the Writer as Re-Searcher, following many paths. From another, he is the Teacher Revisiting Experience, testing its truth, listening to its resonance. From still another, he is the Case Study Method personified. And as if all of that were not enough, he is well loved by his colleagues in this room. Today, we are pleased to make this mentor to all of us an Insider.

                                                                                                   ■

The words were still warm from revising when I delivered them to Don and Minnie Mae Murray and hundreds of well-wishers who "leaked out the doorways into the lobby and adjacent room, where they stood or sat on the floor, listening through open doorways" (Romano 2000). I felt good about the words—especially the Outsider/Insider theme—and Don's broad smile signaled that he did, too. What he didn't know, of course, was that I had just demonstrated part of his composition philosophy, the part about "silence, emptiness, the essential terror of not knowing." Language itself had indeed been my teacher when I finally, belatedly, put other worries out of my mind and paid full attention to the unfolding sentences on my notepad.

So the inner game is one in which we create a discourse structure by making decisions about content and form; but it is also a psychological arena where we either permit ourselves to learn from and enjoy a language experience or, alternatively, submit to an internal litany of critical judgments, self-defeating comments, unrealistic expectations, angry reprimands, distractions, expressions of frustration, and self-conscious worries about how we look or how we're doing.

And the outer game, by contrast, is one in which we string words one after another, left to right in space—a not-so-simple transcription of inner speech; beyond this, however, it is a game in which we enact our intentions by listening to an inner voice, saying what is on our minds or in our hearts, rereading an emerging text, trusting ourselves to keep the flow going, and knowing (like William Maxwell) that we can move the phrases, the clauses, and the paragraphs around until they stick.

My point in sharing the "Outsider in Perspective" text is to put the spotlight on genre. Why? Because I now see, with the clarity of 20/20 hindsight, that although purpose, audience, and situation were clear to me, I lacked a framework—a suitable form—for responding to the demands of this occasion, one that was partly academic, partly ceremonial, and partly personal. Also, of course, in thrashing about and subjecting myself to self-criticism, I mainly succeeded in undermining my own efforts.

In making the case for genre, am I opposing the ideas of Donald Murray? Not really. As a journalist, editorial writer, poet, novelist, conference keynoter, and textbook writer, Murray has genre at his fingertips, which he uses, adapts, and sometimes resists with great facility. He is, above all, a practical man who understands the craft of writing and the ways of making text accessible. For him, genre is a resource, not a straitjacket.

What are the implications for instruction in the preceding narrative? One is to help students understand inner game and outer game concepts as applied to language performances such as speaking, writing, or multimedia production. A second is to help students first comprehend and then cope with self-criticism, the negative judgments of self 1 that so often erode the performance of self 2. A third is to involve students in hands-on genre study so that they can see how the demands of purpose, audience, and situation often find creative expression *within* certain structures.

Crafting Writing Assignments

All too often, regrettably, writing assignments result from urgent efforts to keep students in line. A literature discussion lies in ruins; kids are more rowdy than usual; and a harried teacher has had enough for one day: "All right, take out a sheet of paper!" And so it is that writing gets interwoven with punishment for another group of learners.

Of course, some assignments result from a need to test whether students understand—or indeed whether they have even read—an assigned text. Others emerge from textbooks or inspired summer workshops. And, increasingly, assignments come from standards at district, state, or national levels, such as the New Standards project at the National Center on Education and the Economy (Tucker and Godding 1998). In environments for active learning, standards help chart directions for teaching and learning, and in an era of increasing assessment, they also help ensure job security.

For student teachers and new teachers, the curriculum website of their state office of education provides an overview of the playing field called writing instruction. To achieve balance in the curriculum, it makes sense to ask about local and state standards and then talk with veteran teachers before outlining a course or a school year. Working from such standards, most teachers soon see that the traditional modes of rhetoric have little utility for the contexts in which they teach. A balanced approach, by definition, develops a broad array of language skills in functional, engaging ways.

Let's now consider four broad domains in which writing tasks might occur. For me, the work of Fran Claggett (1996) provides a useful synthesis of the theories of James Britton (1970) and Louise Rosenblatt (1976). My effort to build on Claggett's ideas, using slightly different language and layout, appears in the following framework. Like Claggett, I see expressive writing as foundational to the three upper domains of writing but also as a domain with its own school-based genres. In the framework I list familiar assignments, or school genres, as well as other real-world discourse forms. I believe that the latter forms can often be imaginatively appropriated as we structure school essay tasks.

Four Domains of Discourse

Informative/Functional Texts (Convey information or explain ideas, facts, or processes.)	**Literary/Poetic Texts** (Give imaginative shape to an idea, an experience, or an observation.)	**Argumentative/Persuasive Texts** (Influence or convince another of one's ideas or judgments.)
School Essays Description; profile/ biography; process/ procedures; information report; research report.	*Narratives* Adventure/mysteries; fables/ tall tales; fantasy/sci-fi; historical accounts; realistic stories.	*School Essays* Literary analysis; problem/ solution; controversial issue; evaluation; speculation.
Discourse Forms Brochures; business reports; case studies; charts, graphs; career plans; directions, guidelines; histories; holiday greetings; how-to manuals; minutes; newsletters; overviews; pamphlets; posters; resumes; regulations, rules summaries; surveys, forms tables, etc.	*Poetry* Ballads, songs; concrete, visual; formula verse; free verse; rhyme formats. *Scripts* Dialogues; monologues; radio plays; video skits; hypermedia. *Practical Texts* Letters (all types); newspaper stories; interviews, profiles; parodies, satires; speeches, etc.	*Discourse Forms* Advertisements; awards, tributes; commercials; cover letters; editorials; eulogies; evaluations (others); feature articles; invocations; job applications; marketing; memo petitions; proposals; rebuttals; requests; reviews (all types); self-assessments; warnings, cautions; web pages, etc.

Expressive/Writing-to-Learn Texts (Discover, identify, or clarify ideas or experiences for self and for others.) *This domain is foundational to other domains.*

School Essays
Autobiographical incident; personal reflection; multigenre essay; triptych essay.

Discourse Forms
Lists; sketches; diagrams; journal or learning log entries; notes from reading or interviews; e-mail exchanges; letters of advice, affection, apology, complaint, congratulations, invitation, protest, self-disclosure, sympathy, thanks; responses to literature, etc.

■

Here I want to reiterate a point made in Chapter 7, "Coaching Imagination"—namely, that literary/poetic texts (or "reflective texts" as the Summerfields call them) can be impersonations of "practical" texts (labeled argumentative/persuasive and informative/functional in my framework). Why is this point so important? Because it enables us to approach the practical genres in creative, imaginative ways.

An assignment by Richard Coe (1994) illustrates my point. Working in the domain of informative/functional texts, Coe presents teams of two or three students with a pile of "incompetent brochures" to critique and gives them these directions:

> Your task is to communicate technical or specialized knowledge briefly and effectively to readers who are only moderately literate (below "grade 8" reading ability) *and* have little or no background in the specific subject area. Choose a topic on which you have special knowledge and a specific group of readers who need such knowledge. The choice of subject, purpose, and readership is yours; but the reading occasion must be voluntary, and you are limited to the number of words (and graphics) that can be presented effectively on a brochure folded from a single sheet of legal-size paper (8½″ × 14″). (164)

Such an assignment asks students to examine brochures critically, develop a shared information base, and then craft their language within the given constraints. Clearly, imagination is required to envision the needs and abilities of readers, the occasions of voluntary reading, and the ways in which information might be effectively shared. In other words, good writing assignments often invoke a world that middle school and high school students can enter imaginatively.

The following acronym, *CRAFT*, is useful for creating and refining writing prompts:

C = Context	The situation in which writing occurs.
R = Role	The persona that the writer assumes.
A = Audience	The person(s) who will read the text.
F = Format	The genre features that are important.
T = Topic	The focus for the text in terms of theme.

This acronym can be used to generate the enabling constraints that characterize interesting, thought-provoking writing tasks.

The following is an example of a CRAFT assignment, a culminating activity for a short story unit. With this assignment in the domain of literary/poetic texts, students are asked to focus on a conflict situation from their own experience but to transform the experience into a third-person narrative.

Family Matters Assignment

- Context: Your class has been contacted by the editors of a new anthology of student writing called *Family Matters*. Their aim is to publish a book of realistic, compelling stories that will appeal to students your age and offer insights into family life in the new millennium. Knowing of teenagers' varied reading interests, the editors hope to collect a range of stories—some happy, some serious, some bizarre, some thought-provoking—all emerging from family conflicts. The editors have solicited you and others to submit stories based on real events or incidents from past experience. Their guidelines are described below.
- Role: Write from a third-person viewpoint rather than from an "I" point of view. That is, make yourself a character in your family's story. Although your

story will be based on a real, specific incident, feel free to change the names of characters (including your own!) and to delete or expand details such as dialogue. Choose an incident or an event that you will feel comfortable sharing in a writing workshop.

- Audience: Focus on students your age as the main audience for your story, with teachers representing an important secondary audience since they will select stories for the anthology. A possible *future* audience—twenty or twenty-five years from now—might be your own children, wanting to know what life was like in the "good old days."
- Format: Use a short story (narrative) format, ranging from three to six pages. Refer back to the literature selections in our unit if you have questions about format or story conventions. Also, feel free to incorporate journal writing from in-class exercises if these help you advance the story line in an interesting way.
- Topic: Consider "family matters" as a point of departure for the topic of your choice. The incident you choose will likely focus on a conflict between family members; however, the choice of conflict—and the outcome, of course—will be your decision. Share your topic with your teacher if you have concerns about it.

■

Rubrics can be designed to accompany such assignments. A rubric lists the criteria for success—specific features of writing or qualities essential for success. In the case of the previous assignment, a rubric would be used by the editorial board of the *Family Matters* anthology. Of course, it would also be used by class members as they evaluate strong and weak anthology submissions from past years, by response groups that offer supportive advice, and by students assessing their own texts. Here is a possible rubric for the previous task, one that could be adapted and refined for advanced writing students. The "NS" column stands for "not satisfactory."

Family Matters Rubric

Judging Criteria	Great	Good	OK	NS
Focuses on interesting, realistic conflict among family members.				
Hooks the reader's interest by showing setting and situation.				
Creates vivid sketches of family members involved in conflict.				
Makes effective use of dialog, showing conflict development.				
Resolves the story's conflict in a believable, realistic way.				
Uses descriptive language and third-person viewpoint well.				
Uses conventions correctly (e.g., spelling, mechanics, usage).				

A rubric like this one helps learners because its criteria are specific enough to be useful but broad enough to allow for individual creativity. Obviously, the criteria and headings can be modified to fit many situations. Such a rubric can also help teachers by defining in advance the areas for instruction and providing a framework for assessment. As we check rubric categories, we are probably less inclined to mark or correct the language of the text. This change in orientation can easily double or triple one's reading speed. Moreover, responses can be made in relation to criteria. Time spent in correcting texts that students will not revise—and, in fact, may ignore once the grade is noted—is, as Donald Graves once put it, "like manicuring a corpse."

Sometimes, however, we don't have time to devise a rubric with help from our students—or energy to create a genre-specific one. On such occasions, consider using a general scoring guide such as the Six Trait Analytical Model, developed at the Northwest Regional Educational Laboratory and available as a rubber stamp. In *Creating Writers: Linking Writing Assessment and Instruction* (1997), Vicki Spandel and Richard Stiggins show that clear standards for writing success and a framework of feedback underlie good coaching. On the following page is an abbreviated version of the six-trait rubric, with brief descriptors for ideas, organization, voice, word choice, sentence fluency, and conventions. The six-trait framework can influence students' thinking when it is used regularly in workshops, response groups, and self-assessment activities. Equally important, scores on a rubric can help students understand where they need to invest time and effort.

Genre Practice

To prompt genre practice, I now outline two student-friendly approaches. The first exercise, a lesson on fable, uses a sentence-combining exercise as part of genre modeling. The second exercise, derived from the "Outsider" text, focuses on rhetorical moves within the genre of tribute. Finally, if you seek classroom-tested units dealing with a wide range of genres—most with rubrics or scoring guides—I recommend Carol Booth Olson's *Thinking/Writing* (1992), a compendium of work from thirty teachers in the University of California-Irvine Writing Project. Their approaches provide points of departure for those hoping to explore the brave new world of genre practice.

Fable exercise as genre study

Fables provide an interesting exercise for middle-level students because the genre has well-defined features and abundant exemplars in the work of Aesop and James Thurber. But writing an effective fable is not easy. In fact, considerable planning and craft lie beneath the surface of any memorable fable. In getting started, it helps to have a list of genre features in mind, ones that will be shared with students in workshop settings and used in a rubric (Strong 1991b):

Writing a Fable

- The characters are animals with human qualities.
- The story has some kind of problem or conflict.
- The story is told to make a point (moral).
- The moral comes at the end of the fable.
- The animals may talk to one another in the fable.
- The fable is usually short (one page or so) and fun to read.

	Ideas	Organization	Voice
5	The paper is clear and focused. It holds the reader's attention. Relevant anecdotes and details enrich the central theme or story line.	The organization enhances the central idea or story line. The order, the structure, or the presentation of information is compelling and moves the reader through the text.	The writer speaks directly to the reader in a way that is individualistic, expressive, and engaging. Clearly, the writer is involved in the text, is sensitive to the needs of an audience, and is writing to be read.
3	The writer is beginning to define the topic, even though development is still basic or general.	The organizational structure is strong enough to move the reader through the text without undue confusion.	The writer seems sincere, but not fully engaged or involved. The result is pleasant or even personable but not compelling.
1	As yet, the paper has no sense of purpose or central theme. To extract meaning from the text, the reader must make inferences based on sketchy details. The writing reflects more than one of these problems . . .	The writing lacks a clear sense of direction. Ideas, details, or events seem strung together in a loose or random fashion—or else there is no identifiable internal structure. The writing reflects more than one of these problems . . .	The writer seems indifferent, uninvolved, or distanced from the topic and/or the audience. As a result, the writing is lifeless or mechanical; depending on the topic, it may be overly technical or jargonistic. The paper reflects more than one of these problems . . .

	Word Choice	Sentence Fluency	Conventions
5	Words convey the intended message in a precise, interesting, and natural way.	The writing has an easy flow and rhythm when read aloud. Sentences are well built, with strong and varied structure that invites expressive oral reading.	The writer demonstrates a good grasp of standard writing conventions and uses conventions effectively to enhance readability. Errors tend to be so few and so minor that the reader can easily overlook them unless hunting for them specifically.
3	The language is functional, even if it lacks punch; it is easy to figure out the writer's meaning on a general level.	The text hums along with a steady beat but tends to be more pleasant than musical, more mechanical than fluid.	The writer shows reasonable control over a limited range of standard writing conventions. Conventions are sometimes handled well and enhance readability; at other times, errors are distracting and impair readability.
1	The writer struggles with a limited vocabulary, searching for words to convey meaning. The writing reflects more than one of these problems . . .	The reader has to practice quite a bit to give this paper a fair interpretive reading. The writing reflects more than one of the following problems . . .	Errors in spelling, punctuation, usage and grammar, capitalization, and/or paragraphing repeatedly distract the reader and make the text difficult to read. The writing reflects more than one of these problems . . .

Of course, the human qualities mentioned here are foibles and vices; and it is upon such traits that fables turn as a minimal plot unfolds. This point should be emphasized in teaching. To set up discussion, you might assign small groups of students to work up short readings or even skits to dramatize various fables. You might further develop fable schema by using a sentence-combining exercise like the following one from *Sentence Combining* (Strong 1994) or a second SC exercise (Parable 2) from the same text.

Parable 1

1.1 A Fox saw a Crow.
1.2 The Crow was flying.
1.3 The Crow had some cheese.
1.4 Her beak held the cheese.

2.1 Crow settled on a branch.
2.2 The branch was on a tree.

3.1 Fox wanted the cheese.
3.2 Fox approached the tree.
3.3 Fox spoke to Crow.
3.4 Fox called her Mistress Crow.

4.1 He complimented Crow.
4.2 She looked remarkably well.
4.3 Her feathers were glossy.
4.4 Her eyes were bright.

5.1 Fox then remarked on Crow's voice.
5.2 It was reported to have a sound.
5.3 The sound was sweet and melodious.

6.1 He asked Crow to sing one song.
6.2 He might call her Queen of the Birds.

7.1 Crow preened her black feathers.
7.2 Crow opened her mouth to caw.
7.3 Crow dropped the cheese.

8.1 Fox snapped up what he wanted.
8.2 That thing was the cheese.
8.3 Fox gave Crow some advice.
8.4 "Flatterers can't be trusted."

Students might brainstorm traits (or personalities) they find irritating or ridiculous. Know-it-all types? Airheads? Macho wannabees? Two-faced friends? Follow-the-crowd conformists? Cheats? Then they might identify animals that have metaphoric associations, for example, eager beavers. How do we often think of snakes? Sheep? Pigs? Sharks? Ostriches? Weasels? It is in the links between human traits and animals that the first hints of plot begin to develop. How do each of these animals behave? A fable like "The Ant and the Grasshopper" could be useful in discussing animal behavior.

To further prime the pump, you might think aloud (or at an overhead projector) about ideas for a fable. "I'm interested in bullies," you might say. "So I'm thinking about a bull or a bulldog—or how about a pit bull? They're aggressive. Maybe this pit bull gets loose and terrorizes the animal community. So now we've got a problem. The pit bull is so vicious it attacks without warning, then boasts that it's the 'meanest junkyard dog' in town. So the animals have a meeting, and they're desperate because the pit bull is now extorting money, and nobody can solve this problem. Who, after all, is brave enough to face a pit bull as mean and bullying as this one? And a small voice from the edge of the circle says that she'd be willing to try. And the word goes out to the pit bull that there's a new kid on the block, one who's holed up in a dark cave. And this new kid isn't going to pay extortion money to the pit bull. In fact, the new kids says that pit bulls are sissies. And of course the pit bull barks furiously because his machismo has been questioned. He charges headlong into the cave in his vicious pit bull way, teeth snapping—and ten seconds later he's running for his life. So why the sudden change of heart? Could be he's just gotten a face full of skunk. Or maybe a mouth full of sharp porcupine quills? I mean, fables are supposed to have a *point*, aren't they?"

Working in small groups, students could extend the list of traits and the list of animals, then begin to follow the think-aloud model, brainstorming ideas for possible fable plots. Such work would prepare students for the writing of a fable on their own.

Analytic exercise as genre study

Let's suppose that your students find the ideas in Donald Murray's *Write to Learn* (1993) useful as they prepare to work on the genre of profile writing (a character description), focusing on different individuals in the community. Also, let's suppose that you have read the "Outsider" piece from earlier in this chapter and feel that certain aspects of its structure might interest your students.

Your first task, probably, is to activate background knowledge for the profile genre. Because students may not understand the context of a professional tribute, use familiar examples such as awards, toasts, celebrity biographies, and eulogies. Point out that in such ceremonies the language is usually respectful but not formal or stuffy. Facts about a person's life can contribute to the text structure of a profile, but details must be carefully selected and packaged. What listeners (or readers) probably want to know is "How has this person's life been important?"

Part of a larger text could then be selected to illustrate a specific genre feature or writing strategy. For example, you could draw an SC exercise from the second paragraph of the "Outsider" text, the one that frames the piece, asking students to first combine sentences in clear, natural ways and then pay special attention to the function of this paragraph and to the use of contrast. What words, you might ask, serve as signposts to signal contrast? In small groups, students would put their consensus sentences onto blank transparencies to share with the larger class. If you meet in a networked lab, such sentences might be electronically distributed. Of course, the original text would be withheld from students until sharing and comparing were completed.

The rationale for this method is straightforward: by exposing students to well-written text and by inviting comments about text structure, we inform their language development. It is through such activated awareness that students gravitate toward effective writing over time and begin to appropriate the characteristics of quality texts. What do students notice about the original? Are its sentences as effective as theirs? What about its punctuation? Length of sentences? If sentence variety is one way to achieve interest, what can we say about parallel structure? Following such prompts, students could think about the characters in their profile pieces. Could they adapt the form of what they have just studied to their in-process descriptions?

Students might then brainstorm what they already know about the profile genre. Their list of features, from which a rubric could be developed, might look like this:

Profile Genre

- Has attention getter (brief story, description, humor, surprise).
- Emphasizes an underlying theme for the person's life.
- Selects key facts, with anecdotes or quotes for support.
- Makes strong, clear transitions from point to point.
- Emphasizes the individual's distinctiveness or differences.
- Has a positive ending to tie the text together.

■

Working from such a list of features, you could then use a chart like the one on the following page to give students an x-ray view of the "Outsider" text. This paragraph-by-paragraph analysis would offer a simplified inside look at how rhetorical purposes are realized through various strategies and specific text features; it could be used in connection with an oral reading of the text. Of course, students could be invited to add their own ideas to the chart or to modify it so that it more accurately reflects their reading of the text.

After students understand how to distance themselves from text with the tool of charting, you might offer charts that are only partially filled in—scaffolds for further analytic work. The class could then work in small groups to exercise their x-ray vision, thinking about the specific ways in which writing purposes are accomplished through language. Such a strategy would link analysis to the beginning list of generic features presented earlier and to an evaluation rubric, thus preparing students for writing.

Genre as Shared Expectations

Because this chapter parallels the others, you have come to expect several text features: first, a brief poem; then an introductory section, perhaps with a first-person narrative; next, a middle section, with discussion and professional references; and finally a practical section dealing with classroom applications. These features define the genre called chapter, at least in this book.

A case can be made that we have created those genre expectations together—me by putting material in certain formats and depending on a certain register of language, you by expecting me to be provocative or useful (maybe even *both* at times) and by promising swift, decisive action when I fail to deliver.

This genre is also defined by a rhetorical relationship. You know by now that I often address you directly, use memories for examples, or take risks like the one at this moment—drawing upon the presumption of our shared experience. I say "shared experience"

P	Purpose	Strategies	Text Features
1	Engage the audience; emphasize significance of the work.	Parallel imagery Humor Imagery	"Imagine . . . Imagine . . ." "briefcase" "restaurant" "enormous yawning hole"
2	Establish occasion; introduce Outsider theme.	Tone shift Claim Contrast	"My purpose today . . ." "challenging orthodoxy . . ." "authority did not derive . . ."
3	Develop Outsider theme.	Characterization Contrast Parallel contrast Parallel contrast	"Murray's basic assertion . . ." "He challenged . . ." "dialectic, not unity . . ." "Tradition . . . ; Murray . . ."
4	Develop theme further.	Narration Characterization Claim	"But Murray did more . . ." "As a dropout . . ." "Obviously . . ." "In addition . . ."
5	Emphasize significance of the work.	Tone shift Statistics Claim	"Scary? You bet." "1.5 million teachers . . ." "Murray has helped make . . ."
6	Refocus and restate for emphasis.	Claim Characterization Parallel structure	"Simply put, . . ." "As the Apostle . . ." "He . . ." "He . . ." "He . . ."
7	Refocus and restate for emphasis.	Characterization Contrast	"His is a process . . ." "In place of . . ."
8	Amplify and summarize significance of work; link to Outsider theme.	Characterization Parallel claims Contrast	"Historically speaking . . ." "From one perspective . . ." "make mentor . . . an Insider."

because I am the first reader of this text, and it is therefore written as much for my learning as for yours. What interests me now is the fact that the chapter framework seems to provide an enabling constraint for getting my work done. The bottom-up prompts come from ideas, and the top-down prompts come from genre.

And I therefore find myself thinking: If the constraints of genre can assist me, how might they also assist middle school and high school writers, who often complain of not having anything to say or of not knowing how to accomplish writing tasks?

The emphasis on form in discourse may seem a defense of the five-paragraph theme, the one-size-fits-all genre that so many of us love to hate. Instead, I want to invoke the views of psychologist Howard Gardner (1982) who describes his own use of a specific genre, the letter of recommendation. Ask yourself: "Why are *these* features so important to Gardner?"

> I have a plan that I generally follow in writing such letters. I begin by indicating the circumstances under which I have met the individual, how well I know him, what the nature of our relationship (professional and personal) has been. A second paragraph usually describes the growth of that individual over the period of time I have know him and indicates the kinds of work and issues that occupy a central place in that person's professional life. A third paragraph will review the person's principal scholarly accomplishments so far and his future promise. (An optional paragraph will focus on teaching abilities.) A fourth paragraph will touch on the individual's personal dimensions—what kind of colleague he makes, how he gets along with others, whether he has a good sense of humor, is reliable, responsible, and so on. (An optional paragraph will detail problems or weaknesses.) The final paragraph is summative: it recapitulates what I find most outstanding about the individual, explains (or explains away) any difficulties I have mentioned, and attempts to integrate my assessment of the individual as a scholar and future contributor to the field with his qualities as a person, friend, and colleague. I may also suggest some comparison with others of considerable age, background, and ambition and offer to provide further information. (361–62)

Because Gardner has read many such letters, he appreciates the reader's needs and expectations. He knows that omitted items can prove significant and that his wording will be closely monitored by others. As an abstract representation, his skeletal model is quite adaptable. It has fixed conventions, but it also has flexible slots, in which points can be arrayed. The diverse instances of letters—each focused, by definition, on a single career—have family resemblances. Indeed, he adds, "the realization of each future instance is helped immeasurably by the prior existence of the schema" (362).

Gardner believes that he is hardly alone in using a top-down approach to such composing tasks, including his professional articles. As a well-practiced and prolific writer, he claims to orally dictate entire essays from one-page outlines—this the product of his background reading and thinking—on which he simply lists a sequence of major points. And although he acknowledges that speaking and writing are strikingly different processes, he emphasizes their similarities in what follows:

> Both [speaking and writing] depend upon sufficient mastery of the *forms* of a particular linguistic entity (be it the letter, report, or poem) so that each realization of that form observes its basic rules. Thus in delivering a campaign speech, politicians know the general form and the points they wish to make with sufficient intimacy to present on each occasion an acceptable, if modified, version of "the basic speech." By the same token, the writer of a daily newspaper column—James Reston or Ann Landers, for example—has mastered several forms that such columns usually take and can plug the specific content into the pattern easily and quickly. (260)

Discussing genre in terms of shared expectations may well help middle school and high school students. As listeners, readers, and viewers, their expectations are enacted in every textual encounter. So questions like these seem important: What *are* their text expectations? Where do they come from? And how can a writer *use* genre expectations to communicate effectively? Clearly, such audience questions have the potential to make even a five-paragraph theme assignment more interesting!

If it is true that genre practice enables skilled speakers and writers to work smarter, not harder, we have a strong rationale for paying attention to the constraints of genre in our teaching. Exemplars of genre will be vital for instruction. Rubrics will be tied to genre features. And students will have chances to explore creative approaches with the support of good modeling and peer response. It is thinking like this, of course, that can lead us to create active learning environments (Hillocks 1995), as described earlier in this book. Students themselves help define genre and articulate key features or assessment criteria.

In other words, the constraints of genre need not be stifling. Gardner himself is eloquent on this point as he quotes Igor Stravinsky to conclude *The Unschooled Mind* (1991): "The more constraints one imposes, the more one frees one's self of the chains that shackle the spirit" (264).

Learning Through Language

1. In Chapter 9 you learned more about the concepts of the inner game and outer game of writing, first introduced in "Thinking About the Basics" in Chapter 1. As a teacher, how would you share these ideas with middle school or high school students? Also, consider how you might explain such ideas to colleagues, some of whom may be dubious about coaching language. Describe the resistance you would anticipate in both contexts. Discuss with members of your group.

2. You may agree that the intellectual center of the chapter is the Four Domains of Discourse Framework. In this depiction, expressive/writing-to-learn texts provide the foundation for the other three domains. What are the implications of this idea for process writing instruction in secondary schools? Which school essays or discourse forms were part of your experience as a learner? Write a reflective essay, with your group as audience, in which you consider both questions.

3. According to the chapter, "good writing assignments often invoke a world that middle school and high school students can enter imaginatively." By attending to the CRAFT of writing assignments, you can use creative approaches to practical genres (argumentative/persuasive and informative/functional writing). Develop one such writing assignment, with rubric, for a class of middle school or high school students. Share your assignment and rubric with your group.

CHAPTER 10

COACHING
ASSESSMENT

Grading Papers

Snow whirls in darkness, piles deep at the door;
And inside are papers, white drifts on the floor.
I winnow a blizzard, catch words in mid-air—
Give praise in the margins, note items in error.

Words swirl in flurries, and white fills my mind;
Tracks fill with words as I stumble snow-blind.
Out in the darkness the silence drifts deep—
A strong homeward pull, a long wordless sleep.

Fake Writing, Fake Reading

Sporting curly blonde hair and a winter suntan from weekend skiing, Trudy looked like a kid with typical Utah priorities. What I couldn't fathom after our three weeks together was why my writing course wasn't among them. After all, I had set up workshop-style assignments, moved students into well-coached response groups, and opened my office door to multiple conferences. But now, Trudy's blue eyes avoided mine in class, and I had yet to see a draft for her first assignment, one focused on a significant learning experience. Frankly, I was irritated by her procrastination.

Finally, her name appeared on my conference sign-up sheet, and a two-page draft of her learning experience paper came in, just under the wire, with no title and no paragraphing. Its topic was skiing. I read it once, then went back for a second, closer look, wondering how to coach Trudy. Be positive, I reminded myself. In her two opening paragraphs she had loaded up details in melodramatic fashion; after that came the actual narrative.

Grabbing my Rossignal skis and Scott poles I headed for the lift. I felt the confidence and excitement circulate within my body with each step I took. As I patiently waited in line I glanced up at what I was about to attempt again. The fear of being defeated again by that mighty mountain ate at the lining of my stomach like acid through metal. I said to myself, "today I will not be defeated, I will conquer that run no matter what it takes." As I rose slowly up toward my destination I felt a calmness as the morning sun warmed my face.

Confidence, excitement, patience, fear, resolution, calmness—six emotions in five sentences. What about focus? "Beware of overwriting," I wrote in the margin, then braced myself for more purple prose.

I then looked down upon that treacherous hill in which I saw skiers crash right and left. It was as if I felt an excruciating pain myself. When the ride ended I put on my black gortex gloves and adjusted my boots as tight as possible. I looked down at the run I was about to take once again. It was covered with a foot of fresh powder from the previous nights storm. This would add a new twist to things but I was determined not to let this stop me. I saw only a few moguls as I stood at the top contemplating which way to go.

Trying too hard, I told myself. I corrected the mechanics of the first sentence, checked a few punctuation details, and complimented her on "setting the scene"—modest praise from a fake reader. After another fifteen lines of richly overwrought narrative, with further problems and a sentence fragment or two, came this:

Skiing mogul after mogul I finally reached the peak of difficulty. I was shocked by the strength that my body possessed. Being familiar with what awaited me I pushed myself more and more. I went up, around, down, and beneath the average amount of gravity. My heart was pounding, and I could never have reached a more pleasing and satisfying attitude. A bright, enlarged smile broke across my face as I glanced back at the overwhelming mountain at which I had just mastered.

Another question mark or two in the margin. To me, this seemed like a fake learning experience, not a real one. Although it pretended emotion, the writing felt detached. The sentences seemed warped, oddly misshapen. I reread them and shook my head.

Accomplishing this great task with determination made me realize to never quit or give up. It reminded me of when I was young, I learned that when you get bucked off a horse the best thing to do is climb right back on.

I scanned the paper again. Writing as a Sunday school lesson perhaps? I'd have to raise that possibility—gently, of course—during our follow-up conference. Trudy and I had work to do.

The Assessment Situation

To open this chapter on assessment, I began with "Fake Writing, Fake Reading" because it underscores a key theme of this book: that the coaching of written language causes suffering to teach us humility and then offers unexpected moments of joy to teach us hope and commitment and professional perseverance. The next section continues the story of Trudy's writing. We will focus on my response to an individual student's effort, but I am acutely aware of the other daunting challenges of assessment, such as trying to manage the sheer volume of work from 150 (or more) students.

My aim in this chapter is to continue situating assessment where it belongs—in explicit standards and criteria—and to further describe the conditions that help students self-assess written products as well as their own composing processes. In Chapter 8 we saw how self-assessment exercises and writing conferences create contexts for coaching reflection. In Chapter 8 we also saw how peer response groups offer scaffolds of social support for generating text as well as revising it. In Chapter 9 we saw how rubrics for crafted assignments provide criteria for student writers, peers, and teachers to make formative assessments about writing quality. This chapter considers offering feedback and response as a core activity in an active learning environment (Hillocks 1995)—a key issue for coaching effectively and working smarter, not harder.

A summary of the assessment characteristics for an active learning environment would probably look something like this:

- The criteria for writing tasks are accompanied by various scaffolds, such as exemplars of text, process guides, and workshop activities.
- Ongoing assessments—in checklists, peer teaching, miniconferences, or anecdotal records—are closely linked to the activities of daily instruction.
- Self-assessment activities, in which students keep records, reflect on effort and progress, and monitor their own performance, are highly valued.
- The summative assessments of effort and achievement, beyond the writing task criteria, occur within the context of each student's writing portfolio.
- A teacher periodically confers with students about grades, taking into account daily assessments, self-assessments, and the student's portfolio profile.

The claim of this chapter is that explicit standards, when coupled with expectations for a *shared* process of evaluation, can not only motivate students but also motivate us.

The real challenge, after all, lies in transforming assessment from a dreaded Sunday evening chore to an act of genuine learning, for our students and for us. To coach writing is to help students think and behave in positive ways toward their own potential. It is an audacious, ethical act to invoke or nurture possibility in somebody else. The bottom-line question, of course, is how to create assessment conditions that will enable individuals to grow and learn but will also be practical for large groups.

As a practical matter, many teachers try to increase the levels of feedback to students but decrease the emphasis on grades. How is this done? First, grading standards (or criteria) need to be shared so that students have ways to assess the extent to which their work measures up. Next, students need to engage in daily activities—for assessment and instruction—that will assist them toward the standards. Third, students must reflect on their efforts and share self-assessments with their teacher. Fourth, the teacher needs to discuss an assessment of the text (a grade, in most cases) based upon the available data— the standards, the student's daily efforts and self-assessment, and the student's potential as reflected in the portfolio of accumulating work. Fifth, a grade should not be given if one expects further revision from the student.

"Students will float to the mark you set," according to Mike Rose (1989, 26)—and because of a mixup in school records, Rose himself was placed in a vocational track for two years, "bobbing in some pretty shallow water." When the error was finally corrected, he had honed the skills of "a mediocre student and somnambulant problem solver"—and thus found himself far behind academically (27). Fortunately, "deliverance" from vocational education came in the coaching expectations of English teacher Jack MacFarlane, who "startled" his students with deep immersion in language and lots of work in writing. In the following excerpt, Rose describes how MacFarlane hooked an "at-risk" kid. It might be titled "Essential Elements of Coaching."

> He tapped my old interest in reading and creating stories. He gave me a way to feel special by using my mind. And he provided a role model that wasn't shaped on physical prowess alone. . . . Jack MacFarlane established a literacy club, to borrow a phrase of Frank Smith's, and invited me—invited all of us—to join. (34)

"I now know how subjective grades can be," Rose says, "but then they came tucked in the back of essays like bits of scientific data, some sort of spectroscopic readout that said, objectively and publically, that I had made something of value." Indeed, Rose adds, "these papers with their circled, red B-pluses and A-minuses linked my mind to something outside it. I carried them around like a club emblem" (34).

If Rose is correct that "students will float to the mark you set," the first question we face is where to set the mark and *how* to set it. A second question is how to help students reach toward the mark, not just with abstract admonitions but with scaffolding activities that develop their language abilities. A third question, perhaps the most difficult one, is how to assess individual potential and motivation. Central to the art of effective coaching is knowing when and how to praise or criticize—or when and how to *withhold* judgment. Something like luck plays a huge role in such matters; but it is in the coach's handling of praise and criticism, or its absence, that true art lies.

For Rose, grades became instruments of motivation. A "spectroscopic readout" validated his work and prompted further learning. In fact, it was through the "emblems" of assessment that he learned to "feel special" by using his mind. But, obviously, the same grades do not affect everybody in the same way. Earlier in this book, we heard from learners whose grades had toxic, not tonic, effects on motivation. When students see themselves as capable, low grades can be a wake-up call; yet for other learners, low grades may confirm beliefs about being "picked on" or being "no good at writing." When students make good-faith efforts, as Rose did, a high grade can provide reason to try all the harder; yet the same grade may actually reduce motivation for others, especially those who fake their writing or have inflated estimates of their own abilities.

Later in the chapter, we will consider the tricky issues of praise and criticism in relation to student writing. Many of us draw on our own experiences, using techniques that others used on us. The effects of criticism are old news, but less well understood are the potentially insidious effects of praise, including grade inflation. For now, suffice it to say that criticizing comes naturally for most of us, whereas praise must be learned and practiced as a balancing self-discipline. Perhaps our best hope of resisting critical impulses lies in self-awareness—an inventory of our past experiences and their effects on us as language learners.

Think back to your own experience with genuine praise, the kind that made an investment of effort feel worthwhile; now consider your experience with cool or sarcastic criticism, the kind that tended to undermine your motivation. Understanding the effects of both, you can probably see that praise provides the best packaging for advice that students might interpret as critical. Many teachers therefore try to sandwich criticism between statements of praise. In this way they strive for balance in their feedback.

So much for background. Let's now get back to Trudy.

Real Writing, Real Reading

A day or two later, Trudy knocked at my office door, then slipped inside. Her smile was nervous and polite as I began my chatty teacher routine, hoping to break the ice. Everything about her asked the same question: How bad is it?

I asked about her choice of topic, and she spoke vaguely of a recent ski weekend. The paper had potential, I remarked, but I wondered about its focus, what it was really about. Was she skiing alone or with others? When she spoke of her three companions, I asked whether she had felt embarrassed taking a spill in front of them. Was competition with friends a part of this experience? Her answers would help me see why this learning was significant.

Trudy seemed edgy and unable to deal with this question, so I finally backed off, switching to the problem of overwriting. We discussed William Zinsser's idea that the secret of good writing is to strip every sentence to its cleanest components. I offered suggestions on trimming back description. Turning to the conclusion, I urged her to write simply and clearly about whatever her experience meant. "Don't try to impress your readers," I emphasized. "Be honest and direct. Remember, this isn't a Sunday school lesson. No need for a moral."

A week or so later there was another knock at the office door—Trudy again, just under the deadline. She left a new version of the first assignment before beating a hasty retreat down the hall. This essay had an interesting title, plus conventional paragraphs. As a piece quite different from the skiing narrative, it would answer many of my questions about her earlier effort.

The Easy Way Out

Here I sit at 12:00 midnight. I am trying to revise my English paper that is to be turned in tomorrow. With sunflower seeds in one hand and a Diet Pepsi in the other, I am just now starting my paper. Well, I should say starting my paper over.

English has always been my worst subject in school. Ever since I can remember, I have hated to read and write. This is where all my problems begin because I do not have any confidence in my own writing.

Voice, I thought. This writing sounded real, not like the exaggerated voice of the skiing incident. The sentences were direct and clear. And the word *own* was underlined. I wondered why.

Relieved at the thought of having to take only one more English course, I strolled into William Strong's course. I had missed the first day of class, so I was already a day behind. Our first assignment was a descriptive/narrative learning experience, the assignment I am writing now. Mr. Strong went on to explain the assignment in more detail. The more he explained, the more horrified I got. I said to myself, "I cannot do this. I have nothing to write about."

The class consisted of about twenty students. We all sat in rows facing each other. Everyone commented and asked questions right and left, while I just sat back, still trying to decide how I was going to write this paper.

The following class period focused on evaluations. We were put in groups of three. In those groups, we offered suggestions on each other's papers. Of course, I was not prepared because I had not written my paper. I had put it off because I do not enjoy writing. The following week we started a new paper on two different teaching styles. I put paper number one in the back of my head and went on to paper number two.

Now I was hooked. In three succinct paragraphs, Trudy had neatly folded in background information about her midnight situation—a predicament that resulted from a lack of confidence in her own writing ability. She was doing so many things well here that it was hard to believe she had written the skiing piece.

> A couple of weeks later, I realized I still had that horrible paper to finish. The first thing I did was to try to find an easy way out; next I went to my filing cabinet where I kept all my past class work. I dug out all my old English papers. Thumbing through them, I found a descriptive/ narrative paper on skiing that my roommates had helped me write two years ago that had actually gotten an "A." Actually, my two roommates wrote it, I just typed it and turned it in. I was sure I could just change it a little and turn it into a learning experience.
>
> Sitting at my sister's house the night before my conference was quite an experience. We laughed and stressed over the paper for three hours. It was so dramatic and descriptive that I had to change and eliminate half of it. I was to the point of not caring, and it was getting late so I just hurried and finished it so I could turn it in.

So "the easy way out" referred to strategies that Trudy had used to slip through writing courses. Her pattern had been one of getting by, of faking her work, with some success. The phrase *not caring* seemed significant as I read it again.

> This is where the humiliation began. I turned my paper into Mr. Strong and met with him the following day. Feeling very nervous and scared, I went up to his office for our conference. He invited me in, and we began talking about my paper. We were facing each other, staring at what might be called an English paper. I felt very uncomfortable and knew my paper was a joke. I was sure Mr. Strong knew it, too. He was just too kind to say it. I just sat there and listened while he gave me suggestions. I could tell he could not make sense out of my paper. I felt very embarrassed and just kept making reasons and excuses for why I had written what I did.
>
> Leaving his office twenty minutes later, I was no further ahead than when I had started. My paper needed a lot more work. Where was I going to go now? Who could help me? What was I to do? Maybe I'd try to find another paper. All of these thoughts ran through my head.

I couldn't help but smile as I thought back to Trudy's foot-dragging during our conference. Little did I know that she was on the threshold of insights far more important than a few cosmetic changes.

> None of these thoughts were the solution. By this time in class we were working on assignment number three. My second paper was coming along much better than paper number one. Starting on the new assignment, I put my skiing paper away for the second time. The next week in class Mr. Strong set some due dates for our papers. He sounded a little stern and the class knew he was serious. He told us to quit putting them off and to just get them done and turn them in. Now I was in for it. I had one week to get a final copy of my paper.

A little stern? I recalled quoting from the course syllabus how "procrastination is a writer's worst enemy." For Trudy, then, fear had been a motivator. She had known for whom the bell tolls.

> This takes me back to tonight. It is Wednesday evening, and I returned home at 10:00 p.m. I pulled out my English paper and climbed on my bed. Sitting here, trying to revise my paper, I started giving up after ten minutes. My roommate, who was sitting across from me on her bed, started laughing because I was getting so frustrated. Finally she started to help me.

> As I started reading my paper to her, I could not help but be very embarrassed. I just then realized what a total joke my paper was. For one thing, I was trying to write a simple paper on skiing and was using lines like "unexplainable to mortal man" and "it ate at the linings of my stomach like acid through metal." These were just a few lines, but there were many more just as bad or worse. My roommate said it sounded like I was going to Mars or something.
>
> This paper was the combination of four people's ideas thrown together like a jigsaw puzzle, which might have worked for another situation but I found it very inappropriate for this assignment. Continuing to read the lines, we ended up laughing hysterically.
>
> She was amused by my paper, but I was laughing because of embarrassment. I said to her, "I cannot believe I actually handed this in. He must have thought it was a joke." I continued writing for five more minutes, laughing and trying to change this mess I was trying to call a paper.

I pictured two college girls sharing real laughter over fake writing. The two were an interpretive community, to use contemporary jargon, and their collaboration marked a turning point for Trudy, just in the nick of time.

> Around this time, it was close to midnight. I could not believe how much work I still had to do. But what upset me more was how much time I had wasted because of my procrastination and most importantly my fear of writing. Then I looked up at my roommate and said, "This is the best learning experience ever." This is what I get for trying to take the easy way out, for underestimating my abilities, and lastly for putting things off until the last minute. Now I had something to write about that was true and not being made up.
>
> It is now 1:30 a.m., and I have just finished a very, very rough draft of paper number one, which was assigned five weeks ago. I have definitely learned a great lesson from all of this. Now I know that in the future when given an assignment, I will sit down with my own ideas and write it myself!

I wondered about being seduced by the voice of intimacy here. Was this perhaps a fake confession rather than a real one? Or was Trudy genuinely working toward the truth here? Rereading her paper that afternoon, I realized that real writing had made me a real reader once again.

The Role of Self-Assessment

Obviously, busy middle school and high school teachers cannot confer with individuals to the extent I did with Trudy. However, it is possible to read her story aloud (Strong and Griffin 1993) to introduce the ideas of fake versus real writing as well as the critical role of self-assessment. After sharing her narrative and the self-assessment exercise in Chapter 8, ask learners to recall fakery in book reports, essay exams, or papers copied from the Internet. "Confession is good for the soul," you might say.

Trudy's breakthrough reveals the power of self-assessment. Early in the narrative she and her sister "laughed and stressed over the [skiing] paper for three hours" as they cunningly tried to outwit a writing instructor. Later, however, as Trudy read the skiing paper to a roommate, her laughter had a different ring to it. Instead of being amused by the conspiratorial game of faking her writing, Trudy found herself laughing *about* the text, a critical judgment that showed her finally beginning to consider her essay from a reader's viewpoint. Ironically, her embarrassed laughter signaled that she had begun to take herself—and her writing—seriously.

Students may also be interested in Trudy's final examination, in which she explained what "The Easy Way Out" meant in terms of self-assessment.

> This paper was the beginning of my improvement. . . . In this paper I admitted to myself and my classmates and most embarrassingly my professor what I had done. In writing this paper I realized just how immature I had been. I was sick and tired of not being able to write.

The theme of immaturity linked to fakery is a powerful one for some learners who do not want to think of themselves in these terms. Also provocative is Trudy's feeling of being "sick and tired" about her situation. Many secondary students claim to feel much the same way about game playing in school.

Trudy wrote that her "turn-around in writing" occurred after handing in her confessional essay.

> Two hours later I went back and picked it up. I was so nervous and embarrassed, and I was praying he was not there. I got my paper from him and immediately left. I remember on the front of it, it said, "Applause, very intelligent; let's work on this." I was so pleased because it was my own work. Right then I realized I could do it if I would just try.

However, old beliefs and strategies are not always turned around with a single incident. Thus, when Trudy received positive comments on a second essay, she "could not believe the feedback that was on it." Part of her clung to an old identity, although she wanted to pursue a new direction. In Trudy's words, her "negative attitudes toward writing" still undermined her self-confidence, making her "hesitant." Old attitudes began to change when she changed her writing strategy. Her old strategy was to write with "no outline, no plan, just to get it over with," whereas her new strategy involved freewriting, followed by outlining and drafting, and then peer response. What she came to learn was that "personalizing" the task of writing "makes it much easier."

Trudy's self-assessment was supported by three activities: evaluation from peers, revising on her own, and instructor conferences. This work was full of surprises. As she invested herself in text development, she found that she "really enjoyed sharing her work with others." As she got feedback from others in class, she found that it was "very beneficial to read a rough draft over many times" and that the more she read and revised, "the better the paper was." As she read and revised on her own, she found that she began to enjoy conferences with her instructor: "I wanted help and feedback so I could improve my writing. For once in my life, I wanted to learn about writing."

Middle school and high school students may resonate to Trudy's comment that she had "always tried to write like someone else" because she "always felt that the other person's style of writing was correct and [hers] was wrong." They may nod assent to her point that "when it comes to writing the worst thing you can do is fake it." And they may wonder how it would feel to be "excited, pleased, and satisfied" because of no longer having a fear of writing. As students consider their own work habits and strategies, such topics are useful ones for reflection.

And in this context, perhaps, we can begin to level with our students about the circumstances we face as teachers and what we propose in terms of self-assessment guidelines for each writing assignment. First, the situation we face:

- We have lots of papers to read, and we often face them in stacks of 25 (or more) at a time. Generally, the papers are read after school or on weekends—hardly ideal conditions for reflection. We have to read fast. With only six minutes per paper, it will take 15 hours to read 150 papers—without a bathroom break.

- We often can't afford the luxury of long comments. We have to make quick notes and trust that students will see these comments as genuine efforts to be helpful. Our aim is to read *honestly* because we believe that our students want real readers, not fake ones. We therefore invite students to follow up with us.

Given this situation, we might also say that there are certain ways in which students can be of assistance to us. They can build background for the paper being submitted. Such background is created in two ways:

- Each student can prepare a brief cover letter that tells, succinctly and honestly, about the paper's background, for example, how it was developed and what it tries to accomplish. The letter may point to strong sections as well as problems areas; it can also ask for the teacher's response to specific questions.
- The student can attach a summary of peer suggestions as well as a completed self-assessment based on the assignment rubric. Such moves suggest that the student is truly interested in feedback from others and willing to learn from their comments. Teachers appreciate writers who thoughtfully assess their own work.

And, finally, there is the matter of student response to our teacher feedback, suggestions, and grades. Nothing is more discouraging in human relationships than the feeling that one's good-faith efforts are being ignored or rejected. Therefore, we have certain additional expectations of students:

- We ask students to carefully read our comments (or in the case of audiotape grading, to listen to them). We know that such feedback may not be pleasant. Students should understand that the comments are intended as helpful, honest assistance, not as criticism. Being open to feedback requires emotional maturity.
- For students to prove that they have heard us, we ask for a brief note of response. We want to know what they learned from our comments, how they are reacting to suggestions, and what points they will keep in mind for future writing. We also want to know if they have questions of us, ones that still trouble them.

This last point is so important that I always build it into my lesson plan. Students often have surprises for us. For example, after returning literacy autobiographies to a teacher education class, I got these paragraphs from one student:

When I first read your comments on my reading and writing memory paper, I was pissed. Then I started thinking of how dumb of me to get upset for my own mistakes. Yes, my paper was crap and hard to follow. The mistakes needed to be fixed. I am once again sorry about how my paper was written, and I am glad we were able to meet and discuss the problems of my paper.

I appreciate the time you took to help me start fixing the memories paper. I did go through the paper twice since we met. This time I slowed down and put more thought into the revisions of my paper. I was more careful in that I looked over every sentence, and read it out loud. I also expounded on a few points that I felt did not have enough content when first written.

—Alan Spaulding

Alan's honest response to my feedback suggested his willingness to have an ongoing dialogue with me, one that he would help author. Coaching depends on conversation, and Alan had signaled a willingness to join me on the playing field of language learning.

Taken together, the preceding six bulleted points define an environment for active learning, one in which miniconferences and assessment are companion activities. Students are asked to appreciate the challenge their teachers face, to take on self-assessing roles, and to respond immediately to teacher feedback. Teachers who succeed in securing the cooperation of students along these lines will achieve positive outcomes.

Evaluating Papers

Little can be done about huge classes taken by students whose passions are more often for each other than for writing. However, we *can* craft engaging writing prompts by attending to context, role, audience, format, and topic, and we *can* use exemplar papers tied to rubrics so students have a clear direction for generating and revising text. We *can* learn strategies for guiding peer response groups, and we *can* use oral and written responses that encourage rather than discourage students.

Before responding to the written text of any student, we need to ask some very basic questions. It is by having clear answers to these questions that we increase the likelihood of working smarter, not harder.

First, where is this text in the writing process—at an early, a middle, or a final stage? A cover letter, described in the previous section, can orient us to the paper's development and to the student's needs or expectations. Response to an early stage text will probably emphasize its ideas, development, and voice; response to a middle stage text—assuming that the basic ideas are clear—will probably emphasize its form, organization, and conventions. The response to a final stage text will probably emphasize its overall effectiveness in relation to certain standards. (To correct a final text is a mostly wasted effort in the eyes of many veteran teachers because students are unlikely to use corrections for revision.)

Next, how will we read the text? As teachers, we tend to read papers in four basic ways: (1) we skim certain texts (like cover letters) for background; (2) we scan other texts (like short-answer exams) for specific content; (3) we carefully read major essays that represent major investments of time and energy; and (4) we read for pleasure those texts that are celebrations of achievement—in portfolios, on bulletin boards, or at in-class publishing parties. To a large extent, our reading strategy dictates our response strategy. For skimming tasks, many teachers use check marks (or, in certain situations, a check plus or a check minus). For scanning tasks, many teachers respond with points. For careful reading, many teachers respond with balanced descriptive comments. For pleasure reading, many teachers respond with personal notes.

After deciding how to read the text, we must consider how the response should be communicated. Here are a few possibilities: (1) we can make notes directly on student papers; (2) we can respond on a separate sheet of paper, say, at the bottom of a rubric or in a brief letter; (3) we can use audiotape as a method of response; or (4) we can use electronic response, with comments layered into a text. Scribbling on student papers offers an efficient way to note specific text features, but is such response always effective? Some students claim to value personal response letters, but what are the human costs of such response? Audiotape offers a substitute for one-on-one conferences, but is a substitute approach necessarily the best one? Electronic response offers a new option, but isn't it possible that such comments are even more controlling and intrusive than traditional marking?

We must also consider what we hope to accomplish with our response. In general, of course, our aim is to encourage, not discourage. However, within the context of careful reading, a quick first reading of the paper will probably establish a more specific teaching aim for response. This decision is crucial. For help in making this decision, it is very useful to lightly underline those parts of the text that read well or galvanize our attention and to use a wavy underline for those parts that confuse us or present problems (Strong 1996). These initial responses offer important cues for our second reading and helpful feedback to students. Basically, they help us answer two key questions: What should be praised? What should be taught?

And then we must ask: *How* should texts be praised? One of Donald Murray's favorite methods of response begins with five simple words: "I like the way you . . . " It is hard to go wrong with these words because they invite us to specify some aspect of the text ("described the character's attitude through gestures and dialogue") or some aspect of our response ("caused me to think about this character's motives"). To be effective, praise should be sparing and specific, not gushing and global. Students will remember "this image grabbed me" but often dismiss more global comments such as "effective language use."

On the other hand, how should texts be criticized? Helpful feedback to students should center on one or two points, three at most. The language we use to communicate these points should be clear and personal. For example, one might say, "I'm lost here," or "An example would help me," or "I don't follow this reasoning." Such response offers a clear report of how the text was experienced by *one* reader rather than by readers in general. Global comments like "confusing" or "example needed" or "unclear reasoning" sound like Olympian pronouncements. Above all, students want to feel respect from their teachers. We can communicate respect by using open-ended questions ("How could you introduce this idea earlier?") and other requests ("For final draft, please edit with care").

And finally, how should grades be given? Students come to us with many levels of ability. As suggested earlier, summative assessments of effort and achievement, beyond the writing task criteria, would occur within the context of each student's writing portfolio. Translated, this sentence means that students who are *able* to do more *should* do more. In other words, as we come to understand the abilities of individuals—using the best work in their portfolios as yardsticks—we should hold students to increasingly high standards. In my view, top grades should result only from true effort and achievement; lower grades, on the other hand, should reflect more modest efforts and achievements.

Taken together, the several preceding paragraphs provide a frame of reference for evaluating student papers. I agree with Peter Elbow (1999) that "there is no right or best way to respond to student writing" and that the "right or best comment is the one that will help *this* student on *this* topic on *this* draft at *this* point in the semester" (198). Response, after all, is an art, not a science—a human relationship, not a mechanical act. If we are sensitive to discourse dynamics, as Elbow so clearly is—"I write only in light pencil, never ink" (199)—and if we strive to be "humble" and "strategic" in our comments, describing and reporting our real experiences as readers, we pay students the intellectual respect of treating them as writers. "There is an enormous pedagogical power," Elbow says, "that comes from this truth-telling" (200).

Elbow's method of response deserves further space here because it has been widely used by writing process teachers. First of all, he tries to behave as a reader, not as an editor. For this reason, he prefers to make his comments on a separate sheet of paper with a word processor. He cautions that "relying on only one or two habitual modes of commenting" or "settling for the first thing that comes to mind" leads to poor or misguided commentary (201). The key to good commentary, Elbow believes, is when "our minds fill quickly with *many* different things, even conflicting things, that we *might* say about a paper" (201).

In addition to the use of straight lines and wavy lines, other strategies are useful as prompts for commentary. The following list of starters is adapted from Elbow's essay "Options for Responding to Student Writing" (1999, 202):

- Jot down what happens within, particularly what you feel, as you read the text. Create a movie of the reader's mind.
- Praise the text. Ask yourself about its strengths.
- Describe the text. Identify its genre, topic, key points, pattern of organization, syntax, diction, voice, point of view, and so on.
- Reply to the text as a human being, not as a teacher. In other words, respond to the message, not just to the form.
- Make inferences about process. Inferences are guesswork, but they invite dialogue.
- Praise the text, second try. As Elbow notes, "Well focused praise—even for small successes—produces more learning than criticism of failures (202)."
- Find the fruitful problem. "Try to figure out the one problem that might be useful to work on (202)."

From such mental exercises, Elbow recommends that teachers prepare "an honest process account" of what happened while reading a given text (202). This account, although it may not include all actual reactions, tells truthfully of the experience of one thoughtful reader. "And interestingly enough," Elbow says, "our subjective reactions are often surprisingly universal" (200).

Elbow's style of evaluation balances praise and criticism as it points to specific sections of the text. It invites dialogue and reflection, but it does not provide direct guidance or advice nor does it address issues of usage, mechanics, syntax, or style. At the opposite extreme, of course, is the traditional marking of papers, in which teachers typically change wording or mark errors, make evaluations of text features ("unclear reasoning here"), issue commands ("Use example to develop this point"), offer advice ("I'd organize this chronologically"), ask questions about content or form ("Why do you believe this?"), or provide reflections ("This point seems to contradict the earlier one").

Of course, traditional marking has long been criticized because it rides roughshod over student aims, imposes an idealized text, and takes control in unfriendly or authoritarian ways (Brannon and Knoblauch 1982; Sommers 1982). A traditional directive style is regarded as "masculine" by Elizabeth Flynn (1989) because the teacher assumes the role of "judge"; in contrast, she says, a "feminine" style of response casts the teacher in the role of "sympathetic reader" and "friendly adviser" (50). Finally, Rebecca Rule (1993) expresses well her resistance to the traditional forms of controlling comments on a student's essay:

As teacher, I must be careful not to take over—because the minute I do, the success (if there is one) becomes mine, not his—and the learning is diminished. I can contribute; I can guide; I can brainstorm with him; I can suggest exercises; I can offer models; I can tell him where the comma goes; I can support him wholeheartedly. But I must not take over. (50)

Given these points, it will come as no surprise that I urge an ethos of balance when commenting on student papers. Praise *and* criticism, content *and* form, questions *and* directions—all need to be balanced if our comments on student papers are to be heard by students. Unfortunately, the traditional paradigm for marking papers has tended to emphasize criticism over praise, form over content, and directions over questions. The legacy of such imbalance, of course, is the stuff of legend, a stereotype of the English teacher as "proofreader," "gatekeeper," or "hostile reader," to use Robert Probst's (1989, 73) descriptors.

The concept of balance implies multiple roles for coaches. For some students, the role of supportive facilitator makes sense; but for other learners, what makes more sense is the role of demanding taskmaster. Trudy may need sensitive coaching, but a more challenging style of interchange may work for young dudes with attitude, some of whom prefer clear advice and direction over what they see as "bogus" responses. And as we saw in Chapter 3, under "Workshop-Style Instruction," Nancie Atwell (1998) does see a role for copyediting by the teacher, for making corrections on a student's paper before the final manuscript is prepared. Of course, teacher editing occurs only *after* the paper has been revised and copyedited by the student and her peers; this editing sets the stage for an editing conference, in which one or two items are taught in context.

As in so many other things, problems arise from trying to do too many things at once. Atwell works smart because she doesn't confuse text development activities and content conferences with skill development minilessons and editing conferences. The traditional paradigm, on the other hand, compresses all of these process steps into a single make-or-break event, the submission of the final paper. As tired teachers give advice about vivid examples (a prewriting lesson), clearer voice (a drafting lesson), better organization (a revision lesson), and technical correctness (an editing lesson), they are certain to overload the circuits. A smarter approach, perhaps, is not doing everything at once. It involves crafted writing assignments, explicit standards (rubrics and model papers), peer response and self-assessment, and one-on-one conferences.

Here are several additional ideas and reminders for beginning teachers, assuming that comments or corrections are made directly on the student's paper at various stages in the cycle of text development:

- Remember, the job is to teach the student, not to fix the text.
- Know why you are reading and what your focus will be.
- Be alert to the student's self-assessment questions and requests.
- Use the student's name as you make comments or suggestions.
- Have a grading rubric as a frame of reference for your comments.
- Lightly underline strong parts; use a wavy underline for problems.
- Tell how the text affects *you* as a reader, not readers in general.
- Don't waste time with a text that falls below your basic standards.
- Try to sandwich your criticisms between statements of praise.

- Raise questions to prompt reflection about content or form.
- Couch suggestions in open-ended language (e.g., "Consider . . . ").
- Try to use full, elaborated sentences in your summary comments.
- Use the common code (see Chapter 8) employed by peer groups.
- Circle misspelled words; circle suggested changes in punctuation.
- Limit yourself to a paragraph or two of close editing; then move on.
- Try using smiley faces or other icons to signal responses to text.
- Use sticky notes so that you don't write on the student's text.
- Work as fast as you comfortably can; take breaks to stay focused.
- Ask students to jot down their candid responses to your comments.

Finally, audiotape grading also deserves mention. With this approach, you first skim the text, noting strong and weak sections with straight lines or wavy underlines, and jot down a positive general impression as well as an area for instruction. Then you pop a labeled audiocassette into the recorder and begin your commentary in a friendly, upbeat way. You note strengths of the text and identify problems. All comments refer to line numbers in the margin of the text.

I try to read parts of the text aloud, showing what needs work and what might be done to improve readability. The tone can be encouraging ("Jenny, think back to that great piece from last semester as you revise."), rhetorical ("Would it work, Andy, to put your strongest reason as a clincher?"), stylistic ("Nice use of the opening cumulative sentence to grab my attention, Heather."), personal ("Maybe I'm wrong, Matt, but did you give up toward the end?"), or technical ("Jonathan, mark and fix the run-on sentences that I point out."). When papers are returned, they have no marks on them. The student's task is to listen to comments, make revisions and corrections, and resubmit the piece for a final, graded reading. Of course, a self-assessment sheet should accompany the final paper, describing changes and improvements.

I like audiotape grading because it enables me to work in a personal way with students and because it puts them in a mode of active response. Generally, I say far more with tape grading than I do with traditional methods of commentary. Therefore, the approach doesn't usually save time. If your school has a setup for audio playback in the media center (playback units plus headphones), audiotape response is certainly worth a try—if nothing else, as a change of pace for you and your students.

For an excellent resource on evaluating student papers, I highly recommend *A Sourcebook for Responding to Student Writing* (1999), edited by Richard Straub. The book contains student papers evaluated by many well-known leaders in the profession, showing their different styles and methods of response. Also included are a few essays about evaluation, including a fine one on audiotape response by Chris Anson (1999).

Self-Assessment for Coaches

It's a spring morning, and I'm visiting a class of seventh graders and their bright-eyed student teacher, her blonde hair fluffed in the fashion of her sorority sisters. At the back of the room I watch and listen, trying to get a feel for the quality of discussion. The desks are in rows, and the kids are bored and restless, minimally responsive. She cheerfully asks questions about the assigned short story, but little is happening. It's paint-by-numbers teaching.

I know this student teacher—she's taken two of my courses—and I can sense her edginess. She's been a dutiful student, though no standout. We've talked about my coaching role, how I'm there to help her do well, but she may not believe me. I can still recall my own panic in years past when a supervisor "dropped by" to inspect my work. It's too bad I can't make myself invisible to ease her jitters—and too bad also that my coaching role must inevitably give way to evaluation. But that's life.

With twenty minutes to go, the kids finally shut down. It's a novice teacher's nightmare—time to spare and no activity planned. In leading the nondiscussion, she's already passed up three opportunities to use writing-to-learn activities, ones that might pump some energy into the room. How will I get her to think about such possibilities? I circle the word *reflection* in my notes and hear the student teacher make the classic moves of true desperation. She assigns another story, with time for in-class reading. Most students nap at their desks or pick their noses and watch the clock.

With time on my hands until our conference, I'm thinking about my own student teaching with Rae Dodge, a demanding taskmaster in the early 1960s. I recall the tidal wave of work—stacks of papers at a kitchen table in a one-bedroom apartment, the detailed lessons prepared two weeks in advance, then discussed and modified and discussed again. And I recall an evening phone call to my university supervisor—an announcement, late in the term, that I had decided to quit student teaching.

"You're quitting?" Dr. Brown asked. "But *why?*"

"We had an argument. I'm not going back."

"An argument? About what?"

"That's not important. It's the last straw."

"But you have only ten days to go—and you're doing so well."

I finally explained how my ideas hadn't meshed with Mrs. Dodge's traditional teaching. Pressure had built up during the term and had come to a head late in the afternoon following a grammar lesson she had requested, one on adverbs.

"Adverbs," Dr. Brown said.

The textbook defined adverbs as words that modified verbs, adjectives, and other adverbs, but I had said that some adverbs—those of location—could modify nouns at times. And although I'd used examples of adverbs doing what I claimed—these drawn from my term paper in Freeman Anderson's structural linguistics course—Mrs. Dodge argued that contradicting a textbook would not serve students well. They could learn "newer approaches" to language later.

"I think you need to sleep on this," Dr. Brown said.

"Look," I said. "My mind's made up."

"I know. But at least go back. The three of us will talk."

There wasn't any point, I explained. I'd given teaching a try, and it hadn't worked out. Besides, I didn't want to go back to see the kids and Mrs. Dodge.

"Face your decision," Dr. Brown said. "Don't retreat from it."

I hesitated. Something in this challenge made sense to me.

I'd had free rein at least part of the time, Dr. Brown said. What about using the prescribed vocabulary words as a poetry trigger? The kids had liked that. And hadn't Mrs. Dodge helped me think hard about ways to involve them?

"Right," I agreed. My resolve was weakening.

"I'll see you at school tomorrow," Dr. Brown said. "And for tonight, think about this question: What's more important—an *adverb* or a *career*?"

And the rest, as they say, is history, including an exchange of Christmas cards with Mrs. Dodge over many years. As I finish up my notes for the student teacher, part of me still wonders how I'll handle my follow-up conference with her.

After the bell rings and the kids head for lunch, the student teacher and I confer in the media center, where she feels "pretty good" about the lesson, although the class was "sort of apathetic." It's mid-April, she reminds me, and I know about spring fever. When I ask about the goals for today's short story, she shows me a list of questions. Her aim, I gather, is "a good discussion," nothing more specific. The questions are those offered in the teacher's edition of her anthology, massaged ever so slightly.

"Think back to our classes together," I say. "Do you remember those little quick-write activities, the ones for getting learners to reflect, then trade writing with a partner?"

"Oh, yeah—like the minilesson I did."

"Right, your minilesson. So what's the point of writing-to-learn work?"

"Uhm, to make learning more interesting?"

"Sure. Writing can prompt thinking and talk. Remember, you can always use what students have written as a springboard, to change the rhythm of the class."

"Okay," she says. "That makes sense."

I wait for several beats. There's no move toward follow-up on her part.

"How about directed reading lessons?" I ask. "Those in-class demonstrations?"

"Oh," she replies. "That's like, you know, relating it to the kids, and doing the vocabulary, and setting purposes. There was one other step, too."

"Focusing on a reading skill."

"That's it. The fourth part."

"Right," I say, nodding. "Four prereading steps—all possible ways to set up reading. And what about that first step, you know, relating it to the kids?"

She hesitates. "Well, like their experience, what they know—you could use that. Or maybe current events."

"That's good. Or connecting with something kids have been studying. It's those connections that get students to think about their reading."

She glances at the notes I will soon share with her. It's an odd conversation we're having, this review of material she has studied and assimilated to some degree. She wants to know how well she did in today's lesson. Will I give her a good write-up? Do I have any suggestions to offer? What about class management?

"You know that material pretty well," I nod.

She laughs. "Well, we went *over* it enough."

I pause. "So what do you think? Any chance today to *apply* writing-to-learn or prereading ideas? Say, setting up your reading assignment—to build interest?"

There is another pause. And in that long, lovely moment the blue eyes of the student teacher blink, just once. Somewhere behind those sorority eyes a small blue flame arcs between two parts of her neocortex—the first with information from teacher education classes, the other organizing the learning about real student teaching. For some reason there has been a disconnect between these areas of experience. And in that long moment she perhaps takes a first step to assess herself, honestly, as a teacher. It is a step I myself took at her age, prompted by a supervisor's question.

So maybe today she is a professional who uses self-assessment strategies with her students and can still recall the turning points in her own development—a mid-April morning, say, with anthologies open to a short story and her good-faith efforts sparking far more interest than any teacher's edition activity. And maybe she now sees herself on this page and knows that through clear-eyed self-assessment she has become a truly remarkable teacher, one often praised for her ability to exercise language and coach writing.

At least, it's pretty to think so.

Learning Through Language

1. In Chapter 10 you considered the themes of fake reading and writing versus real reading and writing. Ask yourself whether these ideas make sense, that is, whether you can recall instances of each from your own experience. Next, consider how your experiences or ideas about fake versus real writing might be introduced to students. Finally, write up an account to share with a writing partner, then exchange papers and respond *supportively* to your partner's text.

2. In the "Evaluating Papers" section of the chapter, several ideas are presented as background to evaluation. Find three separate paragraphs, at different points in the section, that especially interest you. Copy a single sentence from each passage. Then in follow-up writing, explain why you focused on each of these sentences. That is, what in this particular language reached you? Be prepared to share your work with others and think about their ideas.

3. The idea of working smarter, not harder has been woven throughout this book. With the theme of balance in mind, develop a set of your guiding principles (personal belief statements) and a plan of action (strategies or steps) for working smarter, not harder, when it comes to grading papers. This document is important to your future coaching success. Take your time with it. Be realistic. Think it through. Publish your coaching philosophy for members of your group.

CONCLUSION:
THE ZEN OF COACHING

The Thing You Must Remember

The thing you must remember is how, as a child,
you worked hours in the art room, the teacher's
hand over yours, molding the little clay dog.
You must remember how nothing mattered
but the imagined dog's fur, the shape of his ears
and his paws. The gray clay felt dangerous,
your small hands were pressing what you couldn't
say with your limited words. When the dog's back
stiffened, then cracked into white shards
in the kiln, you learned how the beautiful
suffers from too much attention, how clumsy
a single vision can grow, and fragile
with trying too hard. The thing you must
remember is the art teacher's capable
hands: large, rough and grainy,
over yours, holding on.

—**Maggie Anderson**

A Matter of Values

It was a gray, rainy morning in early January, three days after my mother's fiftieth birthday, when I got the intercom call. In the school office I stood at the secretary's desk, watching rain drip from a leafless Japanese maple in the courtyard. Its black branches were weeping. On the other end of the line was my father, his voice quavering. He was at home. My mother was dead. She had taken her own life.

Back in class my students wanted to know what was up. The break had been fun, but we'd been having a good discussion, so they wanted to get back into it.

"I have to go," I told them. The principal took over my class.

The windshield wipers beat a steady rhythm across town. In the backyard of the white frame house with a green laurel hedge were police and firemen and the burned-out remains of a two-person camping trailer, a gift I'd given my parents for their twenty-fifth wedding anniversary. Inside the trailer was my mother's body.

"Don't look," someone advised.

TV reporters and camera crews ambushed me under the spreading limbs of a moss-covered walnut tree, its leaves now black in the wet grass. A reporter shoved a microphone in my face and the camera lights went on, a scene framed for the evening news. My rage was unspeakable. I ordered them from the property although I wanted to do more. Then I was in the house.

My father sat at the kitchen table. A few neighbors stood around in the kitchen, helpless. No one knew what to say or do. And neither did I.

It is a sad little tale, this story from 1966. But sadder still, in retrospect, are the days that followed. I know now what I should have done with the time away from my classroom. I should have written about that day and her birthday and the years before her mind began to unravel. Doing so then, I might have recalled Christmas celebrations and homemade ravioli and fresh tomatoes for my lunch. Such details would have led me to remember events in between and how she held a family together during the dark years when my father glowered in the garage, trying to deal with his disability. I might have captured her voice, seen her eyes brighten with laughter, or felt her touch.

Instead, I graded papers. I sat in a fiberglass chair at a round white table in a college cafeteria. The *Macbeth* essays, among others, were folded in half lengthways and bundled with rubber bands. Sipping coffee, I asked questions, offered advice, and made judgments. I marked errors in punctuation, spelling, and usage. I kept the bundles in a stuffed leather briefcase next to my chair.

After the funeral, when I returned to school, I thanked my classes for the flowers and cards they had sent. I didn't talk with them about the meaning of my mother's life or her back-and-forth visits to the state mental hospital or what had happened on the day of her death. Rather, I reached into the briefcase, pulled out a bundle of papers, and handed them back. I had read all the essays from all my classes. For the first time since September, I was caught up.

It was during the early spring of that year that I went to an auction where I paid five dollars for a sturdy pine trunk with metal framing and thick rope handles. Inside the trunk, to my surprise, were hundreds and hundreds of Mother's Day cards. Now I had a millennium supply of Mother's Day cards and no mother to give one to. Students in my classes wrote letters to their mothers that spring, and I supplied cards for all the mothers and grandmothers throughout the school. I gave away cards by the handfuls, and my heart ached.

My father dismantled what was left of the camping trailer. At first I was appalled, but gradually I got used to the idea. Working from the frame up, he built a small utility trailer, one that we used for more than thirty years to maintain the property around his house. We parked it not far from where my mother had died and where TV reporters had made their retreat in the January rain. Finally, in the summer of 1999, I loaded up his wheelchair, furniture, and personal effects, and we made our way to Utah and the new apartment attached to my home there. Today, the trailer sits on a vacant lot next door, with a view of the mountains and the river and the changing seasons. It needs to be rebuilt.

In the years since my mother's suicide, I have sometimes thought of those essays, with their marginal notes and corrections, the ones written in her blood. To characterize my effort as wasted or misguided or stupid would be to understate the obvious. A more valid evaluation might be "unbalanced." The truth of the matter is that no comments at all would have had equal educational effect on my students, most of whom slipped the papers into their notebooks, hardly giving them a second glance. With grades noted and my summary paragraph read, it was time to move on.

Balance, as the Zen masters have long known, is always a matter of values.

Coaching Through Conferences

The computer lab hums with activity. Kids talk, keyboards click, and an ancient printer grinds out paperwork in the corner. The teacher and I move through the room in zigzag fashion, swooping in from time to time to either ask a question or answer one. Most students are well prepared, with notes or handwritten text, but several also seem well behind the curve, still struggling to generate ideas.

Rachel stares intently at her computer screen, then wrinkles her nose. I drag up a chair beside her. "So how's it going?" I ask.

"I don't know," she says. "This part doesn't sound good."

"Which part?"

She's looking at the screen again. "It starts out okay," she says, her voice trailing off. "Do you think it's any good?"

"What are you trying to do?" I ask. Now we're both reading the screen.

"Like we talked about in class: 'The bigger the issue, the smaller you write.' That was such a cool idea."

"So you're trying to use a story opener?"

"Right. I just thought—oh, I don't know."

I let a couple of beats go by. "Your strategy seems fine, Rachel. What's the idea you want to explore?"

Now she looks at me. "The assignment—reflecting on your writing process."

"Okay, but what do you want to *say* about it?"

"Getting started. How much trouble I have."

"That's a great idea to explore. Do you have it down in your notes?"

"Not yet."

"What interests you about the getting started stage?"

"Like if I can get started, it's not that bad, you know? But if I get stuck, it's, like, hopeless."

I'm wondering how much to lead. "I see. So you're thinking about describing the problem—how you *usually* approach a writing assignment—and what happens when you get stuck?"

"Right."

"I notice you don't have any notes to work from."

"Usually I just write it out."

"Are you stuck now?"

Rachel hesitates. "Pretty much."

"Hmmm. So the just-writing-it-out strategy isn't working, and some thoughts and feelings are stirred up. What are they?"

She laughs. "Like being frustrated? Wanting to quit?"

A hand goes up down the aisle. It's time to move on. "Believe me, I know the feeling. But let's say you make a list of those thoughts and feelings so you can write about them. Could be you'd get yourself *unstuck*. What do you think?"

Rachel shrugs. "I guess."

"Give it a try, and I'll come back to see how you're doing. Then we'll look at that other paragraph." As I slip into the downstream current, Rachel flips open her notebook and wrinkles her nose again.

And so it goes. Conferences like that one provide scaffolding for students as they struggle to generate ideas, organize texts, or make revisions based on peer feedback. In fact, for most writing process coaches, miniconferences are central to the game. Why? Because good conferences can reveal whether students are thinking about—or avoiding— the key issues of content, process, and skills in writing.

Although part of my conference with Rachel focused on content—her desire to write about the "getting started" part of writing—much of it dealt with process. Ironically, Rachel was continuing to use a strategy that had not served her well in the past. So it seemed useful to encourage a substitute strategy: making a simple list. Like someone who knows all about healthy lifestyles but strays from the path of regular exercise and good nutrition, Rachel already understood the value of prewriting tools because they were part of her teacher's curriculum. All she needed was friendly encouragement to use what she knew.

Once students like Rachel begin to plan, the content conference becomes easier to manage. To set up such dialogue, a simple preconference tool like the following one can be useful.

Conference Preparation

1. Put your paper's aim in a nutshell, a single sentence.
2. Describe (or attach) your prewriting notes for the paper.
3. Identify, specifically, the strongest parts of your paper.
4. Identify, specifically, the parts of your paper that need help.
5. What are you struggling with right now? Content and ideas? Strategy and organization? Format and expression? Name the issue as best you can.

■

The responder's task in such a conference is to ask questions and listen carefully to the answers. Dialogue provides the writer with scaffolding to clarify goals, ask questions, or articulate possible approaches to the text. Of course, student writers can also share their ideas with partners or small peer groups, and it is in such settings that students can begin to feel genuine interest in their own ideas. Chapter 8 of this book dealt more specifically with these matters, especially the training of peer response groups.

Of course, if students like Rachel have been working with an evaluation rubric as described in Chapter 9, they already have a sense of assignment expectations. A good strategy is to use the rubric to prompt informal self-assessment. Such an activity invites close attention to the text. The dialogue between student and teacher then has direction and structure. If students are nervous in conferences, ask them to tell the story of their paper—how they first came up with ideas and how their thoughts have evolved since they began. This question can provide a foundation for more analytic dialogue.

In my experience, the skills (or editing) conference can be tricky to manage, especially for discouraged, skill-deficient students. For one thing, it can dredge up bad memories. For another, it can gobble up time. I often ask the student to read a few sentences aloud as they should be read. I like to follow along on a copy of the text, checking those spots that present problems. Then the student and I return to the passage, and I point out areas for attention. Of course, students can very quickly become overloaded with editing information, particularly if the text has lots of errors. Nanci Atwell (1998) limits her instruction to two errors in editing conferences. For more about such conferences, see "Three Approaches to Instruction" in Chapter 3.

Physically, it's always helpful for teacher and student to be seated side by side facing a text or a computer screen. This strategy puts the focus where it belongs—on the text as a mutual project. Many teachers also insist that changes always be made by the student. As language experts, all of us can appreciate what it means when a student hands over a paper and we begin to cross out his or her words and insert our own. Such an approach, while perhaps reasonable as a think-aloud demonstration for editing, does not empower students to reflect on their own work or make their text revisions.

We should remember, too, that the lessons already learned about writing—and about themselves as writers—can create static for students: that writing is punishment; that the main purpose is to please the teacher-as-examiner and get a grade; and that taking risks, with content or language, can lead to trouble. To make progress with students, we need to get past these old lessons.

Donald Murray (1982) insisted that students speak first in conferences. To set up conferences, he leveled with students about his goal: to teach the reader (or "other self") within them. It is readers, after all, who study an evolving text, keep track of its aims, and make assessments. Instead of coming to conferences expecting Murray to fix their writing, students began to ask themselves, "Where does this text need help?" and "What ideas do I have?" Here is Murray's take on basic writers, those who need lots of support and assistance:

> The more inexperienced the student and the less comprehensible the text, the more helpful the writer's comments. Again and again with remedial students I am handed a text that I simply cannot understand. I do not know what it is supposed to say. I can not understand the language. But when a writer tells me what the writer was doing, when the other self is allowed to speak, I find the text was produced rationally. The writer followed misunderstood instruction, inappropriate principles, or logical processes that did not work. (70)

In a similar vein, David Bartholomae (1980) urged that basic writing be viewed as an intermediate, often idiosyncratic system, an approximation of language still being learned. He noted that basic writers typically make three types of errors—those that suggest an "interlanguage" (or intermediate) system; those that result from transcribing accidents; and those that stem from dialect interference. He raised the question of why it is that teachers invest themselves wholeheartedly in interpreting difficult literary texts but read student writing as "policemen, examiners, [or] gatekeepers" (304).

The main approach, as described earlier, is to interview students and ask them to name or explain their difficulties as they see them. A second approach is to have them read their own texts aloud so that discrepancies between the spoken and written versions can be studied. To illustrate the approach, Bartholomae uses the following sentence by a basic writer:

> I would to write about my experience helping 1600 childrens have a happy christmas.

The missing word in the sentence (*like*) was supplied by the student in oral reading. As an accidental error, like the substitution of *when* for *went*, it is amenable to direct instruction in proofreading. In the oral reading, the student self-corrected *children* for *childrens*, a repeated error in the text. When asked about the *s* on *childrens*, the student explained that it was "because there were 1600 of them" (315). In other words, this error was not a careless one but a rational one—evidence of the student's intermediate language system at work. Clearly, such insights are useful in middle and high school classrooms, where we often meet students in brief on-the-run conferences.

Of course, for truly basic writers, as opposed to everyday adolescents who are merely lazy or careless about editing or proofreading, we are talking about second language acquisition. And as Bartholomae points out, the "target" language is nothing less than "a discourse whose lexicon, grammar, and rhetoric are learned not through speaking and listening but through reading and writing" (309)—in other words, visually, not aurally. And herein lies the difficulty. Although basic writers need to acquire the schema and the registers for academic discourse, they typically have had little practice with critical reading on the one hand and the skills of two-channel thinking and decentering on the other (Mellon 1981). It is because of such histories that we need to recruit young writers to become cocollaborators in instruction. Bartholomae's approach has this kind of humane rationale:

> By having students share in the process of investigating the patterns of error in their writing, we can help them to see those errors as evidence of hypotheses or strategies they have formed and, as a consequence, put them in a position to change, experiment, imagine other strategies. Studying their own writing puts students in a position to see themselves as language users, rather than as victims of a language that uses them. (1981, 308)

These are coaching words, clear and strong and deeply principled, with positive expectations of students. They invite language awareness.

Aesthetic (Not Athletic) Clubs

In "The Thing You Must Remember," Maggie Anderson gives us something to think about. As we jot notes or confer with students, perhaps it is useful to recall our own student days and the heartfelt cliches from our journal—those lines crafted late at night, with moths fluttering at the window screen, and how much it mattered that a teacher saw our little poem as worthy and said so, with an approving nod or a smile or a small scrap of language. Now, perhaps we see "how the beautiful / suffers from too much attention, how clumsy / a single vision can grow, and fragile / with trying too hard."

Like the art teacher in Maggie Anderson's poem, writing coaches work mainly in the aesthetic domain, not the athletic one. In fact, we often try to get students to see beyond the glittery seductions of athletics as we preach the pleasures of reading and writing in our literacy club activities. The experiences we value involve a surrender of self-consciousness, an exhilarating focus of mind and body that has been described in the psychology of optimal experience as "flow" (Csikszenthmihalyi 1990). This focus may require strenuous physical exertion, as in athletics, or highly disciplined mental activity, as in the arts. Flow occurs "at the boundary between boredom and anxiety, when the challenges are just balanced with the person's capacity to act" (52).

In using the literacy club metaphor, I borrow of course from Frank Smith (1988), who in turn acknowledges his debt to members of the Seminal Thinkers Club—among them Lev Vygotksky, George Miller, Michael Halliday, and Margaret Spencer. What I have done is link Smith's ideas with the metaphor of sport. Viewing our lives and work through a double-barreled metaphor is, of course, a playful sporting activity.

Smith makes a compelling case that "joining the club" is the social act that underlies learning in general, and the learning of spoken and written language in particular. We first become members of the "spoken language club" and then members of the "literacy club"; membership in this latter club confers special privileges, the most important of which is admission to many other cultural clubs, including formalized ones run as active learning environments by language coaches. According to Smith, it is mainly club membership, not instruction, that enables all of us who are neurologically normal to figure out the complex rules, registers, and conventions of spoken and written language. "The learning," he says, "is always (1) meaningful, (2) useful, (3) continual and effortless, (4) incidental, (5) collaborative, (6) vicarious, and (7) free of risk" (6).

To illustrate Smith's points, let's briefly consider three snapshots from a high school course, one that once served as an alternative to the traditional Beowulf to Browning survey for seniors. Grandly titled Literature Seminar by its greenhorn architect, this was an "open admission" yearlong program built around twenty-five room sets of classic and contemporary novels, plus a little Shakespeare to appease the district's curriculum coordinator. Students who elected this course knew about its no-nonsense standards, marketed as a "small taste" of college life.

Scene 1 was any morning, with kids arranging their desks in a circle—a daring innovation—in preparation for discussion and writing or for in-the-round talks and dramatic prompts from their teacher. Within five minutes, most students had fixed themselves a cup of coffee, tea, or hot chocolate from the tall, quietly gurgling pot of hot water that always stood in the corner. It was allowed there, everyone knew, because of special, divinely inspired dispensation from the school principal, and it could go at any time, along with the smuggled treats, if there were any hygiene problems. Teacher and students would settle back, cups in hand, and class would begin.

Scene 2 was a Friday morning, fifteen minutes into the Friday routine of quiet reading in some book—*any* book—not being studied in school. The greenhorn teacher, always exhausted by four days of teaching, had enough sense never to violate the Friday rule, which had been agreed upon by the seminar. On this Friday, students glanced up to see their teacher doubled over at his desk, stifling a spasm of barely controlled laughter. "What's so funny?" someone asked, and he started in again. Finally, they pressed him to read aloud the opening pages from *Lucky Jim* (1954) by Kingsley Amis, and he broke down a third time. It was a book he knew well because in his private hours he was trying to write one like it, but on this particular morning it had struck him as extra funny, this savage work of comic genius.

Scene 3 of the literacy club drama occurred on the following Monday. As the class put their desks in a circle, filled their cups, and heard morning announcements, the teacher was surprised to learn that several of them had copies of *Lucky Jim* in their backpacks. Someone said that Powell's Bookstore in downtown Portland had more on order because their shelves had been cleaned out. Later, one girl with dark shining eyes confided that the book was "okay" but "a little disappointing." It somehow didn't seem as funny as it had the Friday before. "Trust me," the teacher had advised. "It gets better."

Smith might agree that Literature Seminar, at least briefly, met most of the seven conditions listed earlier. Certainly, there was a literacy club community during those unplanned, "incidental" moments when the students sipped from their cups, and I wiped away tears and let brilliantly crafted language take center stage. Of course, I had no idea that I was coaching language or that students were attending to my lessons. For them, the learning was meaningful and useful and without effort. For me, it was a transcendent Zen glimpse of what might be if I could ever get it right again.

Part of getting it right may come from understanding that although my culture celebrates the worth and dignity of the individual and admonishes me to "have it *my* way" with hamburgers and everything else, I am hardly the unique, self-determined teacher of my imagination. I may chant the mantra of self-actualization, but actually I am part of a community, a club of people whose values, actions, and interests are not so different from my own. In understanding how cultural clubs have shaped the ways I talk and think and behave, I can begin to see myself in multiple mirrors at once. Most aspects of my identity—gender, race, heritage, and language, as well as my assumptions about reality and my training in teaching—are unexamined gifts of the various clubs to which I belong.

This perspective defines each of us as a literacy club representative. Our coaching mission, should we choose to accept it, is to follow the lead of Jerome Bruner (1983b) and invite students to join us in genuine explorations of language:

> Language is for using, and the uses of language are so varied, so rich, and each use so preemptive a way of life, that to study it is to study the world and, indeed, all possible worlds. (176)

For confirmation of Smith's ideas in the actual arenas of sport, we need only watch children as they set out to learn something that holds special interest from their point of view, whether skateboarding, surfing, in-line skating, karate, snowboarding, or soccer. First they tag along with the gang, noting how the experts dress, behave, and talk; then, assuming that leaders welcome apprentices, new learners begin to comport themselves in similar ways. They become keen observers of those with more advanced skills and often they team up with friends of comparable (or slightly advanced) ability, who become their collaborators in learning. In the process of mastering the basics, they may invent drill-and-practice games—routines that make certain moves increasingly automatic and unselfconscious. Eventually, they themselves become the experts who coach (or exclude) those seeking admission to their club.

If the previous observations about social language learning seem fair, we might reasonably infer several behaviors for those who coach writing for a livelihood—or as a lifetime sport: They facilitate open admission to individual and team sports within the language arts curriculum. They organize interesting practice activities. They insist on respect for everyone's effort. They demonstrate and model the skills being learned. They laugh at their mistakes and think aloud about how they went wrong. They invite trial-and-error learning as well as questions. They notice and acknowledge changes in performance or effort. They identify learners with advanced skills and focus attention on specific aspects (or subskills) of their performance. They encourage learners, both expert and novice, to work together. They have fun and invite learners to do likewise. They use minilessons to teach. They share glimpses of their own language pursuits.

But easier said than done, of course. It takes courage and self-discipline to approach, listen to, and learn from what Parker Palmer calls "the voice of the inward teacher" (1998, 29). Palmer believes that the voice of the teacher within is not the nagging voice of conscience, a voice focused on what one ought to be doing. Instead, it is a voice of "identity and integrity," of what is right and true for each of us as teachers or learners. "The teacher within stands guard at the gate of selfhood," writes Palmer, "warding off whatever insults our integrity and welcoming whatever affirms it" (31).

Palmer's notion of an inward teacher, the voice that serves as an inner compass, invokes the classical ideal of education, a process of "leading out." And in this context he reminds us of twin truths about teaching: first, that real teaching is about the quality of connections we make with the "inward, living core of our students' lives" and, second, that "we can speak to the teacher within our students only when we are on speaking terms with the teacher within ourselves" (31).

A Replay of Highlights

Let me now review this book's major themes and challenge an idea or two in the new orthodoxy of instruction. Then I will discuss the long-awaited issue of a life of sport, so fundamental to the Zen of coaching.

The role of language coaches, as we have seen, is to welcome and encourage learners, demonstrate skills, design exercises and practices, connect activities to larger goals, oversee student performance, and model adult learning. In the Introduction, I began with the assumption that language learning is the work of a lifetime and that the coaching of writing may usefully be considered a lifetime sport, one that causes suffering to teach us humility and then offers unexpected moments of joy to teach us hope and commitment and professional perseverance.

And how do we meet the needs of diverse learners—150 (or more) per day—and not burn ourselves out? The principle of balance requires that we relentlessly shift the workload for instruction and assessment to learners themselves. Basically, it is by setting up environments for active learning (Hillocks 1995), working with scaffolded materials and activities, and coaching students toward reasonable goals through exemplars and rubrics that we work smarter, not harder. And it is by negotiating standards—for students and for ourselves—that we achieve a sense of centeredness.

The standards come from external sources but also from our assignments. By crafting our assignments, we take a long step toward establishing reasonable goals. And with coaching experience, we acquire good exemplars to put before the class, ones that portray a range of student work. Such papers become a way of showing, not telling our expectations. As students study exemplars and discuss their features, they begin to consider their own responses as audience and to visualize format (or genre) possibilities. They assess the effectiveness of different texts in terms of imagination, voice, paragraphing, style, and sentence conventions. And they begin to plan.

As a practical matter, explicit criteria enable us to guide self-assessment and peer assessment. Rubrics define the playing field for discourse, the markers and goalposts that serve as public reference points. Obviously, the playing fields can be as varied as the universe of discourse. In some discourse sports, students can compete against their own past performances. Practice exercises occur in a context of efforts to achieve performance goals. Response groups also occur in this context. And so do self-assessments, conferences, and final evaluations of papers.

So much for context. Here are some key ideas:

- A balanced perspective underlies the effective coaching of written language in middle schools and high schools.
- With a balanced view, language coaches understand their central role: to set up and maintain an active learning environment.
- The curriculum for an active learning environment gives balanced attention to literature, composition, and language.
- In an active learning environment, writing coaches seek ways to work smarter, not harder, thus reducing the risk of burnout.
- As students study written language, they inquire into topics ranging from syntax and usage to the analysis of genre features and organizational strategies.
- Good coaches set clear, reasonable goals for writing performance and create activities that invite involvement and self-assessment.
- Language inquiry takes many forms, including wordplay, syntactic risk taking, field research, voice explorations, self-assessments, and coauthoring tasks.
- A basic coaching aim is metalinguistic awareness, so that learners know what they know and apply such knowledge to their writing.
- Reading and writing, listening and speaking, critical viewing and computer-based imaging—all are enhanced through language inquiry and practice.
- Written language can usefully be considered in terms of its inner game (psychological) and outer game (physiological) dimensions.
- The concepts of two-channel thinking, decentering, and flow help explain basic processes in written language production.
- Scaffolded instruction—through materials, group activities, and direct teaching— will help improve many skills in written language.
- The writing curriculum offers scaffolded instruction in four broad domains: expressive, informative, literary, and argumentative.
- Crafted assignments address context, role, audience, format, and topic and offer rubrics for peer response and self-assessment.
- Good language exercises invite students to pay attention to text and assume increasing control over their processes of planning, drafting, and revising.

- The idea of enabling constraints underlies many successful writing assignments and language exercises.

Like those teachers who feel queasy about focusing on language structure, I at first hesitated to give exercises such prominence in this book. Why? Because highly influential colleagues in English education sometimes use the term with more than a hint of disdain. For example, in *Uncommon Sense*, an award-winning critique of the status quo in language arts instruction, John Mayher remarks that "even the notion of exercise, so central to schooling, implies that mental workouts are required to ensure the development of both skilled performances and good study habits" (1990, 50). Mayher continues as follows:

> The commonsense equation seems to be that if it's painful, it's productive; if it's fun, it's trivial and a waste of time. This conception of learning provides a rationale for the emphasis in schools on memorization, drills, and exercises as we struggle to learn the parts of speech and to analyze the structure of a model paragraph. And if no one enjoys doing it very much, not to worry, because the competence thus acquired will stand us in good stead when we leave school. (52)

From such broad rhetorical strokes, one might conclude that many teachers are either lazy, stupid, or downright perverse. But the culprit, it turns out, lies not so much in our character as in our unwitting acceptance of behaviorism, which emphasizes careful task analysis and reinforcement, and in our reluctance to question a pair of "controlling myths" in our profession: first, "that students learn what teachers teach" and, second, "that it is possible to determine in advance not only what children need to learn but also the optimum sequence and means through which they should learn it" (57).

Not surprisingly, dire consequences follow from our acceptance of these twin myths. We give students the idea that "school is for boring and meaningless stuff, and real life is where the excitement and action are" (62). We succeed in "making grades determined by teachers and tests the only motive for schooling, at least with those students who continue to buy into the system" (67). And we provide administrators with justification for "dividing subjects into small blocks of time and content, and having classrooms where teachers do most of the talking and ask most of the questions" (72). Here is the root of the problem, as Mayher sees it:

> This organization of content and skills into bottom-up sequences which move from simple to complex takes no account of the students' background or interests except insofar as they are directly concerned with the skills or knowledge being transmitted. The knowledge itself is disembedded from its human context, and its acontextual quality is regarded as a virtue not a defect because it allows for building a coherent sequence entirely on the basis of expert analyses of the structure of the tasks to be mastered or the content to be remembered. The only legitimate student purpose that is recognized is that of the need to learn the material, and this is to be ensured by frequent assessments and the accompanying rewards of good grades on the test. (73)

While I have the utmost respect for Mayher's wide knowledge and perspective, the preceding statements are simply too facile and overstated for me to take seriously, except as a position to be questioned. I acknowledge that I may be yet another mossback unable to cope with postmodern realities; however, I still believe—in my more optimistic moments, at least—that many secondary students *do* learn what teachers teach (myth 1) and that it *is* possible to determine what many children need to learn and to identify reasonable sequences and approaches for learning (myth 2). And I do not think I am alone in this regard.

For example, when I read thoughtfully designed lessons field-tested by George Hillocks (1995) or when I study the research-based paradigms for strategic writing instruction developed by James Collins (1998), I resist blanket indictments. Drawing upon his encyclopedic research knowledge and practical experience, Hillocks says that "a common characteristic of effective teaching of writing is clear objectives, clear not only to the teacher but also to the students" and that "specific descriptions of writing, along with examples . . . , are imperative to determining what those objectives will be and, therefore, to effective planning" (1995, 142–43). With similar attention to coaching fundamentals, Collins defines a strategy as "a sequence of cognitive steps designed to accomplish a particular outcome" and argues that helping students develop "controls over inward processes which result in outward manifestations of skills" can result in significant breakthroughs (1998, 21).

Thus, to help learners find effective language for personal narratives and other genres, Hillocks has developed many gateway activities, each a "complete, interesting, and challenging 'whole language' task in its own right," the summative effect being to enhance student performance (1995, 159). And to test whether ninth graders might assimilate language forms through imitation, Collins (1998) has helped teachers use strategies like "I Wish I Could Write Like That" and found, after once-a-week practice over a semester, clear improvements in writing quality as well as increased variety and control in syntax and paragraph structure (148).

So what Hillocks calls "activities" and Collins calls "strategies," I call "exercises." And here we approach the heart of the matter. Hillocks and Collins urge practice along specific lines, but both are clear that such work must be meaningful, *contextualized* practice. Hillocks (1995) recommends an environmental mode of teaching, one characterized by clear and specific objectives, selection of materials and problems, and instructional supports (simplifications of task as necessary and lots of productive work in small groups). Collins (1998) calls for a "co-constructed" teaching model, one that is explicit, richly collaborative, and connected to context, its steps involving strategy identification, modeling, workshop-style guidance, and "helping students work toward independent mastery of the strategy through repeated practice and reinforcement" (65). For both, the ethos is one of balance, as discussed throughout this book.

To conclude this section, I argue that it is the responsibility of teachers like you and me to take account of students' backgrounds and interests and that bottom-up sequences of content and skills should only provide a backdrop for this accounting. If knowledge is disembedded from its human context, it is our job—and *not* the job of our activities, strategies, or exercises—to give that knowledge a human face. Finally, it is our task—and *not* the task of exercises—to engage in the dialogue that speaks to the "inward, living core of our students' lives" (Palmer 1998, 31) and invites their attention, good-faith effort, and self-assessment.

In other words, the radical (commonsense) idea I choose to advance is that the authority for creating active learning environments resides not so much in instructional materials or in tasks themselves but rather in coaches who help students understand *what* they are learning, *why* the learning is useful, and *how* it might be approached.

A Life of Sport

Let's be honest. Teaching is work that can grind down even the most dedicated of writing coaches. It's easy to get discouraged and to forget the many attractions of our discipline: good books, stimulating ideas, and lifelong language development. Without due diligence, new teachers in particular can lose their balance, a process I described in "A Matter of Values" at the beginning of this chapter. To balance this work, it's absolutely essential to have other outlets.

A "life of sport" may suggest images of the rich and famous, say, cruising a yacht in the Caribbean or gathering polo ponies on the south lawn of the estate. What I want to consider, however, is the serious business of adult language play as implied by the metaphor of sport, that is, "an active pastime; recreation." As writing coaches, we certainly earn the right to our language obsessions, and from time to time, we should therefore indulge ourselves, creatively and unreservedly.

In addition to its in-school epiphanies, a life of sport centers on experiences we truly enjoy and make time for outside the classroom, whether logging on to a chat room, or talking story with friends and family, or reading mystery novels, or analyzing political give-and-take, or going to movie festivals, or telling bedtime stories to our kids, or practicing new jokes, or acting in local plays, or strengthening a marriage through daily talk. Such language events center on our core personal interests. And whether motivated by creative impulses, a quest to know more, or a need for reflection, the life of sport helps make us whole and balanced again and, in so doing, helps prepare us for the in-school coaching game. Sport, in this context, refers to language experiences that feel good, however we define *good*, and to having fun with language, however we define *fun*. It is purposeful adult language, alert and animated, pursuing its own ends.

For one teacher, the quiet discipline of yoga, a language of silence, feels right; for another, the camaraderie of an adult reading group offers welcome stimulation; for yet another, work on a master's degree provides a stressful pleasure. What characterizes this lifestyle is passionate pursuit. "The key element of an optimal experience," writes Csikszentmihalyi, "is that it is an end in itself" (1990, 67). And pursuing such a passion almost always involves an extension or a refinement or a new use of language.

For example, if gourmet cooking and entertaining are obsessions, you cannot help but develop a rich array of conversational graces. If you restore old cars, you are likely to participate in the culture of car buffs, with its social agenda, reading, and arcane jargon. If you find yourself drawn, irresistibly, to the best-seller list or to nature writing or to memoir, you probably enrich your language in serendipitous, unexpected ways as you journey to other worlds. All the diverse forms and functions of language are learned, extended, and refined in context, *as* we use them.

Clearly, a life of sport encompasses both team sports and individual sports, and just as clearly, nobody is limited to a single sport. For most of us, it is the constraint of free time that limits our interests. We insert the bookmark or exit the computer, feeling tired, but refreshed, and say to ourselves, "Until tomorrow."

Part of the appeal of such sporting activities may also lie in their challenge, a testing of self. Like marathon runners, we may pursue a goal not only because it feels good but also because we want to prove something to ourselves. A payoff may come in self-definition—the fact that, having pursued some passion with success, we feel entitled to regard ourselves as a "pretty good punster" or "the literate gourmet" or "Big Mama problem solver" or "word sleuth" or "toastmaster and entertainer" or "wannabe poet." We not only *learn* what we do but, in a very real sense, we *become* what we do.

Thus, poetry aficionados learn how to read a poem every time they pick up *The New Yorker*. Those curious about body language notice intriguing demonstrations in every faculty meeting, no matter how boring the agenda. Those trying to shape the great American novel for young adults find new possibilities in every novel they read. So, whatever our motivation may be, a life of sport helps balance the day-to-day work of coaching writing, making our lives more vital and interesting than before.

That, in itself, should be reason enough to pursue what we enjoy and to make room for ourselves. But if further rationale is needed, remember that vital, interesting teachers are like magnets for middle school and high school students. To the extent we share our lifestyle passions with them, the more *real* we become in their eyes.

Finally, let me mention that most writing coaches who are seriously playful about their work belong to a professional club, one made up of adults whose interests closely parallel their own because they too are responsible for language arts education in middle school and high school classrooms. They stand connected, not isolated.

Admission to a local chapter of the professional club comes either with student teaching, when most of us focus on dress standards, lesson plans, and class control, or during our first year on the job. We all learn quickly how club members are expected to look and act and talk. We come to understand, not long after our initiation—sometimes a baptism by fire—that local club charters make three paths available to us: we can accommodate ourselves to local standards, however enlightened or bizarre; or we can struggle, sometimes in alliance with others, for acceptance of new methods and ideas; or we can become a loner in a lunar landscape, pretending that the self-determined individual doesn't need club affiliation.

Of course, although the larger culture sees our club members as guardians of language and arbiters of usage disputes, we define our mission in other ways: as transmitters and conservators of a heritage; or as trainers of a skilled, competitive workforce for post-industrial America; or as advocates of students' personal growth through project-based, experiential learning. Clearly, there are conflicts among these disparate goals; clearly, too, each tradition has its spokespersons who try to influence members on issues that matter. The lively debate among contesting viewpoints—just a step up from mud wrestling at times—helps explain why the professional club holds such ongoing appeal for many teachers, writing coaches included.

The professional club provides an arena for good sports to come together and share ideas. Club members are expected to observe rules of good sportsmanship in their public conversations, for example, in books like this one. Among other things, it is important to say thank you, which I do now.

Zen Coaching

The bonsai on the bench,
wind-sculpted like memory—
I liked that part.

The path along the river,
and your fingers on my back—
I lived that part.

The quiet of your breathing,
and how you heard your heart—
I loved that part.

ACKNOWLEDGMENTS

In this final section I want to acknowledge first the inspired work of teachers in National Writing Project sites across the land. If this book has utility, it is because it draws upon the balanced practices of smart, informed teachers throughout the country, including my hundreds of colleagues in the Utah Writing Project.

In addition, let me applaud the coaches whose research and scholarship, or whose mentoring and example, have helped me write this book: Dick Adler, Mike Angelotti, Nancie Atwell, Ann Bayer, Donn Beck, Sheridan Blau, Tommy Boley, Ken Brewer, Jim Burke, Rebekah Caplan, Francis Christensen, Fran Claggett, James Collins, Charles Cooper, Chris Crowe, Don Daiker, Rae Dodge, Charles Duke, Nick Dyorich, Kenneth Farrer, Ken Fleming, Ralph Fletcher, Don Gallehr, Ann Gere, Donald Graves, James Gray, Sally Hampton, Dick Harmston, Shelley Harwayne, George Hillocks, Dave Holden, Kellogg Hunt, Lloyd Johnson, Dan Kirby, Bonnie Lesley, Andrea Lunsford, Joy Marsella, Charles Mazer, George McCulley, Larry McKinney, James Moffett, Max Morenberg, Donald Murray, Miles Myers, G. Lynn Nelson, Tom Newkirk, Roy O'Donnell, Carol Booth Olson, Margaret Pettis, Will Pitkin, Linda Rief, Teresa Robinson, Margaret Rostkowski, Kathy Rowlands, Ivy Ruckman, Bill Scannell, James Shaver, Mary Ann Smith, Karen Spear, Kim Stafford, William Stafford, Patricia Stoddart, Jeff Stephens, Marlin Struckman, Geoffrey and Judith Summerfield, Nila Thompson, Nat Teich, Bob Tierney, Fran Weinberg, Jeff Wilhelm, Lynn Williams, Sharon Williams, Patty and Vince Wixon, and Denny Wolfe.

To Tom Newkirk and the editors at Heinemann, I voice my sincere appreciation for assistance during my sabbatical writing. The leave was made possible thanks to the support of the Utah State University and my colleagues in the Department of Secondary Education.

Finally, I must acknowledge the woman who is my true Zen master, not to mention a university professor of the year. If I could coach as well as Carol Strong, I probably would not have needed to write this book. After all, it was during the ninth year of our divorce that Carol sent me a single well-crafted sentence from Garrison Keillor's *Lake Wobegone Days*, one typed on a small blue notecard.

> Some luck lies in not getting what you thought you wanted but getting what you have, which once you have it you may be smart enough to see is what you would have wanted had you known. (1985, 377)

I taped this thirty-seven-word sentence to the blue wall in my Honolulu bedroom, where I worked at a computer each afternoon after my morning field tests of SC exercises with seventh graders. It was complex syntax that expressed a subtle idea. I considered it with care.

A few weeks later in mid-October, just a day or two before what would have been our twenty-fourth wedding anniversary, I sent my reply. It was a blank marriage license, with roses as a footnote. She got the message.

To join me, she traveled to Hawaii. Our two grown children took part in the ceremony. It occurred on the day after Christmas, her birthday, a sunny day filled with the fragrance of flowers and a view of the blue sea that stretched to the far beyond.

And because this is a true story, we lived happily ever after.

We really did.

REFERENCES

Adams, B. 1997. "Tight Focus in Small Places." Interview with Diane Ackerman. *Writer's Digest* 77 (9): 29–34.

American Heritage Dictionary of the English Language. 1985. Boston: Houghton Mifflin.

Amis, K. 1954. *Lucky Jim.* New York: Viking.

Andrews, L. 1993. *Language Exploration and Awareness: A Resource Book for Teachers.* New York: Longman.

Anson, C. 1999. "Talking About Text: The Use of Recorded Commentary in Response to Student Writing." In *A Sourcebook for Responding to Student Writing,* ed. R. Straub, 165–74. Cresskill, NJ: Hampton.

Applebee, A. 1989. *The Teaching of Literature in Programs with Reputations for Excellence in English.* Report 1.1. Albany, NY: State University of New York–Albany Center for the Learning and Teaching of Literature.

Atwell, N. 1987. *In the Middle: Writing, Reading, and Learning with Adolescents.* Portsmouth, NH: Boynton/Cook.

———. 1998. *In the Middle: New Understandings about Writing, Reading, and Learning.* 2d ed. Portsmouth, NH: Boynton/Cook.

Bakhtin, M. M. 1981. *The Dialogic Imagination.* Ed. M. Holquist. Trans. C. Emerson and M. Holquist. Austin: University of Texas Press.

Bartholomae, D. 1980. "The Study of Error." In *The Writing Teacher's Sourcebook.* 2d ed., ed. E. P. J. Corbett, N. Myers, and G. Tate, 303–17. New York: Oxford University Press.

Bossert, S. T. 1988. "Cooperative Activities in the Classroom." *Review of Research in Education* 15: 225–50.

Braddock, R. C., R. Lloyd-Jones, and L. Schoer. 1963. *Research in Written Composition.* Urbana, IL: National Council of Teachers of English.

Brannon, L., and C. H. Knoblauch. 1982. "On Students' Rights to Their Own Texts." *College Composition and Communication* 33: 157–66.

Britton, J. 1970. *Language and Learning.* Harmondsworth, England: Penguin.

Bruner, J. 1966. *Toward a Theory of Instruction.* Cambridge, MA: Belknap Press of Harvard University Press.

———. 1983a. *Child's Talk: Learning to Use Language.* London: Oxford University Press.

———. 1983b. *In Search of Mind: Essays in Autobiography.* New York: Harper and Row.

———. 1986. *Actual Minds, Possible Worlds.* Cambridge, MA: Harvard University Press.

Burke, J. 1999. *The English Teacher's Companion: A Complete Guide to Classroom, Curriculum, and the Profession.* Portsmouth, NH: Boynton/Cook.

Calkins, L. M. 1986. *The Art of Teaching Writing.* Portsmouth, NH: Heinemann.

———. 1994. *The Art of Teaching Writing.* 2d ed. Portsmouth, NH: Heinemann.

Caplan, R. 1984. *Writers in Training: A Guide to Developing a Composition Program for Language Arts Teachers.* Palo Alto, CA: Dale Seymour.

Christensen, F. 1967. *Notes Toward a New Rhetoric: Six Essays for Teachers.* New York: Harper and Row.

————. 1968. "The Problem of Defining a Mature Style." *English Journal* 57: 572–79.

Christensen, F., and B. Christensen. 1978. *Notes Toward a New Rhetoric: Nine Essays for Teachers*. 2d ed. New York: Harper and Row.

Claggett, F. 1996. *A Measure of Success: From Assignment to Assessment in English Language Arts*. Portsmouth, NH: Boynton/Cook.

Coe, R. M. 1994. "Teaching Genre as Process." In *Learning and Teaching Genre*, ed. A. Freedman and P. Medway, 157–69. Portsmouth, NH: Boynton/Cook.

Cohen, E. G. 1994. "Restructuring the Classroom: Conditions for Productive Small Groups." *Review of Educational Research* 64 (1): 1–35.

Collins, J. 1998. *Strategies for Struggling Writers*. New York: Guilford.

Connors, R., and A. A. Lunsford. 1988. "Frequency of Formal Errors in Current College Writing, or Ma and Pa Kettle Do Research." *College Composition and Communication* 39: 395–409.

Cordeiro, P. 1998. "Dora Learns to Write and in the Process Encounters Punctuation." In *Lessons to Share on Teaching Grammar in Context*, ed. C. Weaver, 39–66. Portsmouth, NH: Boynton/Cook.

Csikszentmihalyi, M. 1990. *Flow: The Psychology of Optimal Experience*. New York: Harper Perennial.

Csikszentmihalyi, M., K. Rathunde, and S. Whalen. 1993. *Talented Teenagers: The Roots of Success and Failure*. Cambridge, England: Cambridge University Press.

Dale, H. 1994. "Collaborative Research on Collaborative Writing." *English Journal* 84 (1): 66–70.

————. 1997. *Co-Authoring in the Classroom: Creating an Environment for Effective Collaboration*. Urbana, IL: National Council of Teachers of English.

Dawkins, J. 1995. "Teaching Punctuation as a Rhetorical Tool." *College Composition and Communication* 46 (4): 533–48.

Delpit, L. D. 1986. "Skills and Other Dilemmas of a Progressive Black Educator." *Harvard Educational Review* 56: 379–85.

————. 1988. "The Silenced Dialogue: Power and Pedagogy in Educating Other People's Children." *Harvard Educational Review* 58: 280–98.

Dillard, A. 1989. *A Writer's Life*. New York: Harper and Row.

Ede, L., and A. Lunsford. 1990. *Singular Texts/Plural Authors*. Carbondale, IL: Southern Illinois University Press.

Elbow, P. 1985. "The Challenge for Sentence Combining." In *Sentence Combining: A Rhetorical Perspective*, ed. D. A. Daiker, A. Kerek, and M. Morenberg, 232–45. Carbondale, IL: Southern Illinois University Press.

————. 1999. "Options for Responding to Student Writing." In *A Sourcebook for Responding to Student Writing*, ed. R. Straub, 197–202. Cresskill, NJ: Hampton.

Englert, C. S. 1995. "Teaching Written Language Skills." In *Effective Instruction for Students with Learning Difficulties*, ed. P. Cigilka and W. Berdine, 304–43. Boston: Allyn and Bacon.

Fletcher, R. 1993. *What a Writer Needs*. Portsmouth, NH: Heinemann.

Fletcher, R., and J. Portalupi. 1998. *Craft Lessons: Teaching Writing K–8*. York, ME: Stenhouse.

Flower, L., and J. R. Hayes. 1981. "A Cognitive Process Theory of Writing." *College Composition and Communication* 32 (4): 365–88.

Flynn, E. 1989. "Learning to Read Papers from a Feminine Perspective." In *Encountering Student Texts*, ed. B. Lawson, S. S. Ryan, and W. R. Winterowd, 49–58. Urbana, IL: National Council of Teachers of English.

Freedman, A., and P. Medway, eds. 1994. "Introduction." In *Learning and Teaching Genre*, 1–22. Portsmouth, NH: Boynton/Cook.

Fromm, E. 1956. *The Art of Loving*. New York: Harper and Row.

Gallwey, W. T. 1976. *The Inner Game of Tennis*. New York: Random House.

Gardner, H. 1982. *Art, Mind, and Brain: A Cognitive Approach to Creativity*. New York: Basic Books.

———. 1991. *The Unschooled Mind: How Children Think and How Schools Should Teach*. New York: Basic Books.

Gee, J. P. 1990. *Social Linguistics and Literacies: Ideologies in Discourses*. London: Falmer.

Gere, A. R., ed. 1985. *Roots in the Sawdust: Writing to Learn Across the Curriculum*. Urbana, IL: National Council of Teachers of English.

Gibran, K. [1923] 1975. *The Prophet*. Reprint. New York: Knopf.

Gossard, J. 1996. "Using Read-Around Groups to Establish Criteria for Good Writing." In *Practical Ideas for Teaching Writing as a Process at the Elementary School and Middle School Levels*, ed. C. B. Olson, 240–44. Sacramento: California Department of Education.

Hairston, M. 1981. "Not All Errors Are Created Equal: Nonacademic Readers in the Professions Respond to Lapses in Usage." *College English* 43: 794–806.

Hall, N. 1962. "Individualize Your Spelling Instruction." *Elementary English* 39: 476–77.

Halliday, M. A. K., and R. Hasan. 1976. *Cohesion in English*. London: Longman.

Harris, K. R., and S. Graham. 1996. *Making the Writing Process Work: Strategies for Composition and Self-Regulation*. Cambridge, MA: Brookline Books.

Hillebrand, R. P. 1994. "Control and Cohesion: Collaborative Learning and Writing." *English Journal* 83 (1): 71–74.

Hillocks, G. 1984. "What Works in Composition: A Meta-Analysis of Experimental Treatment Studies." *American Journal of Education* 93: 133–70.

———. 1986. *Research on Written Composition: New Directions in Teaching*. Urbana, IL: ERIC Clearinghouse on Reading and Communication Skills and the National Conference on Research in English.

———. 1995. *Teaching Writing as Reflective Practice*. New York: Teachers College Press.

Hunt, K. W. 1965. *Grammatical Structures Written at Three Grade Levels*. Urbana, IL: National Council of Teachers of English.

———. 1970. *Syntactic Maturity in Schoolchildren and Adults*. Monographs of the Society for Research in Child Development, No. 134. Chicago: University of Chicago Press.

Johnson, D. W., and R. T. Johnson. 1994. "Cooperative Learning in the Culturally Diverse Classroom." In *Cultural Diversity in Schools: From Rhetoric to Practice*, ed. R. A. De Villas et al., 57–73. New York: State University of New York Press.

Keillor, G. 1985. *Lake Wobegone Days*. New York: Viking.

Krashen, S. D. 1984. *Writing: Research, Theory, and Applications*. Oxford: Pergamon.

———. 1993. *The Power of Reading: Insights from Research*. Englewood, CO: Libraries Unlimited.

Kroll, B., and J. Schafer. 1978. "Error Analysis and the Teaching of Composition." *College Composition and Communication* 29: 242–48.

Langer, J., and A. Applebee. 1987. *How Writing Shapes Thinking: A Study of Teaching and Learning*. Urbana, IL: National Council of Teachers of English.

L'Anselme, J. 1967. *The Ring Around the World: Selected Poems*. Trans. M. Benedickt. London: Rapp and Carol.

Lawlor, J. 1983. "Sentence Combining: A Sequence for Instruction." *Elementary School Journal* 84: 53–62.

Loban, W. C. 1976. *Language Development: Kindergarten Through Grade 12*. Research Report No. 18. Champaign, IL: National Council of Teachers of English.

Mayher, J. S. 1990. *Uncommon Sense: Theoretical Practice in Language Education*. Portsmouth, NH: Boynton/Cook.

McPhee, J. 1975. "Travels in Georgia." *Pieces of the Frame*. New York: Farrar, Straus, and Giroux.

Mellon, J. C. 1967. *Transformational Sentence-Combining: A Method for Enhancing the Development of Syntactic Fluency in English Composition*. Ph.D. diss., Harvard University.

———. 1969. *Transformational Sentence-Combining: A Method for Enhancing the Development of Syntactic Fluency in English Composition*. Research Report No. 10. Champaign, IL: National Council of Teachers of English.

———. 1981. "Language Competence." In *The Nature and Measurement of Competency in English*, ed. C. R. Cooper, 21–64. Urbana, IL: National Council of Teachers of English.

Moffett, J. 1968. *Teaching the Universe of Discourse*. Boston: Houghton Mifflin.

———. 1983. *Teaching the Universe of Discourse*. Portsmouth, NH: Boynton/Cook.

Murray, D. M. 1968. *A Writer Teaches Writing*. Boston: Houghton Mifflin.

———. 1982. "Teaching the Other Self: The Writer's First Reader." In *To Compose: Teaching Writing in High School and College* (1986), ed. T. Newkirk, 65–75. Portsmouth, NH: Boynton/Cook.

———. 1984. "Writing Badly to Write Well: Searching for the Instructive Line." In *Expecting the Unexpected: Teaching Myself—and Others—to Read and Write* (1989), ed. D. M. Murray, 37–53. Portsmouth, NH: Heinemann.

———. 1985. *A Writer Teaches Writing*. 2d ed. Boston: Houghton Mifflin.

———. 1990. *Shoptalk: Learning to Write with Writers*. Portsmouth, NH: Boynton/Cook.

———. 1993. *Write to Learn*. 4th ed. Fort Worth, TX: Holt, Rinehart, and Winston.

———. 1995. *The Craft of Revision*. 2d ed. Fort Worth, TX: Harcourt Brace.

Nelson, G. L. 1994. *Writing and Being: Taking Back Our Lives Through the Power of Language*. San Diego: LuraMedia.

Noden, H. 2000. *Image Grammar*. Portsmouth, NH: Heinemann.

Noguchi, R. R. 1991. *Grammar and the Teaching of Writing: Limits and Possibilities*. Urbana, IL: National Council of Teachers of English.

Novello, D. 1977. *The Lazlo Letters*. Vol. 1. New York: Workman.

———. 1992. *Citizen Lazlo. The Lazlo Letters*. Vol. 2. New York: Workman.

O'Hare, F. 1973. *Sentence Combining: Improving Student Writing Without Formal Grammar Instruction*. Research Report No. 15. Urbana, IL: National Council of Teachers of English.

Olson, C. B. 1992. *Thinking/Writing: Fostering Critical Thinking Through Writing*. New York: HarperCollins.

Palmer, P. J. 1998. *The Courage to Teach: Exploring the Inner Landscape of a Teacher's Life*. San Francisco: Jossey-Bass.

Perera, K. 1984. *Children's Writing and Reading*. London: Blackwell.

———. 1986. "Language Acquisition and Writing." In *Language Acquisition*. 2d ed., ed. P. Fletcher and M. Garman, 494–533. Cambridge, England: Cambridge University Press.

Perl, S. 1979. "The Composing Processes of Unskilled College Writers." *Research in the Teachiing of English* 13 (4): 317–36.

Pirsig, R. 1974. *Zen and the Art of Motorcycle Maintenance: An Inquiry into Values*. New York: Morrow.

Postman, N., and C. Weingartner. 1966. *Linguistics: A Revolution in Teaching*. New York: Delacorte.

Probst, R. 1989. "Transactional Theory and Response to Student Writing." In *Writing and Response: Theory, Practice, Research*, ed. C. Anson, 68–79. Urbana, IL: National Council of Teachers of English.

Quirk, R., S. Greenbaum, G. Leech, and J. Svartnvik. 1985. *A Comprehensive Grammar of the English Language*. London: Longman.

Richardson, P. W. 1994. "Language as Personal Resource and Social Construct: Competing Views of Literacy Pedagogy in Australia." In *Learning and Teaching Genre,* ed. A. Freedman and P. Medway, 117–42. Portsmouth, NH: Boynton/Cook-Heinemann.

Rief, L. 1992. *Seeking Diversity: Language Arts with Adolescents*. Portsmouth, NH.

Romano, T. 2000. "The Living Legacy of Donald Murray." *English Journal* 89 (3): 74–79.

Rose, M. 1989. *Lives on the Boundary*. New York: Penguin.

Rosen, L. 1987. "Developing Correctness in Student Writing: Alternatives to the Error Hunt." *English Journal* 76: 62–69.

———. 1998. "Developing Correctness in Student Writing: Alternatives to the Error Hunt (updated)." In *Lessons to Share on Teaching Grammar in Context*, ed. C. Weaver, 137–54. Portsmouth, NH: Boynton/Cook.

Rosenblatt, L. M. 1976. *Literature as Exploration*. 3d ed. New York: Noble and Noble.

Rubin, D. L. 1982. "Adapting Syntax in Writing to Varying Audiences as a Function of Age and Social Cognitive Ability." *Journal of Child Language* 3: 497–510.

Rule, R. 1993. "Conferences and Workshops: Conversations on Writing as Process." In *Nuts and Bolts: A Practical Guide to Teaching College Composition*, ed. T. Newkirk, 40–56. Portsmouth, NH: Boynton/Cook.

Scott, C. M. 1988. "Spoken and Written Syntax." In *Later Language Development: Ages 9 through 19*, ed. Marilyn A. Nippold, 49–93. Boston: College-Hill (Little, Brown and Company).

Shaughnessy, M. 1977. *Errors and Expectations: A Guide for the Teacher of Basic Writing*. New York: Oxford University Press.

Smith, F. 1988. *Joining the Literacy Club: Further Essays into Education*. Portsmouth, NH: Heinemann.

Sommers, N. 1980. "Revision Strategies of Student Writers and Experienced Writers." *College Composition and Communication* 31 (4): 378–88.

———. 1982. "Responding to Student Writing." *College Composition and Communication* 33: 148–56.

Spandel, V., and R. J. Stiggins. 1997. *Creating Writers: Linking Writing Assessment and Instruction*. New York: Longman.

Steinbeck, J. 1965. *Of Mice and Men*. New York: Viking.

Straub, R., ed. *A Sourcebook for Responding to Student Writing*. Cresskill, NJ: Hampton.

Strong, W. 1969. "Why, What Should Be the Fear?" *Media and Methods* (September) 37–70.

———. 1973. *Sentence Combining: A Composing Book*. New York: Random House.

———. 1981. *Sentence Combining and Paragraph Building*. New York: Random House/McGraw-Hill.

———. 1984a. *Crafting Cumulative Sentences*. New York: Random House/McGraw-Hill.

———. 1984b. *Practicing Sentence Options*. New York: Random House/McGraw-Hill.

———. 1986. *Creative Approaches to Sentence Combining*. Urbana, IL: ERIC Clearinghouse on Reading and Communication Skills and the National Council of Teachers of English.

———. 1991a. *Writing Incisively: Do-It-Yourself Prose Surgery*. New York: McGraw-Hill.

———. 1991b. "Writing Strategies That Enhance Reading." In *Effective Strategies for Teaching Reading*, ed. B. Hayes, 153–72. Boston: Allyn and Bacon.

———. 1994. *Sentence Combining: A Composing Book*. 3d ed. New York: McGraw-Hill.

———. 1996. *Writer's Toolbox: A Sentence-Combining Workshop*. New York: McGraw-Hill.

Strong, W., and T. Griffin. 1993. "Breakthrough." In *Peer Response Groups in Action*, ed. K. Spear, 239–50. Portsmouth, NH: Boynton/Cook.

Summerfield, G., and J. Summerfield. 1986. *Frames of Mind: A Course in Composition*. New York: Random House.

Suzuki, S. 1988. *Zen Mind, Beginner's Mind*. New York: Weatherhill.

Swift, J. 1973. "A Modest Proposal." In *The Writings of Jonathan Swift*, ed. R. Greenberg and W. B. Piper, 502–509. New York: Norton.

Tannen, D. 1991. *You Just Don't Understand*. New York: Ballentine.

Taylor, M. 1976. *Roll of Thunder, Hear My Cry*. New York: Dial.

Tucker, M., and J. B. Godding. 1998. *Standards for Our Schools: How to Set Them, Measure Them, and Reach Them*. San Francisco: Jossey-Bass.

Vacca, R., and J. Vacca. 1999. *Content Area Reading: Literacy and Learning Across the Curriculum*. 6th ed. New York: Longman.

Vail, N. J., and J. F. Papenfuss. 1989/1990. *Daily Oral Language*. Levels 1–12. Evanston, IL: McDougal, Littel.

Vygotsky, L. S. 1978. *Mind in Society: The Development of Higher Psychological Processes*, ed. M. Cole, V. John-Steiner, S. Scribner, and E. Souberman. Cambridge, MA: Harvard University Press.

———. 1986. *Thought and Language*. Cambridge, MA: MIT Press.

Weaver, C. 1979. *Grammar for Teachers: Perspectives and Definitions*. Urbana, IL: National Council of Teachers of English.

———. 1996. *Teaching Grammar in Context*. Portsmouth, NH: Boynton/Cook.

Williams, J. M. 1986. "Non-Linguistic Linguistics and the Teaching of Style." In *The Territory of Language: Linguistics, Stylistics, and the Teaching of Composition*, ed. D. A. McQuade, 174–91. Carbondale, IL: Southern Illinois University Press.

Wolfe, D., and J. Antinarella. 1997. *Deciding to Lead: The English Teacher as Reformer*. Portsmouth, NH: Heinemann.

INDEX